AS Level
English Language and Literature

Helen Toner and Elizabeth Whittome

CAMBRIDGE UNIVERSITY PRESS
Cambridge, New York, Melbourne, Madrid, Cape Town,
Singapore, São Paulo, Delhi, Mexico City

Cambridge University Press
The Edinburgh Building, Cambridge CB2 8RU, UK

www.cambridge.org
Information on this title: www.cambridge.org/9780521533379

First published 2003
13th printing 2012

Printed and bound in the United Kingdom by the MPG Books Group

A catalogue record for this publication is available from the British Library

ISBN 978-0-521-53337-9 Paperback

Cambridge University Press has no responsibility for the persistence or
accuracy of URLs for external or third-party internet websites referred to in
this publication, and does not guarantee that any content on such websites is,
or will remain, accurate or appropriate. Information regarding prices, travel
timetables and other factual information given in this work is correct at
the time of first printing but Cambridge University Press does not guarantee
the accuracy of such information thereafter.

ACKNOWLEDGEMENTS

While every effort has been made to contact copyright holders of material reproduced in
this publication, in some cases this has not been possible. The publishers will be glad to rectify
in future editions any errors or omissions brought to their notice.

Contents

Part 2 Advanced Subsidiary Literature in English

General introduction

You are currently studying, or preparing to study, for Advanced Subsidiary (AS) English. This book is designed to help you to do that and to achieve your potential in the examination. There are three syllabuses in which AS English can be gained and this book will be a useful guide, whichever course you decide to follow.

The three syllabuses in Advanced Subsidiary are:

- English Language
- Literature in English
- Language and Literature in English

These syllabuses are all designed to allow you to progress from GCE O level, IGCSE or GCSE syllabuses in English Language and English Literature.

English Language and Language and Literature in English can be gained at Advanced Subsidiary level only. Literature in English can also be gained at Advanced Subsidiary, but can then be used as a progression to Advanced level in the same examination session or at a later date.

If you choose to study for Language and Literature in English, then you won't study for either of the other two syllabuses.

AS English Language

There are two papers in this syllabus, Paper 1 and Paper 2. Paper 1 is Passages for Comment. Paper 2 is Composition. Each paper carries the same number of marks. A detailed explanation of what these papers entail follows in the first part of this book.

AS Literature in English

There are two papers in this syllabus, Paper 3 and Paper 4. Paper 3 is Poetry and Prose. Paper 4 is Drama. Each paper carries the same number of marks. A detailed explanation of what these papers entail follows in the second part of this book.

Progression to Advanced level

If you are studying for AS Literature in English and you wish to progress to Advanced level Literature in English, you will be required to sit a further two papers in addition to the two required for AS level. These two papers are Paper 5, and a choice of Paper 6, Paper 7 or Paper 8. Paper 5 is Shakespeare and Other Pre-20th Century Texts. Paper 6 is 20th Century Texts. Paper 7 is Comment and Appreciation. Paper 8 is Coursework. As already outlined, students may gain Advanced level English in the same examination session or over two examination sessions. Although this book confines itself to Papers 3 and 4, it is useful for Advanced level students, as well as AS students, as Papers 3 and 4 are compulsory for both AS English and Advanced level English.

AS Language and Literature in English

There are two papers in this syllabus, Paper 2 and Paper 9. Paper 2 is Composition, as outlined earlier in AS English Language. Paper 9 is Poetry, Prose and Drama, the equivalent of Papers 3 and 4 in the AS Literature in English examination combined. Each paper carries the same number of marks. A detailed explanation of what Paper 2 entails follows in the first part of this book. A detailed explanation of what Paper 9 entails follows in the second part of this book.

Outline of this book

The first part of the book deals with Papers 1 and 2 and is specifically for students of AS English Language and students of AS Language and Literature in English. The second part of the book deals with Papers 3 and 4 (and so Paper 9, as well) and is specifically for students of AS Literature in English, students of AS Language and Literature in English and students of Advanced level Literature in English.

Each of the two parts of the book takes students through the papers it deals with. The Assessment Objectives of each paper are broken down, explained and explored. Accompanying tasks with sample responses are provided to give practical 'hands-on' work to students. At the end of the units on Papers 1 and 2 revision is offered in the form of examination practice questions. The units on Papers 3 and 4 (and 9) also offer examination practice questions.

Part 1

Advanced Subsidiary English Language

Introduction

Before taking any test or examination, it is a good idea to find out what you are being tested on. You wouldn't try for your driving test or a certificate in, say, a sport or hobby you have without in the first place asking what was expected of you, and finding out what skills you were expected to have. The same is true of any examination you take in school. At the moment you are preparing for Advanced Subsidiary English Language. So what skills and knowledge will you be tested on?

Examiners call the answers to this question the Assessment Objectives. Here are the Assessment Objectives for Advanced Subsidiary English Language:

i Ability to read with understanding written material in a variety of forms, and to comment on its effectiveness.

ii Knowledge and understanding of features of English language.

iii Ability to write clearly, accurately and effectively for a particular purpose or audience.

All of the above taken together seems like a daunting task and yet you already have some foundation in the knowledge and skills referred to in the Assessment Objectives. The aim of this part of the book is to help you to clarify in your mind what you already know from your previous study of English Language, to build on this and to further enhance your knowledge and equip you well for the examination.

The examination

You will have to sit *two* papers. Each of these carries the same number of marks (50) which obviously means that they are of equal importance.

Paper 1

In this paper you will be given three passages for comment from which you are to choose two. For each of the passages you choose you will be asked to write a commentary on the writer's use of language. The passages will be drawn from a variety of sources, for example fiction, or non-fiction such as advertisements, magazine articles, biography or even from spoken language such as a speech. You will then be given a directed writing task based on the passage. You will be expected to write around 120 words. Alternatively you may be asked to produce a piece of writing of around 120 words related to the passage for comment and then asked to write a commentary comparing your piece of writing with the original. You will be given two hours for the paper, and the breakdown of marks is 15 for each commentary and 10 for each piece of directed writing.

Paper 2

In this paper you will be asked to write two compositions. Each composition should be between 600 and 900 words. One must be Narrative, Descriptive or Imaginative, and the other must be either Discursive or Argumentative. You will be offered a choice of compositions in each of the two sections. Each composition carries 25 marks, and you will be given two hours to complete the paper.

You will be tested on all three Assessment Objectives in Paper 1 and on the second and third Assessment Objectives in Paper 2. The units which follow will take you through the examination step by step. At various points there will be tasks for you to work through. Depending on whether you are using this book on your own or in school and depending, where appropriate, on your teacher's advice, you can tackle the tasks on your own, with a partner or in a group.

1 Written material in a variety of forms: genre, writer's purpose and tone

The first Assessment Objective in this examination is to show 'ability to read with understanding written material in a variety of forms, and to comment on its effectiveness'. It seems sensible at this point, then, to explore the idea of variety of forms, and ask ourselves why a variety of forms exists in the first place.

Genre

Even if you are not aware of it, you read a variety of forms of language every day, and not just in the classroom.

Task

Think about and write down the types of written English to be found in your home.

The most obvious types you found would probably be books, which can be divided into two types: fiction and non-fiction. But these can be further divided. There are many types of fiction texts, and the name we give to a type is **genre**.

Task

Make a list of genres of fiction books you know.

Sample response

> Mystery, historical, supernatural, romance, science fiction, war, human interest, adventure, crime.

Task

Now do the same for non-fiction texts.

Sample response

> Biography; autobiography; travel; information on, say, sports or hobbies; history; geography.

Don't forget that ordinary non-fiction texts in most people's homes include cookery books, telephone directories, holiday brochures, magazines, mail order catalogues, instruction manuals for the video recorder, computer, toaster etc. You will almost certainly have newspapers in your home, giving details of recent events and people's opinions of them, or comments or speeches by politicians. You might be surprised by how much we rely on 'written material in a variety of forms' for day-to-day survival in the modern world!

Even if you are not conscious of it, you are already able to recognise forms of written English, not just in an obvious way by looking at a title, but by responding to key features of English language and style. You are now going to be given six short extracts, each from a different genre, with some accompanying tasks. You will be returning to these extracts in unit 2.

Sample responses follow the tasks in a separate section, but don't look at them until you've tried the tasks on your own. This pattern has been adopted in other units in this book. These samples are given as examples of good, rather than bad or average, responses. Rather than suggesting marks for these responses according to examination criteria we offer you samples of good practice, something to aim for. Think big!

Task

Six short extracts follow. For each, identify the genre. You might want to jot down which features of the extract helped you to identify its genre. Don't worry at this stage if you are unsure about the exact words to use for language features; we'll be looking at that later. The six genres used are autobiography, history, women's magazines, travel, speech and crime.

1

Some of the little beaches I have loved are so obscure they have no name. I think of a quiet cove on the coast of Scotland where otters play in the tidal pools. And a tiny bay on the Galápagos island of Santiago where a very sociable sea lion prodded the sole of my foot with his wet muzzle, beckoning me to come in for a swim. And of course there are the windswept wintry walks along the endless seaboard of the Netherlands, guaranteed to clear your head and get your life into perspective.

2

In 1914 Europe blundered into the First World War. From 1870 to 1914 the Germans had built up a military machine of alarming efficiency.

E. L. Black (ed.) *1914–1918 in Poetry*

3

I have been asked to speak on the subject 'The Artist and Politics'. I'll try to do so ... I am an artist by vocation and profession. I am a citizen by obligation and responsibility. And as an actress I am happiest when I work in a play or a film that makes both artistic and social contribution.

Melina Mercouri

4

Most of the Thames Valley Police personnel were ever wont to pounce quickly upon any newspaper clipping concerning their competence, or alleged lack of competence.

Colin Dexter *The Remorseful Day*

were ever wont they had a tendency to

5

Belle – the new moisturiser which is taking over beauty salons all over the country – has now been released on to the sales counters of good department stores. For discerning women who are prepared to spend a little bit extra.

6

I was born on the eighteenth of July, 1918, at Mvezo, a tiny village ... in the district of Umtata, the capital of the Transkei ... My father was a tall, dark-skinned man with a straight and stately posture, which I like to think I inherited. He had a tuft of white hair just above his forehead, and, as a boy, I would take white ash and rub it into my hair in imitation of him. My father had a stern manner and did not spare the rod when disciplining his children.

Nelson Mandela *Long Walk to Freedom*

Sample response

> **1** is travel, **2** is history, **3** is a speech, **4** is crime, **5** is a women's magazine and **6** is autobiography.

Writer's purpose

It is reasonable to assume that any writer has a purpose in the writing which he/she produces. By his/her writing at all, and by your reading what is written, a relationship is set up between you and the writer.

Task

Make a list of different purposes which writers might have in producing a piece of writing. Use the list of genres at the start of this unit to help you.

Sample response

> To persuade, to dissuade, to ridicule, to advertise, to give information, to make you laugh, to puzzle, to scare, to offer a point of view and to offer contrasting points of view.

Being aware of the writer's purpose – that is, knowing *why* he/she wrote what he/she did – will help you to analyse the writing – that is, examine *what* was written and *how*. It will also help you to focus on your own writing skills, which are an important part of this examination.

Task

Go back to the six extracts we have just examined to work out their genre. This time, for each extract, write down what you think the writer's purpose was in writing.

Sample response

- In **1** the writer's purpose is to persuade the reader of the attraction of quiet, deserted beaches.

- In **2** the writer's purpose is to criticise the behaviour of governments which allow a war to begin.

- In **3** the writer's purpose (really the speaker's purpose) is to give information about the link between her work and her politics.

- In **4** the writer's purpose is to entertain and puzzle with a crime story.

- In **5** the writer's purpose is to advertise a particular product and persuade the reader to buy it.

- In **6** the writer's purpose is to give information about his own life and to create sympathy both for the writer as a boy and for his father.

Tone

Before we think about tone when it refers to writing, let us think about what we mean by tone when we refer to speech. It's easy to see that when we speak to other people we might be serious, joking, angry, sarcastic, loving, accusing or persuasive. For example, the tone you would use if you were telling your sister off for borrowing your CD without asking would not be the same tone you would use if you were trying to persuade your parents to let you stay out later than usual.

Task

List four or five recent situations where you have spoken to different people. What tone did you use in each one and why?

Sample response

When I was speaking to a close friend the tone used was informal and/or confidential whereas when I was speaking to the headteacher the tone used was formal and polite. When I was asking for a favour from a parent the tone used was affectionate and possibly ingratiating, but when I was speaking to the ticket collector at the station I used a polite tone. When I was speaking to my next-door neighbour I used a conversational tone.

Written language uses a variety of tones in the same way that speech does. Now we will go back to the six extracts we have already used to establish genre and writer's purpose, and this time we will examine them to think about the tone used in them.

Task

For each of the extracts used earlier (1–6) think about and write down the tone used by each writer.

Sample response

- In **1** the writer's tone is persuasive.
- In **2** the writer's tone is critical and sarcastic.
- In **3** the writer's tone is serious, formal and informative.
- In **4** the writer's tone is humorous.
- In **5** the writer's tone is persuasive.
- In **6** the writer's tone is informative and confidential.

You will have noticed that the tone adopted by each writer is closely linked to the purpose he/she had in writing, and this should hardly be surprising. But what you have done in examining genre, writer's purpose and tone separately is that you have begun to dismantle and deconstruct language in order to understand it better. In the next unit we will be returning yet again to the extracts used in this unit when we come to think about vocabulary.

Exam tip

Before you start to write your commentary on a passage take time to think and possibly jot down its genre, the writer's purpose and the tone the writer is using to make the writing purpose clear.

② Identifying language features: vocabulary

The second Assessment Objective in this examination is to show 'knowledge and understanding of features of English language'.

When we think of the features of any person or thing, we think of what he/she/it looks like, what distinguishes that person or thing from other persons or things. For example, what features do you have which make you different from your friend, different from your sister or the same as your sister? Similarly, a piece of writing has features which make it recognisable. These features might tell you the genre of the writing. They might also alert you to the purpose the writer had in writing it, or the tone adopted in relation to the topic. We examined genre, writer's purpose and tone in the last unit. In this and the following two units we will explore the *language features* which enable us to identify genre, writer's purpose and tone. It is always important to remember that any piece of writing establishes a relationship between writer and reader. We become part of that relationship by responding to the language features used by the writer.

So what constitutes these language features? One way of grappling with this question is to think of language as building bricks. The elements the writer is working with are individual words and they are built up to create the shape and design the writer wants. So it might be helpful to think of language as individual words (**vocabulary**) and shape and design (**structure**).

Vocabulary

We are now going to look again at the six extracts we used when identifying genre. This time there is a different task.

Task

For each extract **a** identify the writer's purpose by **b** isolating and commenting on individual words or phrases – vocabulary – which help you to arrive at your conclusion to **a**. Part **a** of this task has already been dealt with in unit 1. The extracts are given again in this unit to save you having to look back. Sample responses follow but don't look at them until you have finished the task.

1
Some of the little beaches I have loved are so obscure they have no name. I think of a quiet cove on the coast of Scotland where otters play in the tidal pools. And a tiny bay on the Galápagos island of Santiago where a very sociable sea lion prodded the sole of my foot with his wet muzzle, beckoning me to come in for a swim. And of course there are the windswept wintry walks along the endless seaboard of the Netherlands, guaranteed to clear your head and get your life into perspective.

2

In 1914 Europe blundered into the First World War. From 1870 to 1914 the Germans had built up a military machine of alarming efficiency.

3

I have been asked to speak on the subject 'The Artist and Politics'. I'll try to do so ... I am an artist by vocation and profession. I am a citizen by obligation and responsibility. And as an actress I am happiest when I work in a play or a film that makes both artistic and social contribution.

4

Most of the Thames Valley Police personnel were ever wont to pounce quickly upon any newspaper clipping concerning their competence, or alleged lack of competence.

5

Belle – the new moisturiser which is taking over beauty salons all over the country – has now been released on to the sales counters of good department stores. For discerning women who are prepared to spend a little bit extra.

6

I was born on the eighteenth of July, 1918, at Mvezo, a tiny village ... in the district of Umtata, the capital of the Transkei ... My father was a tall, dark-skinned man with a straight and stately posture, which I like to think I inherited. He had a tuft of white hair just above his forehead, and, as a boy, I would take white ash and rub it into my hair in imitation of him. My father had a stern manner and did not spare the rod when disciplining his children.

Sample response

1

a The writer's purpose is to persuade the reader of the attraction of quiet, deserted beaches, which, it is implied, can be found all over the world and are generally unknown.

b The effect is achieved with the words 'obscure', 'quiet' and 'tiny'. The writer creates the attractiveness by reference to friendly, non-threatening animals such as the sea lion, described as 'sociable', and the otter, described at 'play'. Such references make these animals sound as if they have almost human qualities of enjoying company and are like innocent children playing. The social and harmless nature of the sea lion is underpinned by the gentle movements 'prodded' and 'beckoning'. A further attraction of such beaches is created by 'clear your head and get your life into perspective'. This suggests the psychologically calming effect of these places where even the most stressed of individuals can find comfort.

There are other comments that could be made – about structure, for example – both for this extract and those which follow, but we are dealing only with vocabulary at present.

2

a The writer's purpose is to give information about the First World War, and to imply his disapproval of the war and how it was fought.

b The effect of disapproval is created by 'blundered', which suggests mismanagement, that the war was a mistake rather than a thought-out position. The reader is shocked to find that something as huge as war on a world-wide scale could be started, as it were, by accident. The term 'alarming efficiency' is interesting as it is apparently contradictory; normally we would be pleased, not alarmed, by efficiency. This is an example of oxymoron. It suggests that it would have been less harmful if the Germans had turned the virtue of efficiency in other directions.

Don't worry if you haven't heard of oxymoron. You might have spotted the contradictory nature of the expression in question without knowing the terminology. We will discuss specific terminology in the next unit.

3

a The writer's purpose is to give information about the link between her work and her politics.

b The writer (speaker) introduces her topic in a direct way. By contrasting terms associated with her work ('vocation' and 'profession') with terms associated with citizenship ('obligation' and 'responsibility') she establishes both her topic and the contrast between the two elements she has set out to discuss. These terms ('vocation' etc.) are serious and formal ones which underpin the serious nature of the topic and the appropriately serious tone adopted. Beginning the fourth sentence with 'And' introduces a confidential and almost personal note, by which the writer draws the reader (listener) into what she is about to say.

4

a The writer's purpose is to entertain and puzzle with a crime story. In this short section he may also be intending to amuse through the reference in this particular case to the incompetence of the police.

b 'Thames Valley Police' clearly indicates a crime story. 'Pounce' suggests speed and the idea of catching, which is linked to catching criminals. 'Competence' followed by 'or lack of' is humorous as the police are expected to be competent. 'Alleged' suggests accusations linked to police work, wrongful accusations and subsequent conflict.

5

a The writer's purpose is to advertise a particular product and persuade people to buy it.

b Giving the product a French name rather than an English one (Belle) makes it sound exotic and therefore fascinating. 'Taking over' is an image from military campaigns and business deals and makes it seem as if this product has beaten all rivals, as if no other product is used in beauty salons. There is a sense of immediacy and urgency in 'has now been released' as if the product has been a long-guarded secret which is now being shared with others lucky enough to know about it. 'Good' department stores appeals to customers' judgement; by flattering certain stores, those who frequent them are in turn singled out as being 'discerning', which is reinforced in the next sentence. 'Women who are prepared to spend a little bit extra' appeals to people's snobbery – this is a product for those who can afford it.

6

a The writer's purpose is to give information about his life and to create sympathy both for the writer as a boy and for his father.

b The vocabulary is factual and gives the exact date and place of the writer's birth. Thus it is established that giving the correct information is important to the writer. His admiration for his father is shown in 'posture, which I like to think I inherited'. 'Like to think' shows the writer's sense of humour in that he confesses to a little vanity; in addition he is rather afraid to see a likeness between himself and his father, showing that he puts his father on a pedestal. Thus, both the writer and his father become likeable to the reader. Similarly when the boy imitates his father by rubbing 'white ash' into his hair the reader warms to the little boy hero worshipping his father. The reader is made to imagine the little boy watching his father closely ('tuft of white hair just above his forehead') and this shows the importance of the father to the little boy. Reference to his father punishing his children ('did not spare the rod') makes it seem that the boy did not like to fall out of favour with his father. This stresses the huge importance of the father in the little boy's life.

So what have you learned so far? You have learned about genre, writer's purpose and tone. You have learned that vocabulary is carefully chosen by the writer to demonstrate or reinforce the genre of the writing, its purpose, and the tone which the writer has chosen to adopt.

Task

Find short extracts of your own which use vocabulary to demonstrate:

a various genres
b various writing purposes
c various tones.

Exam tip

Before you start to write your commentary on a passage jot down, underline or highlight words and phrases in the passage which help you to see the writer's purpose, or are good examples of the tone used by the writer, or link particularly well with the rubric or question wording.

3 Identifying language features: figures of speech

In the previous unit we saw that writers use particular words and phrases, or vocabulary, to create certain intended effects. We also saw that sometimes these words and phrases can fit a pattern or have a label attached to them. The particular example in the previous unit was oxymoron. We saw that the example of oxymoron could have been spotted, analysed and explained without having the correct terminology. However, if specialised terminology is available our task is made easier if we are able to use it.

When a writer uses a particular device, or trick, with language in order to make it more interesting, we call that a figure of speech. A knowledge of some of the basic figures of speech will not only make it easier for you to analyse and appreciate the craft of writers, thus helping you to comment on passages in Paper 1, it will also enhance your own ability to write in Paper 2. Moreover it will help you in your study of literature.

The first group of figures of speech we will consider is probably the most common type, which we can group together under the heading of **images**. In an image, we see two things which are like each other in some way. The three figures of speech to learn here are simile, metaphor and personification.

Simile

In a simile the writer says that two things are like each other because of at least one similarity between them. Similes always have the word *like* or *as* in them.

Task

In the following short extract, an old woman, Armande, has just had a birthday party in her house near the river. Identify and comment on the two similes in the extract.

I could hear Armande's voice above the rest: her laughter was like that of an overtired child. Sprinkled across the water's edge, the lanterns and candles looked like Christmas lights.

Joanne Harris *Chocolat*

Sample response

'Her laughter was like that of an overtired child' is a simile. Armande is an old lady, not a child, and the simile suggests that Armande has had such a wonderful time that she felt like a little girl again. The second simile is 'the lanterns and candles looked like Christmas lights'. This is effective because it suggests how bright and sparkling the lanterns were, and it adds to the party atmosphere as Christmas is a time of celebration.

Metaphor

In a metaphor the writer goes a step further than in a simile. Instead of basing the comparison on the fact that two things are like each other, the writer actually says that the first *is* the second, because of some similarity between them.

Task

In the following short extract, the writer describes the significance of rice to those who cultivate it. Identify and comment on the metaphor.

Rice is nourished by water, earth and wind and transforms into gold.

Going Places (magazine of Malaysia Airlines) January 2002

Sample response

'Transforms into gold' is a metaphor. Rice is a plant and becomes a food, and people do not eat gold. However, people value gold so the metaphor suggests that rice is valuable because without food we die.

Personification

In personification a thing or object which is not human is given a human characteristic because of some similarity between the thing and a person. It is easy to remember because personification contains the word 'person' inside it.

Task

The following short extract is a continuation of the extract about rice. Identify and comment on the example of personification in the extract.

[Rice] demands the sweat of man. In return, the earth gives birth to a grain that is valuable and precious for human life.

Going Places January 2002

Sample response

'The earth gives birth' is an example of personification as giving birth is a human (or animal) activity, and the earth cannot give birth. The writer wants to stress the life-giving qualities of the cultivated earth and the rice it produces.

> ## Exam tip
>
> The following formulae might be useful for writing about imagery:
>
> - simile: A is like B because of C • metaphor: A = B because of C
> - personification: A (non-human) is turned into B (human) because of C.
>
> In each case C (the detailed comment on the images) is what makes the difference between an adequate and a complete answer.

Now we will move on to two figures of speech which are concerned with sound. These are onomatopoeia and alliteration.

Onomatopoeia

Onomatopoeia is a figure of speech in which the sound of a word suggests its meaning.

> ### Task
>
> Read the short extract below and pick out and comment on two examples of onomatopoeia.
>
> There was a loud clatter as dustbins were blown over in the alleyway. Somewhere in the distance, a dog was howling.

Sample response

> 'Clatter' is an example of onomatopoeia. It seems to copy the loud and strident sounds of the metal hitting the ground. The sound made by the dog 'howling' is also onomatopoeia. It has two syllables and a long *ow* sound; these add to the effect that the noise made by the dog is prolonged.

Alliteration

Alliteration is a figure of speech in which words beginning with the same sounds are deliberately placed close together to achieve a particular effect.

> ### Task
>
> Read the short extract below and pick out and comment on two examples of alliteration.
>
> In the little girl's pocket, wrapped in a crunched-up piece of pale paper, was a rotting apple, brown and bruised.

> 'Pale paper' is an example of alliteration in the repetition of the letter 'p'. As this is an abruptly stopped sound [called a plosive] it is appropriate that it should be used in alliteration as something rigid and crunchy is being described. The second example of alliteration is 'brown and bruised'. Again, hard sounds are used, and this is appropriate as something unpleasant and therefore harsh to the senses is being described.

Contrast

'Contrast' is a common enough word which we all know and use although maybe you haven't stopped to think about its use in language. In using contrast as a figure of speech a writer is placing in close proximity ideas which contrast with each other or seem almost opposites of each other, in order to achieve a particular effect. Another word for contrast is **antithesis**.

Task

Read the extract below and pick out and comment on the use of contrast.

It was the best of times, it was the worst of times, it was the age of wisdom, it was the age of foolishness ... it was the spring of hope, it was the winter of despair ...

Charles Dickens *A Tale of Two Cities*

Sample response

> The ideas of 'best' and 'worst' are contrasted as are the ideas of 'wisdom' and 'foolishness'. There is a double contrast in the third item, between 'spring' and 'winter' and 'hope' and 'despair'. The writer is being contradictory and rather mysterious as if the period being described is problematic, a mixture of different attitudes and events. The effect is to engage attention and make the reader want to read on.

Oxymoron

Oxymoron is another figure of speech which deals with contradictions. In using oxymoron, the writer places two ideas that seem to be directly opposed to one another in close proximity, which, on closer inspection, make sense.

Task

Read the short extract which follows and pick out and comment on an example of oxymoron.

... the star turn in the schoolroom was a massive sandy-haired Highland Major whose subject was 'the spirit of the bayonet' [a weapon]. He spoke with homicidal eloquence, keeping his talk alive with genial and well-judged jokes.

Siegfried Sassoon *Memoirs of an Infantry Officer*

Sample response

'Homicidal eloquence' is an example of oxymoron in that it is an apparent contradiction. The lecturer is clearly comfortable with the idea of killing people in war and possibly derives a certain satisfaction from it; therefore it is appropriate to describe him as 'homicidal'. Because he knows his subject well enough to be lecturing on it, he is also 'eloquent'. It seems contradictory to link killing with being articulate as one seems brutal and inhuman and the other sounds like something associated with well-ordered human beings. This expression is an apparent contradiction only; on closer inspection we can see that the lecturer enjoys both killing and talking about it; his love of killing makes him want to pass on his enthusiasm to others.

Hyperbole or exaggeration

When using hyperbole, a writer draws attention to a particular idea by saying something which cannot possibly be true. Thus the writer is stepping beyond the meaning to achieve a desired effect. This intended effect might be to amuse, shock, puzzle, challenge or impress.

Task

Read the short extract below and pick out and comment on two examples of hyperbole.

I left the house in a hurry, having overslept by ten minutes. Today of all days, I had an important meeting with my boss who was likely to murder me when he discovered I hadn't met my sales targets for the month. As luck would have it this was the very morning that millions of cars were on my stretch of the motorway.

Sample response

It is an exaggeration, or hyperbole, to say that her boss would 'murder' her; such behaviour would obviously be intolerable and out of all proportion with not meeting sales targets. The second example of hyperbole is 'millions'; clearly that is an impossibly high number of cars to be found on a stretch of road. The writer's purpose is to amuse or to impress on the reader the extent of the writer's hostility towards her boss or her boss to her. The sense of frustration in the panic to make up lost time is created by the use of 'millions', as if it seemed to the writer that she would never make it through the traffic.

Rhetorical question

When asking a rhetorical question a writer is either asking a question to which the answer is so obvious that the question is unnecessary or asking a question to which there is no real answer. The intended effect of a rhetorical question is to reshape a statement in order to give it emphasis.

Read this short extract and pick out and comment on a rhetorical question.

She looked anxiously at the clock yet again. How many times had she told her daughter Emma that she should be home by ten o'clock? Sighing, she looked at the clock once again.

Sample response

The writer does not expect an answer to the question. The mother's anxiety is presented in the form of a question in order to emphasise that she had repeatedly told her daughter to be home by ten o'clock.

Repetition

In this figure of speech a word or expression is repeated for effect rather than for meaning in order to emphasise a point or to build up interest or tension, or simply to make the sentence sound poetic or attractive.

Task

Read the short extract below and pick out and comment on the use of repetition.

Standing in the middle of her study, Rachel thought of what she still had to do: Maths homework, Accounts homework, French homework. And that English essay – the hardest homework of all. Her heart sank.

Sample response

The word 'homework' is repeated. It is used four times to give the effect that the amount of homework Rachel has to do is weighing heavily on her. All she can think about is homework when she stands in her study, so that the reader is not surprised that 'Her heart sank'. The repetition is used for effect rather than for meaning.

Pun

A pun is a play on a word or words. This means using a word which might have two or more meanings in order to make a joke or to be ambiguous.

Task

Read the short extract below and pick out and comment on the pun.

'We can't continue like this,' exclaimed the department manager. 'We really need some change.'
   'Will this be enough?' said Jennifer, throwing a handful of coins on to the table.

Sample response

> The pun is contained in the word 'change'. The manager means that reform or alteration is required, presumably to the way in which the business is run. Jennifer's mistake – or possibly her joke – is to think, or pretend to think, that the manager wants some money – just a few coins.

Euphemism

Sometimes when a writer wants to play down some difficulty, problem or unpleasantness, a figure of speech called euphemism can be used. Euphemism seeks to put a pleasant spin on something basically unpleasant.

Task

Read the short extract below and pick out and comment on an example of euphemism.

Everyone knew Claire was a stranger to the truth, and therefore it came as no surprise when she denied ever having seen the strawberry cakes. She wasn't even embarrassed about the red stains all over her chin.

Sample response

> It is obvious that Claire has eaten the strawberry cakes, but she lies about it. Instead of using the word 'liar' the writer softens the idea by using a euphemism and calling her 'a stranger to the truth'.

Irony

When a writer uses irony there is a discrepancy between what is literally said and what is really meant, or a contrast between what the reader expects and what is actually given. When a discrepancy occurs between an expected outcome and a real outcome we have irony. Irony can also be a sarcastic way of speaking or writing in which criticism is disguised as praise.

Task

Read the short extract below and pick out and comment on its irony.

The boss threw my report across the room at me. 'I can see you spent hours on that piece of work,' she snarled.

> It is clear from the boss's actions and tone of voice that she does not think that the employee spent very long on the work at all and that it is in fact a poor effort. The boss uses the expression 'spent hours' ironically to be indirectly critical of the employee.

Idiom

Although idiom is not a figure of speech as such, it is helpful for your understanding of language terms if you understand what idiom is. Idiom is the use of a word or expression which is particular to a language (in this case English) and which would not make sense if it were translated literally into another language. Usually idiom has an informal tone.

Task

Read the short extract below and pick out and comment on the use of idiom.

'I'm over the moon to have Miss Christie as my English teacher,' Emily said.

Sample response

> Emily is expressing her happiness about her teacher. The moon does not have any literal place in what she says. Emily is using an informal, and rather overused, idiomatic expression which is peculiar to English.

A final word about figures of speech

In this unit we have looked at definitions and examples of basic figures of speech. However, it is important to remember that not all interesting writing falls into the category of figures of speech. You will come across a lot of words and expressions which are worthy of comment without their necessarily being able to be 'labelled' as particular figures of speech. But a sound knowledge of figures of speech provides a good starting point for discussion about language.

Exam tip

The key to appreciating figures of speech and to scoring high marks in examination questions is to do more than merely identify the figure of speech. You should be careful to see its effectiveness and comment on that effectiveness, in much the same way as this unit has done in its sample responses. The key is: *identify* and *comment*.

④ Identifying language features: structure

In this unit we will be concentrating on structure. The elements of language are the words actually used by the writer. These elements are put together to create the shape and design desired by the writer, and this is called the structure of the writing. In order to examine structure further, it is useful to sub-divide it into punctuation and grammar.

Punctuation

When we think of punctuation, we think of all the symbols we have been taught which are used to separate words into meaningful groups such as phrases and sentences. Using punctuation competently ourselves and being able to analyse the way writers achieve particular effects with punctuation are two different matters. To examine writers' use of punctuation we must go beyond the mere idea of dividing words into phrases and sentences.

Task

In the following sentence the writer is a young man leaving home in England to travel alone to Spain to live for several months. Comment on the effect created by commas in the sentence.

I carried a small rolled-up tent, a violin in a blanket, a change of clothes, a tin of treacle biscuits, and some cheese.

Laurie Lee *As I Walked Out One Midsummer Morning*

Sample response

Commas are used by the author to separate items in the list of things the boy takes with him. The fact that the author chooses to list them in one sentence emphasises the sense of an inventory.

Task

The following sentence is the same writer's description of a night spent sleeping outside when he reached Galicia, in Spain. Comment on the effectiveness of the colon and the dash in the sentence.

But I slept little that night: I was attacked by wild dogs – or they may have been Galician wolves.

Laurie Lee *As I Walked Out One Midsummer Morning*

Sample response

The colon sets up an expectation in the sentence that the writer will explain why he was unable to sleep. He then goes on to give the expected explanation. The dash leads us to expect additional information, which here adds to the impression that the boy is in danger, wolves being an even more frightening prospect than wild dogs.

Task

Take a random page from a book or magazine you are currently reading and find examples of the following punctuation being used particularly effectively: comma(s), exclamation mark, brackets, question mark, colon, semi-colon, dash. Write down each example in the context in which you find it, and go on to say why it is effective.

Grammar

Many people are discouraged by, or even a little afraid of, the word 'grammar', but you already know a lot about grammar even if you think you don't. If you wanted to examine how, say, your television works, you would need to look at each component and its relationship with the other components. It's the same with language. Grammar is what helps you to do that. The components of grammar are the parts of speech – noun, verb, adjective, adverb, conjunction, pronoun and preposition – and the way in which these are put together. This is called sentence structure.

Task

The following short extract describes the birthday feast of the old woman, Armande. Show how the writer uses particular parts of speech and sentence structure to show that it is a feast.

> Then the *vol-au-vents* [pastries], light as a puff of summer air, then elderflower sorbet, followed by a *plateau de fruits de mer*, [platter of sea food] with grilled *langoustines*, grey shrimps, prawns, oysters and spidercrabs, and atop it all a giant black lobster. The huge platter gleams with reds and pinks and sea-greens and pearly-whites and purples, a mermaid's cache of delicacies which gives off a nostalgic salt smell, like childhood days at the seaside.
>
> Joanne Harris *Chocolat*

Sample response

The writer uses many nouns to create a sense of lavishness. The nouns – 'shrimps, prawns' etc. – are piled up on top of one another, suggesting that the food was too. The abundance of food is reflected in the abundance of nouns. The colours of the food are turned from the normal adjective form into nouns (e.g. 'reds and pinks'). There is no verb in the first sentence and this takes the focus off action, the work of verbs, and concentrates the focus on food.

The adjective 'giant' to describe the lobster is more effective than *large*. The lobster almost certainly isn't 'giant' but it is effective in the context of lavishness to say it is. Thus, exact meaning is less important than atmosphere.

The extract is made up of only two sentences; the sentences are long, and this is appropriate in that the writer is describing an enormous feast, emphasising the great number and variety of dishes on offer.

Task

The following extract suggests possible causes of a fire which destroys a boat at night. Show how the writer uses particular parts of speech and sentence structure to create the effect of catastrophe.

A candle, dripping wax. A cigarette flicked across the water, bouncing into a pile of stovewood. One of their lanterns, the bright paper catching, powdering the deck with embers. Anything could have started it.

Joanne Harris *Chocolat*

Sample response

The writer offers three suggestions as to what might have started the fire. Each of these is a noun – candle, cigarette, lantern. Each is emphasised by being placed in a separate sentence – non-sentences really, as there are no finite verbs. [Finite verbs show tense and person; participles like 'dripping' and 'flicked' do not.] The absence of verbs throws the nouns into sharper focus. In addition, the absence of finite verbs is indicative of the absence of a recognisable agent that could have started the fire, which helps to underpin the final sentence: 'Anything could have started it.' This short final sentence gives an air of finality and stresses in its terse and economical style the frequent imbalance between actions and their consequences.

The following extract describes how the main character has been dreaming and is wakened by her young daughter. Demonstrate how the writer uses parts of speech and sentence structure to show that the character is glad to wake up.

Then I was falling backwards ... with cards spraying out in all directions ... DEATH, DEATH, DEATH ... I held my hands out protectively. I awoke screaming with Anouk standing above me, her dark face blurry with sleep and anxiety. 'Mummy, what is it?' Her arms are warm around my neck. She smells of chocolate and vanilla and peaceful untroubled sleep.

Joanne Harris *Chocolat*

Sample response

The writer uses two verb tenses: the past tense is used when the character is dreaming; the tense changes to the present when she has woken up. The present tense stresses the idea that the character is glad to hang on to the present, and to leave the past of her nightmare behind. The writer uses a build-up of the conjunction 'and' in the last sentence to focus attention on 'chocolate', 'vanilla' and 'peaceful untroubled sleep'. These are all items associated with well-being and pleasure and so are a contrast to the nightmare. The character is pulling herself into the present by focusing on these pleasant things.

Task

From your own reading material, either fiction or non-fiction, or by using the extracts in units 1 and 2, find examples of the following grammar features being used particularly effectively. Write down each example in the context in which you find it, and go on to say why it is effective: build-up of nouns, build-up of verbs, build-up of adjectives, short sentence(s), long sentence(s), single-word sentence(s).

A final word about structure

Although it has not been possible in this short unit to look at many examples of punctuation and grammar, the intention has been to raise your awareness of the craft of good writers in using punctuation and grammar effectively, and to encourage you to examine these more closely in your examination practice.

Exam tip

Before you start to write your commentary on a passage, take time to see whether a particular part of speech or a particular type of sentence structure is predominant in it. If so, jot down, underline or highlight examples found so that you can use the technique of identifying and commenting already established in the Exam tip for unit 3.

5 Writing for a particular purpose or audience

The third Assessment Objective of this examination is to show 'ability to write clearly, accurately and effectively for a particular purpose or audience'. The whole of Paper 2 will be taken up by writing, and we will move on to that later. You will also be required to produce two pieces of writing in Paper 1, one for each of the two passages on which you have chosen to comment. Each of these pieces of writing is directed writing – that is to say, the task you will be given is linked in some way to the passage on which you choose to comment. The original passage provides a stimulus for your piece of writing. We will deal more closely with directed writing in units 7, 8, 10 and 11. The purpose of this short unit is to make you aware of the importance of writing in both Paper 1 and Paper 2, and to start you thinking about some general principles of directed writing.

In directed writing if there has to be a similarity between the style of the original passage and the style of writing you are to produce, return to the original passage on which you have commented. Look back over your comments. Think about genre, writer's purpose and tone. Make a list of language features which you have identified. Remember that these features might be concerned with vocabulary, figures of speech or structure.

Preparatory questions

Before you start to write, answer these questions:

- What genre will I write in?
- Am I clear about the purpose of my writing and about my audience?
- Can I use language effectively to suit my purpose and be appropriate for my audience? What tone does the writer use, and can I achieve that tone in my vocabulary and sentence structure?
- What kind of vocabulary is used, and with what effect?
- Does the writer use particular figures of speech, and, if so, which ones, and with what effect?
- Does the writer use a particular part of speech often, and, if so, which one and why?
- What kind of sentence structure does the writer use, and why?
- Can I copy the language features used by the writer?

Audience

The audience of any piece of writing is the person or group of people for whom the piece is written – those who will be reading the piece of writing. It is always important to establish who these readers are before you begin to write and to keep them in mind throughout your writing. For example, if you were asked to write a description of a country visited on holiday for a travel brochure, it would be different from the description you would write for a primary school magazine. This is because the audiences would be different. For the primary school magazine you would choose a simpler style of vocabulary and probably simpler sentences. In the travel brochure you might use figures of speech like metaphor, hyperbole or pun, the effects of which would be lost on a primary school audience.

Audience is clearly related to purpose. The purpose of the holiday brochure would probably be to persuade and sell whereas the purpose of the primary school magazine would probably be to entertain. Although purpose and audience are obviously linked it is nevertheless a useful exercise to think of them separately when you are planning your piece of writing.

Examination questions

In units 8 and 11 you will look closely at examination questions in which you are asked to produce a piece of directed writing before you write a commentary on a passage. In such cases, the answers to the questions above will still be useful.

It is enough at this stage, when we are thinking about the Assessment Objectives for the examination, to be aware of the possibilities of developing writing skills for directed writing in Paper 1 and for composition writing in Paper 2.

Exam tip

Before you decide which passage for comment to choose from the selection available, look at the directed writing task as well as the commentary instructions. Make the choice which is right for you by weighing up both tasks related to the passage, not just one.

6 Short passages for comment

Now that we have examined some of the key ideas about language and linked them to the Assessment Objectives of the examination, it is time to bring all these ideas together by looking at examination questions. In this unit and in units 7 and 8 we will work with short passages of around 300 words, with their directed writing tasks. In units 9,10 and 11 we will look at longer passages of around the length you should expect to find in the examination.

1 Shanghai childhood

The passage below is written by an English adult, Christopher Banks, describing his memories of growing up in Shanghai with his Japanese friend, Akira.

Task

Comment on the style and language of the passage.

At the rear of our garden in Shanghai, there was a grass mound with a single maple tree rising out of its summit. From the time Akira and I were around six years old, we enjoyed playing on and around that mound, and whenever I now think of my boyhood companion, I tend to remember the two of us running up and down its slopes, jumping right off where the sides were at their steepest.

From time to time, when we had worn ourselves out, we would sit panting at the top of the mound with our backs against the trunk of the maple tree. From this vantage point, we had a clear view over my garden and of the big white house standing at the end of it. If I close my eyes a moment, I am able to bring back that picture very vividly: the carefully tended 'English' lawn, the afternoon shadows cast by the rows of elms separating my garden and Akira's; and the house itself, a huge white edifice with numerous wings and trellised balconies. I suspect this memory of the house is very much a child's vision, and that in reality, it was nothing so grand. Certainly, even at the time, I was conscious that it hardly matched the splendour of the residences round the corner in Bubbling Well Road.

Kazuo Ishiguro *When We Were Orphans*

Organising your response

Think of the key terms you have learned to describe language, and write them down. You should have something like this:

- writer's purpose and audience
- tone
- language features, for example vocabulary, figures of speech and structure.

Now take each of these key terms and try to match them to the passage. Don't think yet about your final answer, just jot your ideas down in note form.

Sample commentary plan

Writer's purpose
This is to entertain and perhaps amuse by his explanation of the confusion in the boy's mind about the size of his house.
Tone
This is nostalgic, looking back.
Vocabulary
Think about and write comments on the following words and phrases: 'mound', 'worn ... out', 'panting', 'close my eyes a moment', 'bring back that picture', 'hardly matched'.
Structure
The central picture in paragraph 1 is the grass mound on which grew one maple tree. A wider picture is given in paragraph 2 because the writer's vantage point is extended to include the garden and the house. It is as if a camera were panning out from a small focus to a larger one. Each paragraph starts with the writer's view as a child and goes on to qualify that childish view with his adult opinion. In terms of punctuation the colon in the second paragraph introduces a list of memories. The inverted commas around 'English' show that the boy's parents were consciously trying to have an English type of garden, but perhaps not succeeding.

Sample commentary

The writer's purpose is to look back on childhood in a nostalgic, sometimes rather comical way. It is incongruous to describe a 'mound' as having a 'summit'. This shows that to small children a slight incline in a garden seems like a mountain. The writer concedes that his memory is exaggerated in the phrases 'even at the time' and 'hardly matched': he acknowledges the 'splendour' of the houses round the corner, which are described as 'residences' rather than merely houses.

A comical picture of little boys is created. Their game is only running about in a garden and yet they are 'worn ... out' and are 'panting', in need of a rest. The gap between childhood and adulthood for the writer is shown in the words 'around six years old'; he does not have an exact memory because it was a long time ago. Nostalgia is created in his closing his eyes 'to bring back that picture', consciously trying to evoke the past. His parents' nostalgia for the England they have left behind is shown in their weak attempt to re-create an 'English' lawn; the inverted commas show their attempt is not entirely successful in the climate of Shanghai.

2 Traveller's check

The passage below describes the writer's journey on the North Borneo Railway.

Task

Comment on the style and language of the passage.

Travel, as we know it today, had its roots with the appearance of trains. The train opened up the countryside and people could head off for a day's outing away from the city.

Thomas Cook was the first travel agent who organised groups of travellers to head off into England's Lake District for some rest and recreation. Since then, we haven't looked back and now there are few areas on the planet where people haven't left their mark.

Some of us still seek out a 'puffin billy' experience as part of our travels. The North Borneo Railway in Sabah, East Malaysia, is the only rail track on the island of Borneo ... these few hundred kilometres of track are a paradise for those who dream of trains. There are two choices – the daily train to the small settlement of Temon or the twice-weekly tourist train to Papar. 'Trainheads' won't need any convincing to do both trips at least once.

The renovated North Borneo Railway operates a journey south from Tanjung Aru in Kota Kinabalu along a narrow rickety train line to Papar some 66 kilometres away. Looking around the train, it's easy to see that some of the passengers fall into the 'lunatic fringe, fanatical steam train devotees' category while others appear to have only a passing interest in the nostalgia of a mode of transport that has slipped into near oblivion ... the train accommodates 180 passengers in fully renovated colonial-style train carriages ... The railway recreates the experience of a bygone era in the land once known as British North Borneo. It's like a time capsule transporting passengers along what was once the lifeline for people living here.

Going Places (magazine of Malaysia Airlines) January 2002

Sample commentary plan

Writer's purpose and audience
This is to persuade readers of the attraction of travel on this railway. The audience is the general public and those interested in travel.

Tone
This is persuasive.

Vocabulary
Think about 'head off', 'puffin billy', 'trainheads', 'rickety', 'lunatic fringe', 'fanatical', 'nostalgia' and 'oblivion'.

Figures of speech
Think about 'traveller's check', 'opened up',' paradise', 'devotees', 'time capsule'. Think also about pun, metaphor, simile, hyperbole, idiom and contrast.

Structure
Think about paragraphing.

Sample commentary

The writer's purpose is to give information about the renovated North Borneo Railway and to persuade readers to try it. The tone is persuasive and relatively light-hearted. The pun in the title establishes light-heartedness: 'traveller's check' is both the possible means of paying one's way in travel and the link with the information to follow about the railway.

The attraction of train travel is outlined in the opening paragraph; the metaphor of 'opened up the countryside' makes train travel attractive by suggesting new discoveries or the revelation of something concealed until now. 'Head off' is light-hearted and gives the idea that travel is relaxing and freedom-giving. The mention of Thomas Cook in the second paragraph gives historical accuracy and therefore credibility to train travel as something tried and tested.

The idiom 'puffin billy' in the third paragraph is informal; the informality gives the passage an easy feel to it, a user-friendly approach. Train travel is for everyone. The metaphor 'paradise' to describe the railway in North Borneo makes the countryside through which it passes seem idyllic, the most beautiful place on earth, or even a beauty which transcends earth. The structure of the rest of the paragraph makes it easy to follow the rest of the passage, because the writer outlines the two options for travel on the railway, which then makes it possible to devote a paragraph to one of them. The idiom 'trainheads' must mean those who love train travel; again, the informal tone makes train travel seem accessible to ordinary people, and the newness of the idiom makes train travel seem modern and possibly an attraction for the young, who are the kind of people to invent new language or slang.

In the fourth paragraph the vocabulary 'narrow rickety' is used to describe the train. Normally, these adjectives would not enhance an overall description, but in this case the train is made to seem attractively old-fashioned, as if the privilege of having such a historical experience makes the discomfort of 'narrow' and 'rickety' more of a pleasure than a pain. The 'lunatic fringe, fanatical steam train devotees' adds a note of humour to the passage; 'devotees' raises train travel to an almost religious level which is clearly exaggeration or hyperbole. 'Lunatic fringe' is humorous because it suggests that those who like train travel are in some way mentally deranged. Contrast is established when the writer goes on to describe the other, completely different type of travellers (those with only a passing interest); therefore it can be seen that train travel is for all, and so every reader is included as a possible traveller, adding to the persuasive tone of the passage. The vocabulary captures the history and therefore the credibility of train travel in words such as 'nostalgia' and 'oblivion' with their connotations of long time scales. A simile describing the train as being 'like a time capsule' makes the train seem old-fashioned, by suggesting that a trip on it is not only through this part of Malaysia but back through history to a time pre-dating our own modern trains. The metaphor 'lifeline' comes from the literal idea of throwing a drowning person a rope with which to be pulled ashore; thus, the vital importance of the railway to people's way of life is underpinned.

You will now be given two short passages for comment which do not give you help in organising your response, or an example commentary plan. You will have to do that yourself following the guidelines you were given for passages 1 and 2.

③ On tracks for big day preparation

The passage below describes the writers' attempts at training to run a ten-kilometre race.

Task

Write a commentary in which you explain how the writers of this passage use language to entertain the reader.

Melanie: Hope springs eternal. I read last week about a woman in the London marathon who took up running a year ago and lost six stones [over forty kilos]. So I will persevere, although I haven't lost any weight yet.

My two dogs have, though. They've grown lean and mean with all the exercise they're getting. I don't know what they will do when I stop running, for as soon as I pick up my trainers, they start ululating [howling] with joy and jumping in the air, all four feet at once.

It is possible to chart some more progress. I am now doing three miles a night and feeling as exhausted at the end as I did, a few weeks back, after two miles.

Does anyone else suffer the same problems getting going?

Even with a warm up, the first half mile is dreadful, like trying to start a seized-up engine. It gets much easier in the middle of the run, before fading at the end ...

Fiona: Nine miles. In one day. In one outing, to be precise. I was exhilarated at the achievement, but completely exhausted. And it was all an accident.

Mr Bionic [her husband] had convinced me to try running five miles – a mile more than I've run before. He had the route planned out. (I couldn't get near the map because 'girls are navigationally challenged'.)

[Her husband got the map wrong and they ran nine miles by mistake.] ... my legs felt like lead ... when I found the estimated distance was nine miles, it felt fantastic (well, mentally, anyway).

The (Glasgow) *Herald* 20 April 2002

Sample commentary

The first writer's purpose is to entertain and create humour by her account of the exhausting efforts made and the discrepancy between her efforts and the results achieved. The second writer also portrays her husband in an amusing way. The proverb 'Hope springs eternal' as an opening suggests the eternal optimism of the human spirit, and suggests the possibility of achievement. However, anticlimax follows in the admission that she has not in fact lost any weight. Humour is derived from the discrepancy between the London Marathon woman's remarkable achievement and the writer's complete lack of it, and suggests that the writer is not really doing very much to lose weight, despite her boasts.

The fact that instead of Melanie the dogs have lost weight is also humorous, for two reasons: dogs do not set out to lose weight as humans do and in any case that was not the point of the exercise. 'Lean and mean' is melodious in its rhyme. 'Ululating with joy' is exaggerated, and the picture of them jumping so that all four feet are in the air simultaneously is both exaggeration and a source of humour – again, the dogs are shown as being ultra-fit, in contrast to the writer.

Further humour is derived from the fact that being exhausted counts as 'progress'. The reader is engaged by the question which makes up the short paragraph 4, and a chatty, informal tone is adopted. The simile 'like trying to start a seized-up engine' is effective in that the writer's lack of fitness is compared to an engine which doesn't function properly. 'Seized-up' gives the impression of being jammed; the contrast between the reality of the writer's body and her wish to be fit is humorous.

The structure of the start of Fiona's section is three short non-sentences. The effect of this is again humorous: it emphasises that the author ran nine miles in one day and in one session, though the reader would hardly have expected her to run nine miles over more than one day. The writer makes the most of the distance travelled, which shows how exhausted she must have been. The 'accident' described is also humorous, especially when set against the arrogance of her husband who would not let her 'near the map'. He is shown to be cocky and foolish. Beginning the 'accident' sentence with 'And' further contributes to the conversational tone of the passage. 'Navigationally challenged' is humorous because it is a term made up by the husband in the style of modern, politically correct expressions using the term 'challenged'. The pompous tone of the husband provides a humorous contrast with his actual ineptitude in the matter of the map. Another simile is found to underpin the writer's lack of fitness in 'legs felt like lead' (i.e. heavy). The addition in brackets of 'well, mentally, anyway' is humorous as it introduces a qualification to what has gone before. In other words, she did not feel physically fantastic, or anything like it. She makes the contrast between her physical and mental conditions. The bracketed text is chatty and adds to the overall informal tone of the passage. The vocabulary of the whole passage consists of fairly short, simple words and the sentences are mainly short. All of this makes 'navigationally challenged' stand out and therefore heightens its pretentiousness and that of the husband.

4 Let freedom reign

Four years after his release from prison, where he spent twenty-seven years for his stand against apartheid, Nelson Mandela was elected president in South Africa's first democratic elections. This is a section of his inaugural address.

Task

Comment on the techniques and the language the speaker uses.

Today all of us do, by our presence here, and by our celebrations in other parts of our country and the world, confer glory and hope to newborn liberty.

Out of the experience of an extraordinary human disaster that lasted too long must be born a society of which all humanity will be proud ...

The time for the healing of wounds has come. The moment to bridge the chasms that divide us has come. The time to build is upon us ... We pledge ourselves to liberate all our people from the continuing bondage of poverty, deprivation, suffering, gender and other discrimination ... We commit ourselves to the construction of a complete, just and lasting peace ...

We understand it still that there is no easy road to freedom ... We must therefore act together as a united people, for national reconciliation, for nation building, for the birth of a new world. Let there be justice for all. Let there be peace for all. Let there be work, bread, water and salt for all.

> Never, never and never again shall it be that this beautiful land of ours will again experience the oppression of one by another and suffer the indignity of being the skunk of the world.
>
> Let freedom reign. The sun shall never set on so glorious a human achievement. God bless Africa ...
>
> Nelson Mandela *The Penguin Book of Twentieth Century Speeches*

Sample commentary

The writer's purpose is to draw the people of his country, and of the outside world, into the celebration of his becoming president after the first democratic elections. He draws his audience into his speech by the use and repetition of 'we', 'us' and 'our' rather than 'you' and 'your'. Thus he personalises what he has to say. At no point does he use the singular form 'I'. So this is a matter for all of the people, not just himself. His vocabulary is optimistic, with 'celebrations', 'glory', 'hope' and 'liberty'. Apartheid is dismissed, by contrast, as 'an extraordinary human disaster'.

In paragraph three he uses the metaphors of healing wounds and bridge building to describe the improved future of his country. He uses a list of nouns associated with the evils of the past: 'poverty, deprivation' etc. He employs a repetitive sentence structure (two sentences beginning with 'The time' and two beginning with the unifying 'We'). This repetition causes a build-up of momentum and underpins the skills of the speaker as orator.

A build-up of ideas is also used in the fourth paragraph, as well as a repetitive sentence structure ('Let there be...'). 'Work, bread, water and salt' are basic requirements, and by suggesting that there was a time when these were not available to 'all' he is stressing the injustices of the past.

The repetition of 'never' at the start of the fifth paragraph gives further momentum to the speech. The choice of the word 'skunk' is dramatic, and contrasts with the rhetoric of the rest of the speech. It also heightens South Africa's sense of isolation in the world during the time of apartheid. The short sentence 'Let freedom reign' is also dramatic and encapsulates the mood of the entire speech. Reference to the sun in the penultimate sentence gives their achievement cosmic significance, as does finishing with a prayer asking for God's blessing not just on their country but on the entire continent of Africa.

Exam tip

Before writing your commentary on a passage, organise your response by jotting down ideas about the writer's purpose and audience, and by jotting down, underlining or highlighting features of language and/or punctuation you want to include in your answer.

(7) Directed writing tasks for short passages for comment

In Paper 1 of the examination you will be given three passages for comment, from which you are to choose two. For each passage you may be asked to write a commentary on the writer's use of language and then to complete a directed writing task based on the passage. Alternatively, you may be asked to produce a piece of directed writing related to the passage for comment, and then asked to write a commentary comparing your piece of writing with the original. In unit 8 you will be looking at the second option, but in this unit you will concentrate on the first option, looking closely at directed writing tasks, trying some of your own and matching your attempts against some exemplars of good practice.

The word 'directed' suggests that the task is prescribed in some way. For that reason it is necessary that you read the task instruction carefully before attempting to write. The task may be imaginative or it may allow you to draw on your own experience. It may require you to write in a particular literary form or genre, for example a letter, a newspaper article or a diary. Your piece of writing might be expected to read like a work of fiction or a work of non-fiction, like a short story or novel, or like an advertisement or a biography. The main rule here is that there are no rules about what might be asked of you!

We are now going to take each of the passages for comment we looked at and analysed in the previous unit, and consider directed writing tasks which could accompany them. For the first two tasks you will be given some preparatory notes to get you started, followed by an example essay. For the third and fourth tasks you will be given an example essay only.

1 Shanghai childhood

The first task was to comment on the style and language of the passage, and was dealt with in the last unit. The directed writing task for the passage now follows.

Task

In the style of the original passage, write about a vivid memory (around 120 words) from your own childhood.

Organising your response

Begin by jotting down in note form the features of the original passage which you have already identified and written about. Look back at our starting point in the last unit under 'Writer's purpose' and 'Tone'. Think about the exaggeration, the misunderstanding, the way in which the writer captures the innocence and partial understanding of children.

Sample directed writing

> I sat on the wall beside my house, dangling my legs, and wondering how long it would be before my feet would touch the ground beneath while my bottom was still in contact with the wall. I studied my new, sparkling white sandals. I had been warned to look after them, but to my dismay I noticed a crack in the stiffness of the leather. A huge shadow fell over my feet. It was Elaine, who, like me, was five years old; my heart leaped at the thought of another exciting adventure with her. Would it be the same as yesterday? A walk to the shop at the end of our street? Sure enough, Elaine was clutching a coin, our passport to delicious sweetmeats. Wordlessly, we set off on the long journey, careful not to stand on any cracks on the pavement, which, we had been told by a big boy, would bring Bad Luck. Today, although I am unclear as to what this bad luck might have been, I recall vividly the deep-down sensation of panic in the pit of my stomach at the very concept.

② Traveller's check

The first task was to comment on the style and language of the passage, and was dealt with in the last unit. The directed writing task for the passage now follows.

Task

As a travel writer for a newspaper, you have travelled on the North Borneo Railway and you were unimpressed. Using the information in the passage, write an article for your newspaper (around 120 words) in which you try to dissuade readers from making the journey.

Organising your response

Begin by jotting down in note form the features of the North Borneo Railway which the writer found attractive. Look back at our starting point in the last unit under 'Writer's purpose' and 'Tone'. Examine the vocabulary used, which, although sometimes potentially unattractive, the writer chose for his own persuasive purpose.

Sample directed writing

> Thomas Cook may have been the first travel agent, and a trip to the Lake District may have been exciting in its day, but nowadays perhaps travellers seek a more fulfilling experience than a train journey. With this in mind, I set off on the North Borneo Railway, on the tourist route to Papar. The railway is limited to two trips a week and the track covers only a few hundred kilometres. The rickety line shook me until I felt sick, and as for my fellow passengers! Never had I seen such a motley crew of misfits, approaching this rail journey as if it were some rare mystical experience. Perhaps Malaysia's past should be relegated to the history books instead of being reproduced in railway carriages, like some sort of time warp. Trains may have their attractions for some, but for me, in this day and age, the scope for seeing the world which is presented by air travel is infinitely preferable. I'm sure Thomas Cook would agree!

③ On tracks for big day preparation

The first task was to comment on how the writers use language to entertain the reader, and was dealt with in the last unit. The directed writing task for the passage now follows.

Task

In the style of the original passage, write a similar article (around 120 words) on an attempt you have made to keep fit, lose weight or both.

Sample directed writing

A little optimism goes a long way. I swaggered into the gym every evening, gaining confidence from my new, squeaky clean sports gear – trainers, track suit, the lot. My aim was improved fitness through classes called, scarily, Body Pump.

Why did Anna seem so much quicker at the movements than I did? Why did I keep looking at her? For the first five minutes I wheezed like an old horse. For the last ten minutes, when we lay on mats to 'wind down', I resembled a beached whale – a small, fit one, of course. I didn't sweat, I perspired daintily.

I persevered for eight classes. Eight one-hour classes. Eight hours of non-stop torture. But meaningfully so. Then the bombshell dropped. My coach told me she thought the exercise was too hard for me and that I should move down a level. I was aerobically challenged by her class, she said. Dreadful, arrogant woman! Insufferable fool who didn't understand me! (Not my exercise needs, anyway.)

④ Let freedom reign

The first task was to comment on the techniques and the language the speaker uses. The directed writing task now follows.

Task

You have been asked to make a speech to the other senior students in your school on a subject about which you have strong views. Write the opening of your speech (around 120 words) in the style of the original passage.

Sample directed writing

My fellow students, all of us show by our attendance at this meeting today that we are concerned about the planet we live on, a planet rich in beauty and resources, but a planet where, alas, these resources are not shared equally. The time has come to commit ourselves to raising awareness in our school of the inequalities in our world. The time has come to educate and inform through posters and seminars. The time has come for the formation of a One World group in the school. Our sisters and brothers in other parts of the world need to know that we stand alongside them and are able to assist them. Through our fund raising, through our awareness raising, through our efforts, let us make our own contribution, however small, on a global scale, to food for all, to water for all, to employment for all, to justice for all. Let us start today.

Don't worry if you are unsure of the layout or rules for a particular genre asked for in a directed writing task (e.g. newspaper article, speech, letter, script, diary). You will be given guidance on this in unit 17.

Exam tip

Before beginning your directed writing task, organise your response by jotting down, underlining or highlighting in the original passage for comment the features of language and structure which you wish to include in your own writing.

8 Directed writing before commentary: short passage

Although the examination question often asks you to write your commentary on the passage before going on to produce your piece of directed writing, sometimes the tasks are given in reverse order. We will now look at such an example, using a short passage.

Task

Read the advertisement below, which promotes short breaks in Scotland.

a In the style of the passage, write another advertisement (around 120 words) which tries to persuade the reader to tour a region or area of your choice.

b Write a commentary comparing your style and use of language with those of the original advertisement.

Scotland is a feast for all your senses

It's time to blow the cobwebs away. Time to make some unforgettable memories. Yes, it's time for a Short Break in Scotland. Now is the time to make it happen, while we're still relatively uncrowded and the days are just made for long walks along empty beaches. Or maybe you fancy exploring your favourite Scottish city – wining and dining, shopping and visiting galleries. How about bagging a Munro you haven't climbed before? Do it. Take a Short Break at home here in Scotland soon!

You know Scotland is special. The scenery looks sensational. People travel from all over the world to enjoy [Scotland] – so get out and enjoy it all! You can feel history in the landscape. And a change of air smells so refreshing after the long winter months.

... Cast your cares aside. Leave your everyday frame of mind in the everyday world and get out and enjoy all the good things Scotland has to offer. You deserve a treat – and maybe you have friends or family who do, too! Stay in a big city hotel and take in a show or a concert. Or retreat to a little hideaway village and fill your days with peace and quiet ... Visit an island you could almost call your own. Keep your eyes peeled for eagles and otters – you never know what you'll see in our great outdoors.

Do it soon. You can pick up some great deals just now ... Before you know it you could be discovering somewhere different and making some new friends and memories for yourself. Apply for your brochure today and we'll enter you into our prize draw. You could win a trip here as our guest! Whenever you take a break in Scotland you can bet it will be sensational in every way!

Munro a mountain over 3,000 feet in height

Scottish Tourist Board, promotional leaflet

Organising your response

The first part of the task is to write an advertisement in the style of the original. It would therefore be sensible to examine the style of the original. Jot down the key features of style you notice.

Sample directed writing plan

Tone

This is persuasive throughout. The writer has one intention, and that is to encourage people to take a holiday, even a short one, in Scotland. The tone is conversational in places, for example 'Yes' and 'You know Scotland is special'.

Sentence structure

The passage is full of short sentences. The aim of these is to hit home, to jolt the reader into paying attention to what the writer has to say. The punctuation is relatively informal, with non-sentences and exclamations throughout the passage. The writer uses imperatives, or commands, for example 'Do it' and 'Cast your cares aside'.

Passage structure

The writer adopts several persuasive strategies. The attractions of Scotland, both countryside and city, are discussed. Appeal is made to the reader's need for rest. The reader is told that the break is deserved, thus appealing to selfishness or a desire to think about oneself. The writer finally draws the reader in by saying that monetary gain is possible if a response is made to the advertisement. Repetition of 'Scotland' is used throughout.

So what have you done so far? You have established the key features of style of this particular piece of writing, and thus you have isolated the features of style which you wish to copy in your own piece of writing. The next task is to decide which part of the world you want to choose for your writing. Remember that you have to write only around 120 words.

Sample directed writing

Get away from it all. You know it makes sense. And what better place than Singapore? Singapore. Where East meets West. Enjoy a trip to Sentosa Island, or a shopping spree on Orchard Road, Asia's favourite shopper's paradise. Shop till you drop! Sample cuisine from all over the world at riverside restaurants in Singapore or try something more traditional at one of our hawker stalls. If the natural world is your thing, watch the lions and elephants on the delightful Night Safari in Singapore. You know you deserve it. What better way to grab some quality time with your family? Singapore boasts hundreds of hotels to suit all pockets, and with this month's special offers there has never been a better time to see this fabulous country! See you there!

Now let us consider the second part of this particular examination question, which is: Write a commentary comparing your style and use of language with those of the original advertisement.

Organising your response

Follow the rules we established in unit 6 where you wrote a commentary before a piece of directed writing. The fact that the order has been reversed here should have no effect on the general principles laid down. Think of the key terms you have learned to describe language and write them down. Take each of these in turn and try to match them first to the original passage and then to your piece of directed writing.

Sample commentary plan

Writer's purpose
This is to persuade and to sell.
Tone
This is conversational and informal.
Vocabulary
Think about 'it's time', 'you know', 'cast your cares aside', 'retreat', 'do it soon', 'apply for your brochure'. And from your own piece of writing: 'get away', 'you know it makes sense', 'your thing', 'grab', 'fabulous'.
Figures of speech
Think about 'blow the cobwebs away', 'bagging a Munro', 'your eyes peeled'. And from your own piece of writing: 'paradise', 'suit all pockets'.
Structure
Think about short sentences and their effectiveness, and the use of repetition.

Sample commentary

Each advertisement is persuasive in tone and its purpose is to convince its reader of the merits of a holiday in the specified location. Each has a conversational tone designed to draw the reader into the confidence of the writer. Each uses imperatives ('Do it' in the advert for Scotland and 'Get away from it all' in the one for Singapore). Each uses short sentences ('You know Scotland is special' in the original and 'You know it makes sense' in my own). Short sentences arrest the attention of the reader and have an immediacy.

Several persuasive strategies are used in each. They give details of the varied attractions of their location, stressing that there is something for everyone (countryside, city, villages in the original, and shopping, animal life and restaurants in mine). Each advertisement stresses that its holiday location is affordable ('great deals' in the advert for Scotland and 'suit all pockets' in the one for Singapore). Each passage stresses the need for rest for its readers ('Leave your everyday frame of mind' in the advert for Scotland and 'Get away from it all' in the advert for Singapore). Each passage appeals to the idea that their readers deserve what they have to offer, and this personal approach links reader to writer. Each uses informal metaphors ('blow the cobwebs away' and 'Keep your eyes peeled' in the original and 'paradise' and 'suit all pockets' in my own). Each uses repetition of the location, Scotland and Singapore.

Exam tip

When the directed writing task comes before the commentary question, organise your response in exactly the same way as you would if you were asked to write the commentary first.

⑨ Longer passages for comment

We have already established that in the examination you will be given three passages, from which you are to choose two and write a commentary. In unit 6 we looked at four passages of around 300 words in order to work out some general principles for writing a commentary. Now is the time to think about longer passages.

① Keeping your cool

The writer is a British journalist living in New York. He describes the problems of high summer temperatures in New York, and recalls an interview with a politician in the heat of New Delhi.

Task

Write a commentary in which you show how the writer uses language to entertain his audience.

'Hot here,' he says, 'how about you?'

'Well, much the same,' I say.

'Do you get out much?'

'No,' I say, 'I'm under house arrest.'

'What?' in the ferocious hissing tones of a Victorian villain – and it takes some ferocity to hiss the word 'what'.

One of the problems, I find, of transatlantic telephone calls is that of picking up the emotional tone of the speaker. Don't try humour, don't try irony.

'Under house arrest? I don't understand.'

'Well,' I said, 'I'm confined here to my air-conditioned cell.'

'Good lord,' he said, 'on whose orders?'

'The doctor.' I said.

In other words this has been a hideous week in which, from the rock-bound coast of Maine to the tip of the Florida Keys, it has been over 100 degrees in, if you can find it, the shade.

A huge crew of city workers, recruited from the hospitals, the sanitation department, firemen and so on, have been cruising the poorer sections to help old people install fans, renovate air conditioners, get new ones – the problem there was that by mid-week the suppliers of even the most modest air conditioners cried: 'Hold, enough' – for the first time they could remember, their inventories were exhausted.

Now, of course, I'm talking about New York City only. The same stories can be told in a hundred cities across this burning land. I looked at a weather map ... the colour kind ... in which parts of the country below freezing were white, up to 50 degrees green, over 70 yellow, over 80 orange, over 90 scarlet.

Well, any day this week you could look at the whole map of the United States, about three quarters was scarlet, most of the rest orange. There was a green patch up in Alaska. In fact I'll break down and simply say that this continent has, except for September and October, for the most part the most hideous climate – bone-crushing cold winters and rancid summers. Goodbye!

But this experience of house arrest – may I just throw in for any tabloid reporter who might have just tuned in – it's a joke, son. The way I live now, which for the past ten days has been confined, as I said, to my air-conditioned study, reminds me vividly of when I sat down to write about a similar scene 36 years ago in a small study – much like mine – cool and serene at 70 degrees while only ten paces outside it was 107 degrees.

This was in New Delhi in 1963 ... I was sitting in the study of an Indian politician, alone ... waiting to interview him ... the only sound the ticking of the clock. The only moving sight the second hand slowly inching round and up to 7 pm. At which precise moment entered my host.

This was meant as a courtesy visit of a roving journalist to a distinguished statesman. I'd been told, by one of his aides ... 'The minister will, 20 minutes into the meeting, offer you a lemonade. Please accept. About 15 minutes later he will offer you a cigarette. It will be time to say: 'Thank you, prime minister, I'm afraid I have to go.'

Well the script was followed almost to the last minute. But just before the offer of the poisonous cigarette the host remarked on the blessings of air conditioning and mentioned it had come very late to India.

'We used to have,' he said and he made a whirling motion in mid-air.

'Same in the United States,' I said until, I suppose, the late 1950s when air conditioning took over in public buildings, theatres, restaurants and shops and so on. Aeroplane propeller fans were the thing, on the ceiling.

Well one little recollection led to another. [It was two hours before the author finally left].

BBC *Letter from America* 14 July 1999

Sample commentary

The passage opens on an informal note, caused by the ellipsis ('Hot here' not 'It's hot here'), and informality is often linked to entertainment. The reader is entertained by the misunderstanding described in the opening dialogue. The writer's London friend does not know that he is joking with him and using a pun in 'house arrest'. He thinks his friend has been in trouble with the police. There is further humour in the suggestion that the word 'what' can be hissed when it cannot. The writer is also humorous when he suggests that his friend is unable to pick up his joking nuances because of the difficulties of transatlantic phone calls. He realises that he has made an error in trying to be funny: 'Don't try humour, don't try irony.' There is also humour in the contrast between the friend's idea of 'hot' in London and the heat experienced by the writer. The use of dialogue is chatty and informal, and appropriate in a passage intended to entertain.

The chatty tone continues in paragraph two at 'if you can find it' to describe the shade. The reader is entertained by the frantic purchasing of air conditioning to the point where nothing is left to buy: even cheap and inferior systems have been bought.

The conversational tone continues in the paragraph which starts 'Now', which engages the reader, as does the 'Well' in the next paragraph. The concession that there was a 'green patch' might be of comfort, but it is lessened by 'up in Alaska', which creates an anti-climax which is entertaining. The valedictory 'Goodbye!' at the end of the paragraph makes it sound as if the writer is beating a hasty retreat from the climate of the United States, which is entertaining. The metaphor 'bone-crushing' underlines the coldness of the winters in the United States.

The writer returns to his joke about 'house arrest' at the start of the next paragraph and amuses the reader with the suggestion of reporters looking for scandal to write about, and of the scandal link with tabloid newspapers. He goes on to use flashback for the second part of his article. The link which leads to the flashback is the topic of oppressive heat and air conditioning, and the common setting of a study. The description of the clock in the politician's study is atmospheric: the silence which makes the clock so audible, and the apparent slow passing of time, are emphasised by the metaphor 'inching round'.

The fact that the politician conducts all interviews according to a formula is entertaining. The writer has been told what to expect and all details are synchronised. The 'poisonous' cigarette is amusing; it is ostensibly being offered as a gesture of hospitality and yet the opposite is true – it is a signal to leave. The forthcoming interview is described as a 'script', showing that it will not be an interview at all in the real sense of the word, but rather a formality. The direct speech in this paragraph adds an informal note.

The reader is entertained by the fact that the 'script' does not go according to plan. The unscripted topic of air conditioning causes a change of direction. The use of miming instead of language is entertaining – the politician makes a 'whirling motion in mid-air'. Aeroplane propeller fans being 'the thing' is informal, like a fashion accessory. The twist that the scripted and timed interview overruns by two hours is entertaining, and the passage is nicely rounded off in that the overrun is caused by the politician's interest in air conditioning.

Estha

As a young boy, Estha has had a traumatic experience which has left him withdrawn and troubled.

Task

Show how the writer uses language to describe Estha's difficulties and to engage the sympathy of the reader.

Estha had always been a quiet child, so no one could pinpoint with any degree of accuracy exactly when (the year, if not the month or day) he had stopped talking. Stopped talking altogether, that is. The fact is that there wasn't an 'exactly when'. It had been a gradual winding down and closing shop. A barely noticeable quietening. As though he had simply run out of conversation and had nothing left to say. Yet Estha's silence was never awkward. Never intrusive. Never noisy. It wasn't an accusing, protesting silence as much as a sort of dormancy ... the psychological equivalent of what lung fish do to get themselves through the dry season, except that in Estha's case the dry season looked as though it would last for ever.

Over time he had acquired the ability to blend into the background of wherever he was – into bookshelves, gardens, curtains, doorways, streets – to appear inanimate, almost invisible to the untrained eye. It usually took strangers a while to notice him even when they were in the same room with him. It took them even longer to notice that he never spoke. Some never noticed at all ...

Estha finished school with mediocre results, but refused to go to college. Instead, much to the initial embarrassment of his father and stepmother, he began to do the housework. As though in his own way he was trying to earn his keep. He did the sweeping ... and all the laundry. He learned to cook and shop for vegetables. Vendors in the bazaar, sitting behind pyramids of oiled, shining vegetables, grew to recognise him and would attend to him amidst the clamouring of their other customers. They gave him rusted cans in which to put the vegetables he picked. He never bargained. They never cheated him. When the vegetables had been weighed and paid for, they would transfer them to his red, plastic shopping basket (onions at the bottom ... tomatoes on the top) and always a sprig of coriander and fistful of green chillies for free. Estha carried them home in the crowded tram. A quiet bubble floating on a sea of noise.

Once the quietness arrived, it stayed and spread in Estha. It reached out of his head and enfolded him in its swampy arms. It rocked him to the rhythm of an ancient, foetal heartbeat. It sent its stealthy, suckered tentacles inching along the insides of his skull, hoovering the knolls and dells of his memory, dislodging old sentences, whisking them off the tip of his tongue. It stripped his thoughts of the words that described them and left them pared and naked. Unspeakable. Numb. Slowly, over the years, Estha withdrew from the world. He grew accustomed to the uneasy octopus that lived inside him and squirted its inky tranquilliser on his past.

When Khubchand, Estha's beloved, blind, bald, incontinent seventeen-year-old mongrel decided to stage a miserable, long-drawn-out death, Estha nursed him through his final ordeal as though his own life somehow depended on it.

After Khubchand died, Estha started his walking. He walked for hours on end. Initially he patrolled only the neighbourhood, but gradually went further and further afield.

People got used to seeing him on the road. A well-dressed man with a quiet walk. His face grew dark and outdoorsy. Rugged. Wrinkled by the sun. He began to look wiser than he really was. Like a fisherman in a city. With sea-secrets in him.

... Estha walked all over Ayemenem ... Some days he walked along the banks of the river ... Other days he walked down the road. Past the new, freshly baked, iced ... houses built by nurses ... and bank clerks who worked hard and unhappily in faraway places. Past the resentful older houses tinged green with envy, cowering in their private driveways among their private rubber trees.

Arundhati Roy The God of Small Things

Sample commentary

Immediate sympathy is evoked for Estha because no one could remember even the year that he stopped talking. This seems incredible to the reader. 'No one' is vague and suggests no particular adults, in particular parents, were looking after him. The non-sentence 'stopped talking altogether' shows that he had hardly ever spoken even before he became silent. The metaphors 'winding down' and 'closing shop' suggest, firstly, a mechanical clock in need of attention and, secondly, a business shutting for the night. Each metaphor has a finality which suggests a stopping in Estha. The repetition of 'never' at 'never awkward. Never intrusive. Never noisy' emphasises his silence, his blending into the background, an effect that is also created by the short non-sentences which, barely communicative themselves, are something like Estha. The metaphor of the 'dry season' is effective to describe Estha's silence, as later the river banks are mentioned as being one of Estha's walking places.

The reader sympathises with Estha in the second paragraph when he is described as being of such little importance that he was 'almost invisible to the untrained eye'. This makes him seem like a rare biological or botanical creature, less than a human being. The fact the some people failed to notice him at all adds to our sympathy for him.

Estha's 'mediocre' exam results create sympathy, as does his being an outsider who likes to do work stereotypically done by the opposite sex. Obviously he has qualities which evoke sympathy in others, for example the bazaar vendors, and this in turn evokes the reader's sympathy. He is an outsider who stands apart from other customers; he doesn't bargain. In turn he has an innocence or simplicity which causes the vendors to look after him, to treat him with a tenderness not reserved for others (the gifts of coriander and chillies), which transmits itself to the reader. The fact that Estha is withdrawn from society is shown in the metaphor 'quiet bubble floating on a sea of noise'. A bubble, like Estha, is fragile, and a sea is vast, and so the noise on the tram is shown in contrast to Estha's quietness; too much noise might destroy him, unless he is able to keep detached from it.

Many metaphors are used in the next paragraph to describe Estha's silence. It is something growing inside his head which embraces him like a friend or lover, thus giving him comfort. However, 'swampy' introduces a sinister connotation, and is linked to the idea of the river already mentioned. The silence also cradles him like a baby; thus the security which he finds in silence is emphasised. It becomes an octopus-like creature with 'tentacles' which 'inch' and are 'stealthy', and so again there is a sinister overtone, as if the silence will eventually be harmful to Estha. The metaphor of the vacuum cleaner removing memories from Estha suggests that these memories are debris and therefore undesirable or even harmful. Personification is also used in this paragraph. Silence is personified in 'sent', 'dislodging', 'whisking' and 'stripped', making it seem that Estha is defenceless against the power of silence. The single-word sentences 'Unspeakable' and 'Numb' emphasise this. The metaphor of the octopus is powerful. It also represents Estha's silence, which stretches around his mind as an octopus might stretch its tentacles; the 'inky tranquilliser' of silence helps him to forget the past in the same way as an octopus emits a dark liquid to confuse and scare away its assailants.

The reference to Estha's unfortunate dog in the next paragraph heightens our sympathy for Estha; to lose this ally seems a cruel blow to someone already in distress himself, and we are sympathetic to someone who would nurse a sick animal, as Estha does. The picture of Estha as the lone walker, without companionship, gains the reader's sympathy. The simile of the fisherman with secrets makes Estha seem like an outsider in his society, as a fisherman would be in a city.

The final paragraph describes the houses Estha sees on his walks. The houses of 'nurses ... and bank clerks' are described metaphorically as if they were fancy cakes, which shows how attractive and ornate they are. The 'older' houses are personified as being 'green with envy' of the other houses and 'cowering'. Thus the contrast in the areas walked through by Estha makes us sympathise with him as it stresses how isolated he is from every social grouping and their petty material concerns.

3 Friendship

The writer discusses the nature of true friendship.

Comment on the writer's use and style of language.

I've just had an old friend to stay and I feel as if I've had the emotional equivalent of a break at a luxury health spa! Alison and I go back a long way. As children, we joined the local church choir together, sharing the excitement of being allowed to stay up late to sing at Midnight Mass. We went for walks through the countryside where we lived, talking about the strange new things that were happening in our lives ... We faced the tough transition from primary to secondary school, and shared the ups and downs of being teenagers. In short, we grew up together.

During her visit we worked out that it had been more that 30 years since we had last spent any real time together ... without the distractions of husbands, children or other friends. We were horrified. Where had the years gone? And then we hugged, and crammed that lost time into two days.

So what did Alison's visit do for me? If I had to sum it up I would say that she made me feel complete, as though I were gathering up all the bits of me, past and present, that have made me into the person I am now. There's something infinitely comforting about being with someone who remembers you in an Aertex shirt and navy gym knickers. And it was the same for her. We validated each other in a way that perhaps only friends – real friends – can.

The feeling stayed with me for several days and it made me look at my friendships in a new light. What is it that marks out a 'special' friend? What separates the many acquaintances we make at work, say, or on the school run, from the lasting and life-affirming relationships that nourish the soul?

... Dr Valerie – a psychologist – who has made a particular study of friendship, explains why it is that friends increase our feeling of well-being. 'One of the central features of a good friendship is that your self image is enhanced', she says. 'If you regard your friends as good and successful people whom you respect, and who value you, it provides a great boost to your self-esteem. It's not articulated, but you feel a sort of glow.' Exactly!

... That brings me to the ultimate test – my favourite definition of a true friend is someone you can call on at three o'clock in the morning. It also embodies one of the cardinal qualities of friendship: trust. If you ring someone in the middle of the night it probably means you're in trouble or despair. You need to be able to trust that person not only with your burden but with the imposition itself. It's a good exercise: run through your friends in your mind and see how many you could call at a very unsocial hour.

If you find that you can count the answer on the fingers of one hand, that's a good sign! Between two and five friends is about right – any more than that and you're spreading yourself too thin.

... Many friendships end up having a bit of guilt attached to them (have you ever tried to avoid someone when you're out shopping because you know you haven't phoned them for weeks?). But maybe we need to look at the source of that guilt. If a friend is far from our mind, perhaps it isn't just because our lives are frantic – maybe that friendship has run its course. Long-standing friendships can become a habit. What we once had in common with someone may no longer be important because we have moved on. I admit to doing an occasional 'spring clean' of my friends ... Life's too short to waste on third-division friends.

Health and Beauty (Boots magazine) Spring 2002

Sample commentary

The passage is reflective and confidential in tone. The writer relates her own personal experience and draws the reader into her reflections. The opening sentence is conversational in its use of the exclamation mark, which establishes informality and a kind of camaraderie between writer and reader. The rest of the first paragraph describes some of the key memories of childhood and this shows old links between the writer and her friend. The final sentence of the paragraph sums up the memories as growing up. 'In short' shows that it is a summary, and it is appropriate that this summary sentence in itself should be short. It has a conclusive tone.

In the second paragraph 'horrified' is exaggeration or hyperbole; they could not have felt real horror at the discovery of such a relatively inconsequential fact, but the use of the word emphasises their desire to get to know each other again on a more personal level. The paragraph's rhetorical question adds validity to the way the writer feels about the fact that it has been a long time since she spent time with her friend. The next sentence is short. It makes an emphatic bridge between the section of the passage about the writer's past and the section to come about her present time spent with her friend.

The third paragraph begins with a topic sentence in the form of a question. This invites an answer, which the writer then details in the remainder of the paragraph. The metaphor of 'gathering up all the bits of me' is effective as it suggests a coming together of memories, thoughts and ideas about herself which make her feel good. It has a harvesting feel to it. The sentence beginning with 'And' is informal and therefore pulls the reader into the writer's confidence. The dashes around 'real friends' remind the reader that it is the nature of true friendship which concerns the writer, not the idea of mere acquaintance.

The writer moves on in the fourth paragraph to reflect on the nature of true friendship. She asks two questions. This time they are not rhetorical questions but questions which require an answer which will be very difficult to find. The reader is enabled by these questions to enter into the thought processes of the writer, to share her deep desire to find an answer to these questions and therefore to be reflective him/herself. The expression 'nourish the soul' is an emphatic one which shows how important the writer feels friendship can be.

The writer continues by validating her own personal opinions with the professional opinion of a psychologist. Thus her own feelings are given weight which they would otherwise not have had. The psychologist is quoted, which gives the passage at this point a mixture of formal professional validation and informal conversational tone. The last word of the paragraph is a single sentence exclamation – 'Exactly!' – which shows in a friendly but emphatic way that the writer knows that what she said is true.

Beginning a sentence with 'That brings me to' is informal and conversational which makes an easy, gliding transition from one point to the next. The writer is probably at her most serious in this and the next paragraph in that she is discussing issues such as trust and despair. She is also making some serious points about true friendship. And yet she keeps an informality about this by using colloquial language such as 'count the answer on the fingers of one hand' and 'spreading yourself too thin', an informal metaphor linked to spreading butter on bread or something of that nature.

The final paragraph deals with friendships coming to an end. The parenthesis 'have you ever tried to avoid someone...' is an informally added reflection, designed to pull the reader in by asking him/her to draw on his/her own experience and reflect on it. The use of the first person 'we' also draws the reader into the passage, particularly as it is extended in phrases such as 'maybe we need to look at' and 'far from our mind' into the next section of the paragraph. The metaphor 'spring clean', suggesting discarding old friendships in the way we would discard old clothes, is informal. Similarly, 'third division' is an informal metaphor drawn from the world of sport.

Exam tip

Be alert to the rubric, that is the wording of the task. Organise your response to longer passages in exactly the same way as you would your response to shorter, more manageable passages for comment.

(10) Directed writing tasks for longer passages for comment

You will be well aware by now of the relationship between passages for comment and directed writing. In this unit we will go back to the longer passages dealt with in unit 9 and work on the directed writing tasks which accompany them.

1 Keeping your cool

The first task was to write a commentary in which you showed how the writer uses language to entertain his audience. The directed writing task now follows.

Task

You have been kept indoors recently because of extremely hot weather conditions. Write a letter (about 120 words) to a friend complaining about how unhappy you are. Base your letter closely on the original passage.

Sample directed writing

> New York
> 3 July 2003
>
> Dear Gerry
>
> Help! I'm imprisoned in my own home! No, I haven't robbed a bank. It's the heat here. Be thankful you live in the relative cool of England, where it doesn't hit 100 degrees day after day after day, which is the situation in New York at the moment. The good news for the air-conditioning salesmen is that they're in big demand; the bad news is that they've now run out of systems to sell. And it's not just New York. I used to think those coloured maps were silly – you know the ones with green for cool, orange for hot, red for murderous. Well, at the moment most of the country is bright red! Lucky green Alaska! If your dad glances at this letter – don't worry Dad, I'm not really in jail, just a bit cooped up. Even an aeroplane propeller fan on the ceiling, as in way back in the 50s, would be no bad thing!
>
> I'll be in touch,
> Julia

② Estha

The first task was to show how the writer uses language to describe Estha's difficulties and to engage the sympathy of the reader. The directed writing task now follows.

> ### Task
>
> In the style of the original passage, continue the story (around 120 words).

Sample directed writing

> The people in the houses knew better than to talk to Estha. For some, fear prompted them to avert their look, to purse tight their lips, at the sight of him. Invisible people. Ghosts. For others it was even easier. They hadn't seen him at all. Propriety, good taste, social necessity empowered them to look through Estha. He became part of the riverbank. Part of the decor of the wedding cake houses with their twin tiers of white rooms. Sugar houses. Invisible Estha. And then there were the people who sensed Estha's otherness, that he carried a knowledge which they would never share. His silence was deafening to them. It smelled of foreboding and suffering. It spoke to them of a life which both fascinated and repelled them.

Friendship

The first task was to write a commentary on the writer's style and use of language. The directed writing task now follows.

Task

In the style of the original passage, write an account (about 120 words) of time spent with a special friend.

Sample directed writing

I spent the day with an old friend last week and I feel really refreshed! Alexandra and I as a team have a long history. We made our shy introductions on our first day at primary school and since then we've shared many high – and low – points in our respective lives. We joined the local youth club together, we walked and talked and went shopping together. We discussed each other's boyfriends. In a nutshell, we grew up together. So, why do I feel refreshed? Because my day with Alexandra restored my well-being, my happiness, my sanity. It made me reflect on the nature of real friendship – having someone who values you for what you are. Just that! Acquaintances can come and go – and should – but real friends stand the test of time.

Exam tip

Remember that in directed writing you are being asked to write only around 120 words, so use your words wisely by organising your response in the ways already outlined.

11 Directed writing before commentary: longer passage

In unit 8 we looked at a question in which you were asked to produce a piece of directed writing before going on to write a commentary comparing your style and use of language with those of the original passage. The passage around which the tasks were based was a short one. We will now look at a longer passage, of around the length you will find in your examination. As in unit 8, the directed writing task comes before the commentary task.

Task

Read the passage below, in which the writer describes the London Marathon.

a Imagine that you are one of the 'fun' runners described in the passage. In the style of the passage, write an account (around 120 words) of your own marathon run.

b Write a commentary comparing your style and use of language with those of the original.

If you read this piece before April 14, then spare a thought for the thousands of soft-headed fools who have been spending the last three months – or more – dragging themselves into sweaty old running kit and out on to the pavements of Mother Britain. Never mind the conditions, be they sleet, snow, rain or wind, they will be out there, desperately preparing for the race of their lives and the chance to raise some much-needed cash for hundreds of different charities.

To want to run the marathon is, without doubt, a form of clinical madness. The doctors might not agree but most of them are batty anyway. Agreed, there are a few people in the world, most of them wafer light Africans or southern Europeans, whose build enables them to motor across the tarmac treadmills at a disturbingly fast rate but most of those who plod around Peckham Rye on a Saturday morning do so with the goal of simply trying to finish ...

The top guys have other things on their mind like world records and bumper booty. The men's world record for the 26 miles and 385 yards of road is two hours, five minutes and 42 seconds – that is a pace of around 13 miles an hour or one mile every four minutes and 40 seconds.

One mile every four minutes and 40 seconds. Think about it. We still talk in hushed tones of breaking the four-minute mile – and Roger Bannister only had to run one. If you still cannot get a grip on this pace then do as one of my colleagues did recently and try it in the privacy of your own gym. Bumbling away on the treadmill, he pushed the pace rate up to 13 mph. For a couple of seconds he powered like an Olympian. Then he went flying off the back of the treadmill and collided with a rather attractive young lady who was minding her own business on one of the bikes.

Of course, most of this year's 32,000 runners will not be running that pace. Most won't even be running half that pace. But for each of them, the race is just as important as it is for the elite runners. Talking before the event last year, Derartu Tulu, the

Ethiopian runner who won the women's race, spoke passionately about the atmosphere of the London Marathon and in almost awed tones about the 'fun' runners – as ridiculous a phrase as you can find for the masses whose every step is shod in pain.

'We are not the real champions of this race,' she insisted. 'They are. We get paid to do this and we get to train thoroughly and professionally. But these people do it because they want to achieve something ... And they raise a lot of money for charities across the world. Everyone who runs this race is a champion.'

As routes go it is also one of the most interesting in the world ... London uses the event to parade a plethora of tourist attractions ... Tower Bridge remains a beacon of the promised land. Reach here ... and there are just four miles to go ... By the time the runners reach the Houses of Parliament ... they have just a mile to go. A dog-leg right turn in front of Buckingham Palace is the cue to unleash that astonishing sprint finish which lifts our man to 14,786th overall.

So, like I say, if you are reading this before April 14, spare a thought for the lonely runner pounding his beat. But, if you are reading this after the race, then you can keep your sympathy. The hard work will have been done and everyone who has crossed the finishing line ... will not just have earned membership of a special club but they will have earned the right to be just a little bit smug. Let them enjoy it.

Skylines (British Airways magazine) April 2002

Sample directed writing

My best friend told me I was mad even to consider running the London Marathon, but, as he is a doctor, I reckoned he had no place to comment, being a member of a mad profession himself. For months I wore out the pavements around my home trying to forget that my build was not exactly slim or athletic. Not for me the lure of fame or fortune; I had committed myself to this to raise money for Cancer Research. 26 miles and 385 yards: don't even think about it, I told myself, as I sweated on the treadmill in my local gym. 26 miles and 385 yards! I tried – unsuccessfully – to think of it as fun, but that was stretching my imagination a bit too far; how could all that pain be described by anyone in their right mind as 'fun'? Still, now that it's all over, I do feel just that little bit superior – and what a great tour of London!

Now let us consider the second part of this particular examination question, i.e. 'Write a commentary comparing your style and use of language with those of the original.'

Sample commentary

The original passage contrasts the 'fun' runners who run to raise money for charity or simply for satisfaction with the professionals who want to break records or win prize money. The 'fun' runners are described as being mentally deficient in some way to want to do this ('soft-headed', 'clinical madness'), and yet the tone is affectionate towards them, so that they become the real heroes. The professionals want 'bumper booty'; this alliteration makes the runners sound greedy and grasping. They are also described rather dismissively as 'guys'. My passage picks up the madness idea, which is dismissed when the doctor friend's credibility is also dismissed; the credibility of the medical profession has already been dismissed in the original passage.

The original passage talks of 'wafer light Africans or southern Europeans'. This implied contrast suggests that the writer is not in the best of physical condition and establishes a humorous tone. Mine tries to do the same by disparaging the runner's build; it also says that the runner 'wore out the pavements', which is a humorous exaggeration. Both pieces of writing spell out the exact length of the marathon, down to the number of yards, and thus the difficulty of such a long run is stressed. The original deals humorously with the 'fun' runner training in the gym, 'bumbling away' and causing an accident. My passage has the runner sweating on the treadmill.

There is a conversational note in the original passage when an interview with a top runner, Derartu Tulu, is recorded. The writer emphasises the physical pain of marathon running in 'every step is shod in pain'. This idea is picked up in my passage in the rhetorical question starting 'how could all that pain...'. The real status of the 'fun' runners is emphasised by Derartu Tulu when she insists that they are the 'real champions'. The passage uses the metaphor of the 'promised land', thus linking the finishing line in the marathon with the biblical idea of something really desired but still out of reach. My passage refers to the 'tour' of London; the exclamation suggests that the route followed is both extensive and interesting.

The original passage uses irony in the penultimate paragraph when the writer describes the 'astonishing sprint finish' that is unlikely from the exhausted participant. That all of this effort should put the runner '14,786th overall' is humorous; why would it be an achievement to end up in such a position, and why would anyone be counting positions at that late stage? My passage picks up the answer to these questions: it is the personal satisfaction of completing the run at all which is rewarding, making the runner feel 'smug' in the original and 'superior' in my own.

Exam tip

Remember that whether the examination question is commentary followed by directed writing or vice versa, the importance and method of organising your response remain the same.

(12) Paper 1 exam practice

1 Dancing classes

The extract below comes from an autobiography. The writer recalls childhood experiences which were stressful to her.

Exam task

a Comment on how the writer uses language to create mood and to entertain in the extract.

b In the style of the extract, write about a stressful childhood experience you remember (around 120 words).

Dancing class was the worst of the social events which I dreaded as a child. It was worse than Parties ... It was the indignity of it that I minded so much, not only the terrible waste of time, or the dressing-up, bad though that was. In the abstract, so to speak, I thought my white frock and pink sash extremely beautiful; but *not on me*. When I wore them I felt a fool, and I went on feeling a fool all the time I had them on. I knew I was fat and clumsy and plain, and the white frock made it worse. And, on top of that, the fiendish Dancing Woman wanted me to hop, and wave my arms about, and stick out my legs, and do idiotic things with skipping ropes and castanets, in public. Degrading antics. I always felt exactly like a lion at a circus, when he is made to ride a bicycle with a pink ribbon round his neck; and I resented it exceedingly.

Strangely enough many of the other children seemed to like the class; and even my cousins, whom I admired more than anyone else in the world, didn't mind it much ... But I felt a shame for them which they didn't feel for themselves. Sometimes one of the best dancers, generally Dolly, would be called out to do a star turn in front of the class; and when she had finished, Miss Ratcliffe's voice would rise in a long crescendo scream, with a drop at the end, as she called:

NOW CHILDREN ALL TOGETHAR

It was then that I hated her worst of all; and I stood there wishing death and ... torture on the poor lady.

So, in revenge, I did it all as badly as possible; kicked the heels of the child in front of me when we were marching; and toppled over sideways when we were kneeling on one knee and supposed to be making graceful semicircles with our arms. But when we came to the polka or barn dance, I used to relieve my feelings by choosing a congenial partner and getting round the room as fast as we possibly could. Then we would be sent out of the room for 'racing'; but I liked that. Or I would divert myself by squabbling with one of the boys who disgraced his manly sex by wearing yellow plush [velvet] trousers and girl's shoes. The lynx-eyed mothers and nurses sat around the room, with shawls on their laps and rivalry in their hearts, while the jangly piano unceasingly churned out jiggetty tunes. Last indignity of all, fuzzy, tickly, Shetland shawls were put over our mouths, so that we should not catch cold when we went home through the Cambridge fog; and the wool got full of little drops of water from our breath.

Gwen Raverat *A Cambridge Childhood*

② A modern constitution

Tony Blair became the leader of the British Labour Party in 1994 and set about speeding up the modernisation of the party. The following extract is taken from his first speech as leader to the party conference.

Exam task

a Comment on the techniques and the language the speaker uses.

b You have been asked to prepare a speech about an issue where improvement can come about only through change. It can be a global, a national or a local issue. Write the opening of your speech (around 120 words), using some of the techniques you have commented on in your answer to **a**.

A belief in society. Working together. Solidarity. Cooperation. Partnership. These are our words.

We are the party of the individual because we are the party of community.

Our task is to apply our values to the modern world ... It is time to break out of the past and break through with a clear and radical and modern vision for Britain.

... Today's politics is about the search for security in a changing world. We must build the strong and active society that can provide it.

That is our project for Britain.

Market forces cannot educate us or equip us for this world of rapid technological and economic change.

We must do it together.

We cannot buy our way to a safe society. We must work for it together.

We cannot purchase an option on whether we grow old. We must plan for it together.

We cannot protect the ordinary against the abuse of power by leaving them to it, we must protect each other.

That is our insight.

The people of this country are not looking to us for a revolution. They want us to make a start.

I want you with me in that task. I want you with me. Head and heart.

Because this can only be done together.

Leaders lead, but in the end people govern ...

We are not going to win despite our beliefs. We will only win because of them ...

We should win because of what we believe.

The task of renewing our nation is not one for the faint hearted, or the world weary, or the cynical. It is not a task for those afraid of hard choices, for those with complacent views, or those seeking a comfortable life ...

We have changed. We were right to change. Parties that do not change die, and this party is a living movement not an historical monument. If the world changes, and we don't, then we become of no use to the world. Our principles cease being principles.

Change is an important part of gaining the nation's trust ...

Are we not right to reach out and touch the people in this way, to show them that politics is not some game ... played out over screeds of paper in wintry meeting rooms, but a real and meaningful part of their lives?

Let us say what we mean and mean what we say.

Not just what we are against. But what we are for. No more ditching. No more dumping. Stop saying what we don't mean. And start saying what we do mean, what we stand by, what we stand for ...

We are proud of our beliefs. So let's state them. And in terms that people will identify with in every workplace, every home, every family, every community in our country.

And let this party's determination to change be the symbol of the trust they can place in us to change the country.

That is our hope. Not just to promise change – but to achieve it.

Tony Blair The Penguin Book of Twentieth Century Speeches

③ Ann and Ben

The following passage is taken from a novel in which the main character, Alice, is critically ill after a suicide attempt. Her parents, Ann and Ben, make the journey to her bedside as quickly as possible.

Exam task

a In the style of the original passage, continue the story (around 120 words).
b Write a commentary comparing your style and language with the original.

Ann and Ben take a taxi from the station. It's an uneven journey, the taxi travelling swiftly at first, tarmac rumbling beneath them; then they hit a traffic jam where they sit for what feels like ages, the engine churning over, the back of the cab filling with sour fumes, the red meter flicking. Ann sits bolt upright, the tendons in her neck visible beneath her skin, staring out of the windscreen ... Ben shifts in the leather seat. His clothes have wrinkled under him during the train journey. He hardly ever comes to London and always forgets how brash he finds it. He cranes his neck out of the window to see the obstruction, and the whitish, level light of the street makes his eyes smart. The sun ... seems harshly bright, picking out people's outlines, making the colours in their clothes shout. He feels the heavy air around his head churn and a cyclist whizzes past, his face obscured by a pollution mask and mirrored visor, the tread of his wheels crunching as he weaves in and out of the stationary cars. Ben brings his head back into the cab and winds up the window. He will never understand why Alice left Scotland to come here.

They could have taken the tube. Maybe it would have been quicker. But the tube to both him and Ann is a fearsome thing: a horrible machine into which you get sucked, dragged down by crowds and escalators, spat out onto blackened platforms where trains arrive and leave with alarming speed, and all you have to find your way is a map of tangled, coloured wires and strange-sounding names. In his breast pocket is the address of the hospital and the name of the doctor. They dictated it to him down the phone that morning. He puts his hand to the pocket, listening out for the crack of the paper to reassure himself, and as he does so, the taxi eases its way into a moving lane of traffic.

They begin speeding through streets, almost without stopping. Ben gets the sensation they are heading uphill. Fragments of shouts, conversations, music, car horns are snatched from the air and whirled into the cab ...

The hospital is large and grey, crouched on a hill. Even before they get out of the taxi, when Ben is still counting change into the man's hand, he can hear the muted roar of its workings – air-conditioning, electrical generators, incinerators. Going up the steps, they hold hands like they did when they were first engaged. Ben is holding a roll of newspaper unnaturally high against his chest. In it, the heads of some late-flowering yellow roses nod to the rhythm of his walk.

Maggie O'Farrell After You'd Gone

④ The World Cup

The passage below is taken from a magazine article written in 2002 just before the competition took place. In it the writer gives some reasons for the universal appeal of football.

Exam task

a Write a commentary on the writer's use of language.
b In the style of the original passage, write a short article (around 120 words) for a school magazine on any hobby, pastime or sport of your choice.

This year's World Cup in Korea and Japan will be the world's biggest sporting event, with more viewers, more hype, more television money, and more sponsorship than ever before. In viewing terms, the World Cup is twice as big as any other sporting event on the planet. And the corporate giants will be pitching to be seen as part of the game. 'It was our biggest sports marketing event worldwide ever,' said Chuck Fruit, Coca-Cola's senior vice president for worldwide media.

But just because it's big doesn't mean it's beautiful. Football can bring out the worst in people, particularly men. It can make them boorish, boring, beerish, obsessive and intolerant of others. It can flirt with the darker side of the mob ... It can breed violence and fanaticism. It has become ugly with money, with spoilt-brat millionaire players and cynical club owners serving up the passions of the crowd as an appetiser for the sponsors' guests in the corporate boxes. Which makes it even more surprising that football has never lost its appeal. So why do so many find football irresistible?

I believe the secret of football is its ability to be whatever you want it to be. It is the ultimate chameleon, weaving itself into the culture of countries that couldn't be more different; appealing to people who have almost nothing in common, but who each think of football as being their own personal passion. There are heroes and villains, moments of hope and disaster, skill and skulduggery, a whole miniature war with flags and armies, all packaged into 90 minutes.

So why should football have spread so easily? Perhaps it is because the game feels instinctive, something that, if it hadn't been there, someone would have needed to invent. If you were hostile to football, you could see it as one of those superbugs that can adapt to any environment.

Forgetting the glitz of the professional game, the basic structure of football is spectacularly simple – two opposing sides attempting to push an object into the other's goal. And for informal matches, it is infinitely flexible, with no particular need for set numbers of players, no expensive kit and no particular type of pitch. All you need are feet, jumpers for goal posts and a roundish object for a ball.

... The ability of football and the media to feed off each other has been another ingredient in its survival. Mass literacy and mass circulation newspapers meant that football results, league tables and match reports could be brought to a wider audience. And even if people aren't interested in football as a sport, it has its own life as a soap opera and public spectacle.

Television and football have gone hand in goalkeeper's glove with each other. Television has turned players into celebrities and pumped unprecedented amounts of money into the game. In return, football has helped pull in advertisers and sell subscriptions for ... television companies ... And the overall effect has been for football to remain the most visible sport in the world.

Times Educational Supplement 19 April 2002

5 The cone gatherers

The following passage is the beginning of a novel about two brothers, Calum and Neil, whose job is to collect cones from fir trees in order to propagate more trees.

Exam task

a In the style of the original passage, continue the story (around 120 words).

b Write a commentary comparing your style and use of language with the original.

It was a good tree ... with many cones and much sunshine; it was homely too, with rests among its topmost branches as comfortable as chairs.

For hours the two men had worked in silence there, a hundred feet from the earth, closer, it seemed, to the blue sky round which they had watched the sun slip. Misted in the morning, the loch had gone through many shades of blue and now was mauve, like the low hills on its far side. Seals that had been playing tag in and out of the seaweed under the surface had disappeared round the point, like children gone home for tea. A destroyer had steamed seawards, with a sailor singing cheerfully. More sudden and swifter than hawks, and roaring louder than waterfalls, aeroplanes had shot down from the sky over the wood, whose autumnal colours they seemed to have copied for camouflage.

... From the larch could be glimpsed ... the chimneys of the mansion behind its private fence of giant silver firs. Neil, the elder of the brothers, had often paused ... and gazed at the great house with a calm yet bitter intentness and anticipation, as if ... he was waiting for it to change. He never said what he expected or why he watched; nor did his brother ever ask.

For Calum the tree-top was interest enough; in it he was as indigenous as a squirrel or bird. His black curly hair was speckled with orange needles; his torn jacket was stained green, as was his left knee visible through a hole rubbed in his trousers. Chaffinches fluttered round him, ignoring his brother; now and then one would alight on his head or shoulder. He kept chuckling to them, and his sunburnt face was alert and beautiful with trust. Yet he was a much faster gatherer than his brother, and reached far out to where the brittle branches drooped and creaked under his weight. Neil would sometimes glance across to call out: 'Careful!'. It was the only word spoken in the past two hours.

The time came when, thrilling as a pipe lament across the water, daylight announced it must go: there was a last blaze of light, an uncanny clarity, a splendour and puissance; and then the abdication began. Single stars appeared, glittering in a sky pale and austere. Dusk like a breathing drifted in among the trees and crept over the loch. Slowly the mottled yellow of the chestnuts, the bronze of beech, the saffron of birches, all the magnificent sombre harmonies of the decay of autumn, became indistinguishable. Owls hooted. A fox barked.

It was past time to climb down and go home. The path to the earth was unfamiliar; in the dark it might be dangerous. Once safely down, they would have to find their way like ghosts to their hut in the heart of the wood. Yet Neil did not give the word to go down. It was not zeal to fill the bags that made him linger, for he had given up gathering. He just sat, motionless and silent; and his brother, accustomed to these trances, waited in sympathy ... He did not know what Neil was thinking and never asked; even if told he would not understand. It was enough that they were together.

Robin Jenkins *The Cone Gatherers*

(13) Narrative writing

In Paper 2 you will be required to write two compositions: one must be narrative or descriptive or imaginative and the other must be discursive or argumentative. In this section of the book we will look at each type of composition in turn, establish some rules for good writing and look at some exemplars of good practice. We will begin with narrative writing.

Narrative writing is writing which narrates, or tells, a story. Its purpose is to entertain or hold the attention of the reader. You are engaging with the reader in the same way as the writers of the passages for comment which we have already looked at. It is important, therefore, to establish and be aware of your audience before you begin to write.

Genre

The genre of your narrative writing will usually be established by the task set in the examination question you have chosen.

Task

Make a list of genres which fit narrative writing.

Sample response

> Mystery, historical, supernatural, romance, science fiction, war, human interest, adventure, crime, childhood.

This is a useful, though not exhaustive, list of genres which you might be asked to write in in your examination. Each genre has its own hallmarks, or characteristics, which make it fit its type. Each genre has typical characters, settings, plots. For example, a story about the supernatural might be set in a castle; it could also be set in a supermarket, but that isn't what you would expect. You might expect to find a scientist in a science fiction story; you might find a fashion model, but that would be unexpected.

Task

For each of the above genres, make a list of:

a characters you might expect to find
b settings in which you might expect to find them
c plot details you might expect to find.

Before you begin writing, then, it is important to have a firm idea of the genre you intend to produce and a firm idea of the hallmarks of that genre in terms of character, setting and plot. Some of these may be built into the examination question for you anyway, but where that is not the case you have to work out those details yourself. This is necessary if you are to produce a convincing piece of writing in the chosen genre. There are various techniques to learn and work on if you are to produce a good piece of narrative writing. We will now examine each in turn.

Characters

Having thought about the type of characters which fit your selected genre, choose the character or characters you wish to make central to your piece of writing. It is important not to clutter your writing with too many characters; it is much better to take one character and trace his or her development, or to take two and develop their changing relationship with each other, than to try to deal with several. If you try to deal with several, the result will be an insubstantial and unconvincing piece of work with numerous sketchily described characters. The number of characters may be specified by the examination question you have chosen, or you may have a free choice. Either way, the key is economy. A short story or narrative is not a mini-novel with many characters whose lives are interwoven.

Task

Go back to your list of genres and for each genre write down two types of characters you might expect to find. (Try to choose characters other than those you chose in the last task on genre.) For example, in a crime story you might expect to find a policeman, or someone who needs money so desperately he is prepared to steal it, or someone wrongfully accused.

Character description

Confine your description of characters to what is necessary for your piece of writing. For example, it might be useful to point out in a crime story that the thief is quick-thinking, but not that he has brown hair, unless that became a necessary detail in his identification by the police.

Task

For each of the characters you have created in the last task, write down two details of appearance or personality which might be necessary to the development of your story. Now for each character write down two details which would make no difference to the development of your story and which consequently should not be included in it.

Plot

Just as important as keeping the number of characters to a minimum is keeping the plot simple. Your piece of writing is to be 600–900 words. You are not writing a novel and it is a mistake to think you should try to condense the hallmarks of the plot of a novel in your chosen genre into 700 words! You can't get a murder and a bank robbery into your piece of writing, at least not convincingly. It is much better to deal with a single, simple event which throws light on, develops or changes the main character or characters (and we have already established that there won't be many of them). Often it is more convincing to deal with simple events which are within the range of your own experience, although that would depend on the genre. You are the writer and so you have to be in charge of the plot and not let the plot become out of control so that it seems to be in charge of you. Clearly you must have an idea of the development of your plot before you begin. It's not enough to wait for it to take care of itself as you write. As with characterisation, the key is economy (which means simplicity).

Conflict

A feature of many, though not all, plots is conflict and you may wish to give this consideration when planning your narrative. There may be conflict, or discord, or disagreement between the two main characters. The conflict may or may not be resolved at the end of the story. The conflict may begin at the start of the story, or it may have already started before the narrative opens. There may clearly be a villain and a hero/heroine, but, given that real life isn't usually as simple as that, there may be something to be said both in favour of, and against, each of the characters involved in the disagreement.

Task
Choose six genres and for each write a very brief plot outline.

Setting

Again, your setting may be prescribed by the examination question, or you may be given a free choice. Either way picture the setting in your mind and ask yourself what aspects of the setting will enhance your piece of writing. Remember that setting is both time and place. The setting may be suggested by the genre. For example, you might expect a childhood story to be set in a school but not in a forest (although it might be). It might help the development of your piece of writing if, having imagined your setting, you insert small, helpful details of it into your story in order to help the plot along, or to build up appropriate mood or develop character.

Task

Go back to your list of genres and for each genre write down and briefly describe two settings you might expect to find in each. Remember to think about time as well as place.

Endings

Not all examination questions will ask you to write an ending. Sometimes you will be asked to write only the opening or a section of a story. But in cases where you are asked to write a whole short story, you must be clear in your mind before you begin what your ending will be. As with the plot, it's not enough to hope for the best and wait for the ending to take care of itself. There are several types of endings we might consider at this point. You don't need to use one of these types of endings, but if you are aware of them it gives new possibilities to your writing.

Twist

In this type of ending, the reader is startled by the unexpectedness of the final section of the plot. For example, a horror story ends with the object of fear being nothing more than a small insect. Conversely a small innocent-looking insect turns out to be the carrier of a deadly disease, or a husband in a seemingly happy marriage has been planning his wife's murder for years. The key to producing a convincing twist is to lay down clues throughout the story, so that the reader, although surprised at the ending, realises with hindsight that the story was heading in that direction all along. A twist must never be just an 'add-on', the effect of which is a stilted, contrived and unsatisfying piece of writing.

Task

For each of four genres, write a brief outline of a plot, including an expected ending. Now take each expected ending and give it a twist. (Don't worry about characters or details of plot; the focus here is on endings.)

Cliffhanger

In this type of ending the reader is left in suspense as to how the story might end. In a sense, the reader is left to draw his/her own conclusions as to how the story ends. For example, at the end of a love story the two characters quarrel. The female character leaves in tears. Will she be back? Will her boyfriend chase after her?

Task

For each of four genres (try to choose genres different from those chosen in the last task), write a brief outline of a plot, including an expected ending. Now take each expected ending and turn it into a cliffhanger.

Ambiguity

In this type of ending the reader is unsure of the writer's plan for the character(s), which is deliberately unclear. This is slightly different from a cliffhanger, where the reader is left to make up his/her own mind about the ending. In an ambiguous ending, the reader is given an ending, but does not understand the writer's plan, which is kept consciously and tantalisingly unclear. For example, in a detective story, the policeman leaves the police headquarters to make an arrest, but each of the two other characters has a motive for the crime already established by the writer. It is unclear to the reader who is guilty. In a well-written story with an ambiguous ending, the reader might be quite certain one day that, say, the guilty party is character A and the next day be equally certain that the guilty party is in fact character B. This example is for crime stories, but ambiguity can be used in all genres of narrative writing and can be very effective if handled with skill.

Task

For each of four different genres, write a brief outline of a plot, including an expected ending. Now take each expected ending and describe how that might be made ambiguous.

Dialogue

Because short stories involve characters, and because people in real life talk to one another, it can be effective to include dialogue in your piece of writing. The first key to effective use of dialogue is to use it sparingly and only to enhance plot or character. For example a long piece of dialogue in which characters discuss the weather could be out of place and redundant in a mystery story, unless of course the weather is the key to unravelling the mystery. The second key to effective use of dialogue is its appropriate placing in the piece of writing. For example, a short story which opens with a short section of dialogue can be very effective in establishing character, setting or plot, or indeed a combination of these. The third key to effective use of dialogue is to be able to punctuate it correctly. If you are uncertain, look at any novel you have and you will see numerous examples of correctly punctuated dialogue. Remember to use quotation marks round the words actually spoken and to start a new line for each new speaker.

Task

Take six different genres. For each, write short sections of dialogue (no more than four lines) which would work as an eye-catching opening to a short story, by giving a flavour of either plot or character.

Sequence

The sequence of your narrative writing means the order in which you choose to relate the events of the plot. The most obvious order in which to write a story is to start at the beginning, move on to the middle, and then to the end. Such a sequence follows the time-lines of the story and therefore the order is **chronological**. But why be obvious? It is possible to tell your story in ways other than the chronological. For example, you might start at the end so that your story is then revealed as a **flashback**. Your opening might be a short section of dialogue between the two characters after their difficulties have been resolved or at a chance encounter years after the events of the plot or whatever. Your opening might indicate a flashback by the tense of the verb, for example a pluperfect tense (e.g. He *had been* there before).

Here are some examples of flashback openings:

- 'I don't believe it!' she exclaimed. 'Not after all these years!'

- If only I hadn't left the house that day. If only I had gone to work an hour later.

You might deviate from a chronological sequence by beginning in the middle of your story. For example, there might be conflict between characters in the middle of the story which takes the rest of the narrative to be resolved. By starting with the conflict, you might give your narrative an interesting and dramatic focus and add something unexpected to its structure. Here are some examples of openings which begin in the middle of the story:

- At that point her patience crumbled. Enough was enough and he had to be made aware of it.

- It seemed as if she had been travelling for days. Was it only four hours?

Task

Choose four genres and for each write brief chronological outlines of a plot. Now take each plot outline and reshape it to produce:

- an outline which uses flashback
- an outline which begins in the middle of the plot.

Openings

Although the opening is obviously what you write first, it should not be what you think about and plan first (which is why it does not come first in this unit). If you are confident that your plot will work and that you know both your plot and your ending, your opening should come relatively easily if you follow certain basic principles. The key to a good opening is that it should be eye-catching; it should engage the reader's attention and make the reader want to read on. It should not make the reader switch off or, worse, bore him/her. So how are you going to make your opening eye-catching?

One possible way has already been dealt with: a short section of dialogue can make the reader curious by giving a flavour of the plot, setting or character. Another possible opening is a single-word opening. Curiosity would be aroused by a narrative which begins in one of these ways:

- Crash!

- Cats.

- Silence.

Or you might have a slightly longer, but nevertheless short, opening, for example:

- Terror washed over me.

- She grinned at him.

- Everybody likes peace and quiet.

Or you might open with a rhetorical question, for example:

- Is there anybody who doesn't like peace and quiet?

- Why did I agree to look after my friend's two children?

- Why was she grinning at him, he wondered?

Another effective opening is a flashback. We have already thought about flashback in the previous section and looked at examples of flashback openings. Likewise we know about opening with a section of narrative from the middle, rather than the beginning, of the story and have looked at some examples.

When thinking about openings and their importance in creating interest in the reader, it might be helpful to think about *poor* openings as these are clearly the kinds of openings we wish to avoid. Here are some examples of poor openings:

- It all started when I got up and ate my breakfast.

- I have been asked to write a story about a boring story writer.

Each of these examples shows students who just don't know where to start, have little confidence in their own ability and have never considered that they can learn to write stories the way they learned to do lots of other things.

Task

Choose six genres. For each genre, write an opening using:

- a single word
- a short sentence
- a rhetorical question
- a short section of dialogue
- a flashback.

Person

Think of stories or novels you have read. Most of these are written in the **third person**. This means that the writer, not a character, tells the story. Third-person writing uses the pronouns *he, she* and *they*. The writer and his characters are quite distinct. The advantage of this is that the writer maintains control over character and plot; when he tells us, say, that the character is in love, we know this must be the case.

Sometimes stories are written in the **first person**. This means that the writer has told the story through the eyes of, and hence through the mouth of, one of the characters, usually the main one. First-person writing uses the pronoun *I*. The advantage of this can be an easier identification with the character by the reader, who empathises with the character's joys, sorrows, fears etc. The disadvantage can be that the reader sometimes gets a limited perspective on the events of the plot or the nature of the other characters.

In your own writing think about the possibility of varying the person in which you write. This may be limited by the examination question chosen, but where you have a choice think about exercising it. For example, a crime story will take on a new slant if it's told through the eyes of the policeman or the eyes of the criminal. A love story takes on a new dimension if told through the eyes of the wronged or broken-hearted lover.

Task

Choose six genres. For each write a brief plot outline to be expanded in the third person. Now take each plot outline and choose a character to tell the story in the first person. Describe the ways in which the story might now become different from its third-person equivalent.

Exam tip

In narrative writing have only a few characters and work out your plot outline before you begin writing, paying particular attention to its opening and ending. Picture the setting in your mind and try to develop it in your piece of writing.

14 Exemplars of good narrative writing

It is impossible in one book to give many examples of good practice in narrative writing, but the purpose of this unit is to draw together some of the techniques discussed in the previous unit and to link the theory to real-life practice.

Openings, setting, character and genre

Each of the following openings to short stories (extracts 1–5) has an accompanying task and is followed by a short commentary. Copying this good practice will help you in your own writing.

Extract 1

Task

Write a short commentary on this opening, referring to these features:

- plot
- genre
- character
- means of narration
- setting
- person.

It was the strangest murder trial I ever attended. They named it the Peckham murder in the headlines, though Northwood Street, where the old woman was found battered to death, was not strictly speaking in Peckham.

Graham Greene 'The Case for the Defence' from *Twenty-One Stories*

Sample commentary

The narrative opens with a short sentence. It establishes the genre of the story, namely crime, and vicious crime at that. It is a first-person narrative; we therefore expect the narrator to present events from a perspective which may be limited but which will be truthful as he sees it. The fact that the narrator was at the trial rouses our curiosity as to why that was; perhaps he is a reporter, or a lawyer or a policeman. As Peckham is in London, the setting is established as inner city.

Extract 2

Task

Write a short commentary on this opening, referring to these features:

- direct speech
- characters
- setting.

'They say he's worth a million,' Lucia said. He sat there in the little hot damp Mexican square, a dog at his feet, with an air of immense and forlorn patience.

Graham Greene 'Across the Bridge' from *Twenty-One Stories*

Sample commentary

The story opens with a short section of direct speech. Two characters are mentioned: Lucia and the man of whom she speaks. This raises the reader's curiosity as to which character is the more important. The man is established as an enigmatic character on account of his wealth and the fact that he seems to be an outsider. The setting is created, its oppressive climate and rather depressing atmosphere a surprising setting for a man of great wealth who might have chosen to live in more congenial surroundings. The nature of the man interests the reader – why is he patient? A man who might have been able to attract friends, at least by his wealth, is alone, and this surprises us. For all his wealth, there is little sign of happiness.

Extract 3

Task

Write a short commentary on this opening, referring to these features:

- character
- method of narration
- sentence structure
- setting.

Peter Morton woke with a start to face the first light. Rain tapped against the glass. It was January the fifth.

Graham Greene 'The End of the Party' from *Twenty-One Stories*

Sample commentary

> The story is a third-person narrative, which gives the writer control over characters and plot. The extract is made up of three short, simple sentences. The staccato effect of this structure arouses the reader's curiosity in its terseness and economy. The setting in time is established; it is wet winter weather.

Extract 4

Task

Write a short commentary on this opening, referring to these features:

- sentence structure
- genre
- character
- person.

I had stuck closely to him, as people say like a shadow. But that's absurd. I'm no shadow. You can feel me, touch me, hear me, smell me. I'm Robinson.

Graham Greene 'A Day Saved' from *Twenty-One Stories*

Sample commentary

> The pluperfect tense 'had stuck' indicates that the story has started before the narration, that what we read here is not the real beginning. Therefore we might expect to read later what happened before the opening. The story, therefore, is probably not being told in chronological order, but through at least one flashback. We might guess that the genre is espionage or crime, as it involves the secret following of a character. There are two characters established, Robinson and the man being followed, and the reader's curiosity is aroused as to which of the two might be the more important. The short sentences make for compelling reading; the economy of ideas makes the extract exciting to read and fits the genre of spying or crime. The use of the first person helps the reader engage more closely with the character who is the narrator.

Timescales and flashbacks

Bernard MacLaverty's short story 'Secrets' tells of how, as a young boy, the main character lost the trust of his aunt by looking through her old love letters when she was out of the house. The story opens with the boy, now a young man, being called to his aunt's death bed years later and recalling his betrayal of her years earlier.

Extract 5

Task

Write a short commentary on the following two sections from the beginning of the short story, referring to these features:

- sequence
- character.

He had been called to be there at the end. His Great Aunt Mary had been dying for some days now and the house was full of relatives.

His aunt had been small – her head on a level with his when she sat at her table – and she seemed to get smaller each year. Her skin fresh, her hair white and waved and always well washed.

Bernard MacLaverty 'Secrets'

Sample commentary

The pluperfect tense in which the story opens establishes that this in fact is not the real beginning, that there is a story yet to be told which has already taken place. Two characters are established in the opening two sentences: the young man and his aunt. Although the aunt is about to die, the pluperfect heralds the possibility of finding out about her earlier life. The second section also begins with the pluperfect, this time indicating a flashback to an earlier timescale than that in which the story opens. The reader is interested in moving back and forward through time, and that combines with the title, 'Secrets', to arouse the curiosity of the reader, who wants to find out what these secrets are and whether they belong to the boy or to the aunt. Something of the aunt's fastidious character is established by the description of her skin and hair.

Endings

It is obviously difficult to consider the ending of a narrative without looking at the whole narrative and we do not have space to do that in this book. However, it is hoped that extracts 6 and 7 and their commentaries may throw some light on what constitutes a good ending.

The short story 'Don't Look Now' by Daphne Du Maurier is about a couple, John and Laura, on holiday in Venice shortly after the accidental death of their little daughter. Laura returns to England because their son is taken ill at home, but John remains. He is told by a blind clairvoyant that he is in danger in Venice, but he is sceptical. He sees his wife, the clairvoyant and her sister going to a funeral, although it seems he must be mistaken because Laura is in England. At the end of the story, he sees what he thinks is a child who reminds him of his dead daughter. He follows her only to find that she is a very small, insane woman who has been responsible for recent murders in Venice. She plunges a knife into his throat. As he dies, he realises that the clairvoyant was correct to tell him he was in danger, and that he himself also has second sight, having witnessed earlier in the day his own funeral. The final paragraph of the narrative is reproduced below.

Extract 6

> **Task**
>
> Write a short commentary on this ending, referring to the feature of *twists*.
>
> And he saw the vaporetto [boat] with Laura and the two sisters steaming down the Grand Canal, not today, not tomorrow, but the day after that, and he knew that they were together and for what sad purpose they had come. The creature was gibbering in its corner. The hammering and the voices and the barking dog grew fainter, and, 'Oh God,' he thought, 'what a bloody silly way to die...'
>
> Daphne Du Maurier 'Don't Look Now'

Sample commentary

The first twist revealed in this ending is that John in fact did see Laura and the sisters going to a funeral, but it was his own funeral. Thus the mystery is solved of how he saw Laura when at that particular point in time she was in England. The second twist is that the small female character dressed like his dead daughter is in fact not an innocent child but an evil, homicidal maniac. The third twist is that he realises that the clairvoyant was right to tell him he was in danger. The fourth twist is his realisation that he himself is a clairvoyant. The short and incomplete dialogue which forms the final sentence of the narrative points to the futility of John's death, making it seem a dreadful waste. This ending cannot fail to make a strong impression on anyone who reads the entire story.

For the next ending we will go back to Bernard MacLaverty's short story 'Secrets'. Unlike the previous story, which involved a murder, this story has a much gentler plot. (It is important to understand that narrative writing can be about ordinary events.) The flashbacks nearer the beginning of the narrative have revealed that both the boy and his aunt have secrets. The aunt's secret is that she was once engaged to, and is still in love with, a man who renounced her so that he could become a priest. The boy's secret is that when his aunt was out one day he opened her locked bureau and read her love letters. She never forgave him for what he did and he bitterly regrets it. The aunt dies and her sister, the young man's mother, clears out her personal belongings and burns her letters – without reading them. The final section of the story is reproduced below.

Extract 7

Task

Write a brief commentary on this extract, mentioning these features:

- mood
- dialogue
- character
- conflict.

'Mama,' he said.
 'Yes?'
 'Did Aunt Mary say anything about me?'
 'What do you mean?'
 'Before she died – did she say anything?'
 'Not that I know of – the poor thing was too far gone to speak, God rest her.' She went on burning, lifting the corners of the letters with the poker to let the flames underneath them.
 When he felt a hardness in his throat he put his head down on his books. Tears came into his eyes for the first time since she had died and he cried silently into the crook of his arm for the woman who had been his maiden aunt, his teller of tales, that she might forgive him.

Bernard MacLaverty 'Secrets'

Sample commentary

The dialogue is simple but evokes the mood of fear of having being found out. The young man's crime and guilt are heightened by the fact that his mother would not dream of reading her dead sister's letters. The final paragraph evokes the mood of remorse, that the young man is desperately sorry for what he did, but time has now run out for a reconciliation with his aunt. There is a sense of unfinished business, of something he should have had the courage to deal with by at least attempting to resolve the conflict, but it is all too late. This sense of lateness gives a particular poignancy to the ending of the narrative. The conflict between the characters has been taken into death. There is also a sense of loss about the aunt, in that she went with her unrequited love to the grave. A wealth of powerful emotions are tapped into in this story, although its plot is utterly simple.

Practice openings and endings

Extracts 8, 9 and 10

Some short extracts follow. Each is an opening to a short story, a novel or a chapter. There is not sufficient space in this book to offer commentaries, but use the task below as an opportunity to practise the skills you have developed in this unit.

Task

Examine each of the extracts to establish why it might be an effective opening.

8 The boys, as they talked to the girls of Marcia Blaine School, stood on the far side of their bicycles holding the handlebars, which established a protective fence of bicycle between the sexes, and the impression that at any moment the boys were likely to be away.

Muriel Spark *The Prime of Miss Jean Brodie*

9 In the fine new sunshine of April which fell upon her through the window, Emmeline Mortimer adjusted her glasses and smoothed her blouse.

Muriel Spark 'Memento Mori'

10 For a temporary shorthand typist to be present at the discovery of a corpse on the first day of a new assignment, if not unique, is sufficiently rare to prevent its being regarded as an occupational hazard.

P. D. James *Original Sin*

Extracts 11 and 12

The extracts are endings to either a novel or a chapter.

Task

Examine each extract to establish why it might be an effective conclusion.

11 'I can't help worrying,' I said. 'It's my nature. There's nothing I can do about my nature, is there?'
   'No,' said George, his hand upon the door. 'No, nothing.'

Margaret Drabble *The Millstone*

12 The eyes in the swollen face stared up at me ... They seemed to hold all knowledge in their depths, and all despair.

Daphne Du Maurier *Not after Midnight*

Exam tip

In narrative writing, remember the value of economy in the number of characters and simplicity of plot. Be aware that not all narrative writing needs to be chronological.

(15) Descriptive writing

When you are asked to produce a piece of descriptive writing, you are obviously being asked to describe something or someone. The range of subject matter is extensive. You might be asked to describe, for example, a place you know well, a person you know well or an event which you attended. These pieces of descriptive writing would be based on some degree of personal experience. On the other hand, it is also possible that the topic for description exists wholly or partly in your imagination. For example, you might be asked to describe an imaginary place, person or event. Another topic might exist only in some abstract way, for example if you are asked to describe an emotion or the feelings evoked by, say, a colour.

What all descriptive writing has in common is that it is an attempt to paint a picture, to leave the reader with a clear impression of the subject matter. The writer has to use language to do this. In order to build up a profile of good descriptive writing, we will work on some short tasks. We will start with topics which draw on personal experience, before tackling more abstract topics later.

Descriptive writing based on personal experience

Task

Describe a person who was important to you in early childhood. Try to make the mood nostalgic.

Organising your response

- What build or stature was he/she?
- What kind of things did he/she often say to you?
- What kind of voice did he/she have?
- What kind of feelings did you have when you heard his/her voice?
- What kind of clothes did he/she wear?
- Can you describe a single favourite or typical outfit he/she wore?
- Are there any special smells associated with him/her?
- What are the most memorable activities you associate with him/her?

Sample essay

Grandad
I loved to sit on my great-grandfather's knee while he read me stories for what seemed like hours. He never tired of reading to me and it would never have occurred to me that

he would refuse to do so. His voice was deep, gruff but comfortable; it was his reading voice just for me. Sometimes I took a peek at his face; his skin was wrinkly and I liked to trace with my eye particular lines as they meandered from one side of his face to the other. He had a white, bushy moustache which curled up at the edges and twitched as his lips moved over the mysterious symbols on the page which I did not understand but loved to listen to. I had to sit very still as his clothes – always a suit – were scratchy and made my legs red if I moved too much. My great-grandfather smelled of soap and tobacco; he seemed to bring his own smell with him from the room at the end of the house which was his own special territory. I watched for him to emerge from it every morning so that I could say 'Story, Grandad?' and wait for the delightful answer.

Commentary

The essay starts with some basic questions, as listed on page 75, about Grandad and it answers them. It tries to evoke his importance to the writer as a child, which was what the task asked for. Therefore the information is selective. It does not give details of, for example, Grandad's hobbies or the colour of his hair or the size of his feet, as none of these details would contribute to the overall mood which is called for by the task. The mood is established not by a lot of detail but by selected detail and carefully chosen language.

Task

Describe a place you know well. Try to make the mood humorous.

Organising your response

- What place is it?
- What kind of person spends a lot of time there?
- What does the place say about the personalities of those who spend time there?
- What colours do you associate with the place?
- What feelings does the place evoke in you?

Sample essay

Catherine's study
Catherine's mother can't remember the colour of the carpet in her daughter's study, although she stands in that room most days. A view of the carpet is obscured by piles of books and papers, piles of clothes, the odd yogurt carton and spoon, and of course Catherine's compact disc collection. Catherine's mother knows of the existence of that collection because assorted singers can be heard wailing from the closed study at all hours of the day and, unfortunately, night. The books and papers look like so much debris, and yet the miracle is that if even a single sheet of paper is moved by a centimetre, Catherine knows immediately by a mere glance around her study that some intruder has been there. It's necessary, of course, to raid the study from time to time to retrieve the teaspoons, when it becomes clear that the kitchen is bereft of tea-stirring utensils. The walls were painted yellow at one time, although there is little evidence of

that. The passing of time and the numerous posters of Catherine's favourite film stars have seen to that.

Commentary

The essay starts with some basic questions, as listed on page 76, about the place and then answers them. It tries to be humorous, which was what the task asked for. Therefore the information is selective. It does not give details of, for example, the dimensions of the room, its furniture, or number of windows, as none of these details would contribute to the overall mood which is called for by the task. The mood is established not by a lot of detail but by selected detail and carefully chosen language.

Task

Write descriptive paragraphs on the following topics:

- A garden I am familiar with
- A favourite relative
- A town I know well
- The city at night

So what have we already established about good descriptive writing? We have established the two main principles that descriptive writing should use:

- selected detail
- carefully chosen language.

Selected detail

Before beginning to write, link the topic for description to the tone or mood you intend to create. Sometimes that tone or mood will be established by the question set, as in the examples given earlier. At other times it will be up to you to decide what tone or mood you intend to create. You might need to work out the tone by thinking about the genre you have been asked to write or have decided to write. Once you are clear about tone or mood, select the details which you wish to include in your piece of writing, and jot them down. These should then be developed through carefully chosen language.

Carefully chosen language

One useful strategy for selecting appropriate language is that of **word banks**. A word bank is a group of words linked around, and evocative of, a particular mood or tone or topic. For example, a word bank for the topic 'A Night in the City', if the chosen or directed genre is the threatening nature of city life at night, might be: *menacing, humid, quietening, neon lights, music, taxis, oppressive, threatening, claustrophobic*. On the other hand, if the chosen or directed genre is the party atmosphere of city life at night, a word bank for the topic might be: *carnival, couples, camaraderie, greetings, warmth, starry sky, balmy, lively*.

Task

Make up word banks for the following descriptive topics:

- The countryside in summer and the countryside in winter
- A favourite teacher and a teacher of whom you were afraid
- A familiar, friendly house and a forbidding, unfriendly house

Descriptive writing based on your imagination

So far, we have been dealing only with descriptive passages which draw on personal experience. Now, we will move on to descriptive writing which draws more on the imagination. It is important to bear in mind that often our imagination is coloured by and affected by our personal experience. So if you were asked to describe an imaginary place in, say, a topic entitled 'My Ideal Town', it would be reasonable that you would begin by thinking of the characteristics of a real town that you know and like. The principles already established for descriptive writing based on personal experience apply also to descriptive pieces calling for an imaginative response. These principles, as we have seen, are selected detail and carefully chosen language. The added dimension might be the overlaying of personal experience onto the imaginary person, place, event or whatever you have been asked to describe. For example, if the topic is 'A Haunted House', it is unlikely that you would be able to write from personal experience. However, it would be useful to draw on your experience of an unfriendly or forbidding house, possibly from your childhood. Was there a house in your neighbourhood which seemed a little scary? Was there an unfriendly neighbour of whom you were a bit afraid? If the topic 'The Countryside in Winter' has to rely on your imagination rather than your personal experience, think of another experience you might have had which will help. For example, have you ever seen a painting of a countryside scene in winter? Have you read any novels which feature the countryside in winter? Are these experiences which might be of assistance to you in forming a picture in your mind which will then lead you on to a word bank?

Task

Write descriptive paragraphs on the following topics. Each of them will probably, although not necessarily, require you to draw on your imagination rather than on your personal experience. But try to draw on something in your personal experience in the first instance. Make up a word bank for each before you begin writing.

- Describe a town after an earthquake.
- Describe the thoughts of a nurse as he/she looks after a ward of patients.
- Write a description of a view from the top of a hill. Try to make the mood peaceful and happy.

Organising your response

Taking the final topic as an example, ask yourself:

- If I have never been on the top of a hill, have I had another peaceful and happy experience? What was this experience?
- What made me feel happy?
- Have I seen a picture or read a novel which helps to show what the view from the top of a hill might be like?
- Where is this hill?
- What kind of terrain is around it?
- What do I want to imagine in my particular view?
- What will I select?

Sample essay

The view from the top of a hill
Still panting a little after the exertions of the ascent, she closed her eyes and breathed deeply. Opening her eyes, she looked around in a wide arc at the expanse of countryside beneath her. The stone walls of the farm at the bottom of the hill zigzagged across the fields, in which small pinpricks of white were sheep. Smoke spiralled from the farmhouse chimney into the blue, blue sky. The ground below her was scrubby with patches of stone, but further down were profusions of bright yellow flowers, the names of which she did not know. Resolving to find out as soon as she could, she smiled contentedly and lay down, again savouring the sweet air of this wonderful day.

Commentary

The essay starts with some basic questions, as listed above, about the topic and answers them. It tries to evoke a feeling of peacefulness and happiness, which was what the task asked for. Therefore the information is selective. It does not give a lot of information, but develops what is selected to suit the tone directed by the task. The language is carefully selected to build up the required picture and establish the directed mood.

Descriptive writing based on abstract ideas

In this sort of writing you might, for example, be asked to describe an emotion or a colour. The general principles established for descriptive writing would apply here in the same way as in other types of descriptive writing we have looked at. These principles are selected detail, carefully chosen language and, where possible, the application of personal experience. For example, if you were asked to describe the emotion of fear, you might think about times when you yourself have experienced fear. You might think about novels you have read which involve characters in fearful situations. You would draw up a word bank of words associated with fear and fearful situations.

Write descriptive paragraphs on the following abstract topics. Try to draw on your personal experience in the first instance. Make up a word bank for each before you begin writing.

- Describe a room full of love.
- Write a description of the thoughts of a piece of coral lying on a beach.
- Describe the colour yellow.

Organising your response

Taking the final topic as an example, ask yourself:

- What things do I like which are yellow?
- Are there any things which I don't like which are yellow?
- Are there any things which are abstract and therefore don't have a colour for which I think yellow would be a good colour?
- As the mood or tone is not directed here, what mood or tone do I think would best suit the colour yellow?

Sample essay

Yellow

Yellow makes me happy. It is the taste of ripe bananas and the feeling of squinting my eyes at the sun. It is fields of sunflowers and Van Gogh's paintings of them. Flute music and knowing I have passed my English examination are yellow. My baby niece's skin smells yellow, like a bowl of yellow plums. Weekends are yellow, but Monday mornings aren't. Yellow roses grow in my garden, the colour of July. Midsummer's day is yellow, and fairies' wings have yellow dots. Yellow makes me happy.

Commentary

The essay starts with some questions, as listed above, and then answers them. Given the imaginative nature of the topic, the questions themselves have to draw on the imagination of the writer if he/she is to proceed with confidence. The writer tries to evoke the mood of happiness, which, although not directed by the question, was chosen by the writer as his/her personal response to the colour yellow. The yellow features selected are in part real and in part imaginary. The writer has achieved this by drawing on the five senses and not just the obvious one of sight. The mood is established by selected detail and carefully chosen language.

Descriptive writing tools

Person, tense and openings can all be useful tools for improving your descriptive writing.

Person

The nature of descriptive writing topics means that in general it will be possible to choose between writing in the first person (using *I*) and writing in the third person (using *he*, *she* or *they*). Examples of both can be seen in the four pieces of writing we have just examined.

Tense

The nature of descriptive writing topics means that it will often be possible to write in either the present or the past tense. As always, of course, you must be directed by the actual question set, but often that will be open-ended enough to leave the choice of tense up to you. Examples of both tenses can be seen in the four pieces of writing we have just examined.

Openings

As with narrative writing, it is important to engage the interest of the reader by establishing an interesting or eye-catching opening to your piece of writing. Look back at what we said about openings in unit 13. Not all of the guidelines laid down there apply to descriptive writing, but some of them do. For example, a single-word opening can be effective:

- Yellow.
- Silence.
- Grandad.

Or you might have a slightly longer, but nevertheless short, opening, for example:

- I had reached the summit!
- Catherine's carpet must be there somewhere.

A question might also be an effective way of beginning a piece of descriptive writing, for example:

- Was there a carpet on that floor?
- What was so special about Grandad?

Exam tip

Be aware of the importance of your own experience in descriptive writing even if it can be applied only in an indirect or abstract way.

16 Exemplars of good descriptive writing

As with narrative writing, it is impossible to give many examples of good practice in descriptive writing in one book, but the purpose of this unit is to attempt to bring together some of the main points made about descriptive writing in the last unit. Remember that these were selected detail, carefully chosen language, person, tense and openings. Below you will find some extracts of good descriptive writing preceded by a task for you to try. Each extract is followed by a short commentary which is intended to help you to copy this good practice in your own writing.

Extract 1

Task

Write a short commentary on this descriptive passage, picking out features of detail selected and language chosen in order to achieve the intended mood.

Each afternoon, when the whole city beyond the dark green shutters of their hotel windows began to stir, Colin and Mary were woken by the methodical chipping of steel tools against the iron barges which moored by the hotel café pontoon. In the morning these rusting, pitted hulks ... would be gone; towards the end of each day they reappeared, and their crews set to inexplicably with their mallets and chisels. It was at this time, in the clouded, late afternoon heat, that customers began to gather on the pontoon to eat ice cream at the tin tables, and their voices too filled the darkened hotel room, rising and falling in waves of laughter and dissent, flooding the brief silences between each piercing blow of the hammers.

Ian McEwan *The Company of Strangers*

Sample commentary

The sleepy effect of rest time is continued with the implied darkness of the shuttered hotel room. The stillness and darkness inside are contrasted with the increasing activity and brightness outside. Outside activity and noise come from the detail of the workmen's mallets and chisels chipping on iron; there is another noise outside, that of voices of café customers. A further contrast is established between the noise of the tools and the sound of human voices; these sounds seem to be in competition with one another. The colour of the shutters is dark, which suits the restful mood of the room interior. The voices 'flood' the silence, which emphasises the increasing noise outside. Work and leisure are contrasted with the workmen on the barges and those eating ice cream at the café. 'Late afternoon heat' suggests the languor of a hot climate. The mood achieved is one of a city coming alive after a period of silence and inactivity.

Extract 2

Task

Write a short commentary on this descriptive passage, picking out features of detail selected and language chosen in order to achieve the intended mood.

Although it was their hottest day so far, and the sky directly above was closer to black than blue, the sea, when they finally came to it down the busy avenue of street cafés and souvenir shops, was an oily grey along whose surface the gentlest of breezes pushed and scattered patches of off-white foam. At the water's edge, where miniature waves broke on to the straw-coloured sand, children played and shouted ... Large families sat round trestle tables preparing lunches of bright green salads and dark bottles of wine.

Ian McEwan *The Company of Strangers*

Sample commentary

The time is established as the middle of the day, with lunch being prepared. A feeling of heat is also established. The bustle of a tourist area is created by the phrases 'busy avenue' and 'souvenir shops'. There is a sense of safety in the 'miniature' waves, which suits the family beach setting, as does the perfect 'straw-coloured sand'. Family meals suggest harmony, and the colourful salad and wine are attractive. The mood established is harmonious, safe and full of activity.

Extract 3

Task

Write a short commentary on this descriptive passage, picking out features of detail selected and language chosen in order to establish the relationship between the mother and her baby.

Octavia was an extraordinarily beautiful child. Everyone said so, in shops and on buses and in the park, wherever we went. I took her to Regent's Park as often as I could face getting the pram up and down in the lift. It was a tolerable summer, and we both got quite brown. I was continually amazed by the way in which I could watch for hours nothing but the small movements of her hands, and the fleeting expressions of her face. She was a very happy child, and once she learned to smile, she never stopped; at first she would smile at anything, at parking meters and dogs and strangers, but as she grew older she began to favour me, and nothing gave me more delight than her evident preference.

Margaret Drabble *The Millstone*

Sample commentary

The mother's love for her baby is established immediately with her claim that Octavia was not only beautiful but 'extraordinarily' so. This must surely be a subjective rather than an objective judgement. The use of the conjunction 'and' to list the places where the narrator was complimented on her child gives the impression of an accumulation of places and people, and therefore an accumulation of compliments. 'We both' suggests unity, as if this is a pair of friends or equals, rather than mother and child. The narrator's delight in her baby is shown in the fact that she was 'continually amazed' at very ordinary things about her; she is caught up in wonder. Her happiness with her baby is stressed at the points where the baby is described as being happy, and then as smiling all the time and at everything she saw. The reader is amused and charmed by the innocence of the baby smiling at parking meters, and gradually learning about the importance of her mother. Vocabulary with connotations of happiness is used: 'happy', 'smile', 'delight'.

Extract 4

Task

Write a short commentary on this descriptive passage, picking out features of detail selected and language chosen in order to establish character.

Madame Defarge, his wife, sat in the shop behind the counter as he came in. Madame Defarge was a stout woman of about his own age, with a watchful eye that seldom seemed to look at anything, a large hand heavily ringed, a steady face, strong features, and great composure of manner. There was a character about Madame Defarge, from which one might have predicated that she did not often make mistakes ...

Charles Dickens *A Tale of Two Cities*

Sample commentary

> The overall impression is of a strong, intelligent and rather frightening character. The paradoxical notion that she had 'a watchful eye' but 'seldom seemed to look at anything' suggests that in fact she is watchful and misses nothing. A mood of mystery is created: what is she watching for? A ruthless quality is established in the idea that 'she did not often make mistakes'. 'Stout' and 'large hand' are details selected to suggest a large woman, adding to her rather frightening description. Economy of language is used to create the impression that here we have a strong character who will have an important role to play.

Extract 5

Task

Write a short commentary on this descriptive passage, showing how the use of the first person throws light on New York and/or the character.

In the early morning the sun threw my shadow westward as I hurried down the white chasms of lower New York to the Probity Trust. I knew the other clerks ... by their first names, and lunched with them in dark, crowded restaurants on little pig sausages and mashed potatoes and coffee ... I began to like New York, the racy adventurous feel of it at night, and the satisfaction that the constant flicker of men and women and machines gives to the restless eye.

F. Scott Fitzgerald *The Great Gatsby*

Sample commentary

> The narrator is clearly impressed and possibly a little overawed by New York. He sees the tall buildings as 'chasms' on either side of him; he feels a sense of the vastness of the city. He is doing his best to be sociable by having lunch with his colleagues. The fact that he mentions he is on first-name terms with his colleagues might mean that he is surprised to have got to that stage, and so maybe he is shy or insecure. He himself is 'restless'. New York is huge, impersonal and full of activity, an impression that is enhanced by the use of a first-person narrator confronting as an individual the variety and freshness of New York life.

Extract 6

Task

Write a short commentary on this descriptive passage, showing particularly how the use of the present tense enhances the atmosphere of the party which is being described.

By seven o'clock the orchestra has arrived, no thin five-piece affair, but a whole pitful of oboes and trombones and saxophones and viols and cornets and piccolos, and low and high drums ... the cars from New York are parked five deep in the drive, and already the

> halls and salons and verandas are gaudy with primary colours ... The lights grow brighter as the earth lurches away from the sun, and now the orchestra is playing yellow cocktail music ... Laughter is easier minute by minute ... tipped out at a cheerful word.
>
> F. Scott Fitzgerald *The Great Gatsby*

Sample commentary

A mood of affluence is created in the vast array of objects being described. Instead of writing merely 'musical instruments' or 'the instruments of an orchestra', the writer chooses to list the instruments, joining up the items in the list by the repeated use of 'and' where a single 'and' would have sufficed. Cars 'parked five deep' emphasises numbers, and suggests the activity and bustle of many people arriving after their journeys to the party. By describing the instruments and the cars in the present tense, the writer creates an immediacy about the proceedings; the party seems to be happening before our eyes and we are caught up in it. Sunset comes as 'the earth lurches away from the sun'; again the graphic present tense, combined with the dramatic word 'lurches', is effective as it portrays a sudden sunset, as if even the elements want night to fall and the party to get into full swing. The writer returns to the idea of music with the reference to 'yellow' music; this is clearly metaphorical, suggesting brightness and happiness, made brighter and more immediate by the use of the present tense. 'Laughter is easier' is also present tense, again drawing the reader into the immediacy of the party, as if it is happening on the page even as we read.

Exam tip

Be selective with detail in descriptive writing. Include only detail which evokes the mood called for by the examination question.

17 Imaginative writing

When we are asked to write a story, or narrative, we are producing a piece of imaginative writing. In other words, we are producing a piece of writing for which the ideas for plot, character, setting and theme have been created by us, in our own imaginations. But there is a wider focus for imaginative writing in that it allows the writer to explore genres of writing other than a story.

Task

Make a list of types of writing other than stories, or narratives, which could be classified as imaginative pieces of work.

Sample response

Letter, diary, script, newspaper or magazine article, biography, speech.

In each of these types of writing you are required to draw on your imagination and also to follow particular rules of style if your work is to be convincing. We will now look at each of these types of writing in turn.

Letter

If your piece of imaginative writing is a letter, two key factors you must be aware of are **punctuation** and **tone**. Each of these will in part be settled by the type of letter you are asked to write. This in turn will be determined by the recipient, or reader, of your letter. All recipients can be divided into two broad types; the recipient who is known personally to you (although remember that he/she need only be known to you in an imaginative way, for example an imaginary brother) and the recipient who is not personally known to you, even in the imaginary scenario into which you must project yourself (for example the editor of a national newspaper). When the recipient is known personally, we call this an informal, or friendly, letter. When the recipient is not known personally, we call this a formal, or business, letter.

Punctuation

To punctuate any letter, whether formal or informal, you must give five pieces of information apart from the actual message, or body, of the letter. These five pieces of information are as follows:

1 address of sender   **2** date   **3** salutation and name of recipient
4 farewell   **5** name of sender

There is a sixth piece of information which appears on a formal letter only, and not on an informal letter, and that is the address of the recipient. Apart from the address of the recipient, which should appear beneath **1** in a formal letter, points **1** to **5** are written in the order in which they are given here. The address of the sender and the date appear on the right-hand side of the page; the salutation and the name of the recipient appear on the left-hand side. The farewell and the name of the sender appear on the right-hand side. Your layout should look like this:

20 Rose Road
Cambridge
CB1 7UP
20 September 2003

Dear Anna

Lots of love,
Grandma

Notice the need for capital letters in each line of the address, and the need for the address to be either blocked (aligned on a straight vertical line, as above) or indented (sloping evenly inwards to the right). The farewell can take many forms in an informal letter ('Lots of love' in this example).

The added information needed for a formal letter – that is, the address of the recipient – should be blocked on the left-hand side of the page below the address of the sender, and should look like this:

The Editor
The Guardian
119 Farringdon Road
London
EC1R 3ER

The correct farewell in formal letters when the recipient's name is unknown is *Yours faithfully*. If the name is known, the farewell should be *Yours sincerely*.

Tone

You must establish the appropriate tone for your letter in your mind before you begin writing. This will often largely be established by the task set. For example, check at the outset whether your letter is formal or informal; this is the single most important factor in establishing tone. You might find it helpful to prepare a word bank of terms appropriate to the letter you are about to write.

Task

Imagine you are a grandparent of a teenager. Write a letter to your grandchild in which you both share news and ask for news, showing that you understand the concerns felt by a young person beginning to experience the adult world.

Discursive/argumentative letters

Although we have dealt with letter writing here under the heading of imaginative writing, it is worth remembering that sometimes you will find an examination question asking for a letter under the section entitled discursive/argumentative. This is because the content matter of some letters can best be described as such. However, the principles established in this chapter about punctuation and tone apply equally to letters in the discursive/argumentative section. An example of this sort of letter is given in the task below.

Task

Your local newspaper has recently published an article describing teenagers as lazy and irresponsible. Write a letter to the editor in which you complain about the views expressed in the article.

Diary

Probably the most helpful information to bear in mind about a diary is that it is very personal. Even if you have never kept a diary yourself – and it would be helpful if you have – you will know that the keeper of a diary does so in order to record his/her innermost thoughts, reflections and experiences. So the two factors to be aware of in writing a diary are **content** and **tone**.

Content

You may be asked to write a single diary entry or a series of entries. The task may be flexible and allow you to choose. The main pitfall in this type of task is to settle for just a general ramble which advances neither plot nor character. Remember everything that was said earlier about narrative writing and apply it to a diary. Before you begin writing, jot down what you hope to achieve in your work. Do you want to show a development in the character who is writing the diary? Do you wish to trace a plot in the diary entries, to unravel a story centred around the character who is writing the diary? These lines of thought will clearly produce a better piece of writing than a string of information about going to school, or what the character had for dinner or watched on television.

Tone

The key to correct tone in diary writing is confidentiality. The reader must feel that the writer is sharing secrets, not necessarily of a momentous nature, but observations about him/herself or other characters with whom he/she is in contact. It might be possible or effective to combine confidentiality with humour; after all, we are usually more candid in our own minds than we are with all but the most intimate friends. Humour might be drawn from the contrast between the public and the private, between what the character you create in the diary writes and how the character is constrained to behave in real life. Conversely, diary writing is an excellent opportunity to use a tone of pathos to engage the reader in the trauma or suffering of the character created.

Task

- Write a series of diary entries for a teenager experiencing difficulties at school.

or

- Write a single diary entry for someone for whom an important relationship has just changed in a serious or dramatic way.

Script

You will be familiar with the term 'script' from your study of drama. It is useful at this point to remember what you learn from the study of drama. As well as being entertained by it, you are caught up in the development of the plot or story, or the revelation or development of characters, or both. The setting might be important, although it would not need to be. The writer might be exploring a particular theme. When you write your own script you are writing a little play. There are also rules to be observed for the layout of a script. So the five factors to be aware of when you write a script are **plot**, **character**, **setting**, **theme** and **layout**.

Plot, character, setting and theme

The number and type of characters might be determined by the task set, as might the storyline or plot, or there may be an element of choice. As it is important in diary writing not to produce merely a ramble which has little purpose, so in script writing it is important to establish at the outset what the purpose of your script is. Do you intend to develop a plot? Do you intend to develop a character? Do you intend to interweave plot and character to produce a surprising or ambiguous ending? What is your setting, and how important, if at all, is it to the outcome of the script? Before you begin writing, jot down answers to these questions. Write a little character study of your characters, and a brief outline of the plot. Describe the setting. As with narrative writing, your plot might involve conflict, but it doesn't have to. You might have a particular theme in mind. Some or all of the above – plot, character, setting and theme – might be prescribed by the examination question, or you might have a wide choice.

Layout

In order to show that a character is about to speak, write the name of the character in capital letters, followed by a colon. (An example is given below.) The layout of a script is much easier than the punctuation of direct speech in narrative writing. Although a script should be mostly dialogue, there will be occasions when you will need to show actions rather than words in order to advance the plot or show something about character. These actions are called stage directions. A stage direction might be just one or two words, to show the way in which a character speaks the dialogue, or it might be a sentence or group of sentences which are necessary for understanding plot or character. Stage directions are shown in a way which differentiates them from dialogue, by being written within brackets. Stage directions are always written in the present tense.

Sample script

> (A letter is pushed through the letter box of the family home. Emma rushes to pick it up.)
> JENNIFER: Whose letter? I was expecting a letter from Chris today.
> EMMA (moving upstairs): No, it's mine. It's nothing really. Anyway, mind your own business.
> JENNIFER (shouting): Mum! Emma's got a letter and it seems to be a big secret. I hate secrets, and anyway ...

The script you are asked to write in the examination may not involve dialogue; it may be a monologue, in other words have only one speaker. But the above rules on plot, character, setting, theme and layout still apply.

Task

- Write a script of a family discussion which begins with a letter arriving for one member of the family.

or

- Write a script based on the idea of revenge.

Newspaper or magazine article

When you write an article, either for a newspaper or for a magazine, you must establish your readership. This will have implications for the tone you adopt. There are also certain rules for the layout of a magazine which you must bear in mind. So in article writing the two factors you should be aware of are **tone** and **layout**.

Tone

You would obviously write differently if you were a journalist on your local newspaper than you would if you were a senior student writing for your school magazine. Think of the intended reader of the article before you begin. This will establish whether your tone should be more or less formal, chatty or conspiratorial. Are you writing for an unknown group or for people whom you know even in a general way or with whom you can easily identify? As with letter writing you might want to make up a word bank of terms appropriate to your intended readership.

Layout

Real articles in newspapers are normally written in columns, but you would not be expected to emulate this in an examination. But there are other conventions of newspapers which you should try to employ. A headline is an obvious one.

Real headlines are short and eye-catching, often encapsulating alliteration or pun. (If you are unsure about these terms, look back at unit 3 on figures of speech.) Sub-headings will be used to divide the newspaper article into sections. The events will not be described in chronological order, but in order of importance. For example, an article about a bank robbery would start with the fact of the robbery and then move on to the getaway car; it would not start with the robbers getting into their car to drive to the bank and then give an account of the robbery. Newspaper articles will also often have interviews with key witnesses; such interviews need to be punctuated properly using inverted commas for words actually spoken, although there is no need to take a new line for a new speaker. Similarly, magazine articles will have headlines. The paragraphs will be ordered according to topics, although that will depend on the task set.

> ## Task
>
> Write an article for a school magazine in which you describe a recent school trip in which you took part.

Discursive/argumentative articles

We have been treating newspaper and magazine articles as imaginative writing so far, as we did with letters. Sometimes, however, as with letter writing, you might find a newspaper or magazine article – though most likely a magazine article – being asked for in the discursive/argumentative section of the examination paper. A magazine article might belong more obviously under this section because its content matter is discursive/argumentative in nature. An example of a magazine article topic which belongs in the discursive/argumentative section of the examination paper is given in the task below.

> ## Task
>
> Write an article for a local newspaper in which you discuss a local issue which interests you.

Biography

Biography literally means 'writing about a life' of someone other than yourself. Biography comes under the heading of imaginative writing in that you might be asked to write about the life of an imaginary person, or, even if the person is real, you might not personally know very much about him/her and so would be drawing on your imagination when you write. Probably the most important factors to think about when writing biography are **tone** and **content**.

Tone and content

The key to correct tone in biography writing is assuming a position of knowledge or inside information. People read biographies out of curiosity. Your choice of content can assist in this. Include personal details of character or events which are not likely to be widely known. Examples might be the person's favourite foods, or details of their disagreements with others or plans for the future. Little stories from the person's life – anecdotes – help to create this confidential tone.

Task

Write the opening of the biography of a famous person. You may choose a real famous person or invent one of your own.

Speech

If you are asked to write a speech, the key factors are **tone** and **delivery**.

Tone

In order to achieve the correct tone in a speech, it is probably best to draw on what we have already said about biography. Your speech might be on a personal experience and if so you would want to establish a confidential tone in order to draw in your reader. Speech writing is artificial in that you are committing to paper what should be delivered orally. You need to make the words rise from the page as if they were being spoken. Do you want to be humorous? Or serious? Or sarcastic? Your chosen style – for example, humorous, serious, sarcastic – combined with a confidential or conspiratorial tone will produce a good speech.

Delivery

Given the artificial nature of speech writing, you will have to show the way in which you would deliver a speech orally through the way in which you write it. Begin with a speech introduction, for example 'Ladies and gentlemen' or 'Good morning, everyone'. Your introduction and its tone will be decided by your audience, which in turn will be decided by the nature of the task. Always bear in mind that you are writing a speech, so pepper your writing with expressions which belong particularly to speech. Signposts in formal speeches might include 'I put it to you', 'Do not let us forget' and 'It has been said many times but it is worth repeating …'. Less formal speeches might use expressions such as 'Well' and 'As you might imagine' or contractions such as 'won't' or 'can't'. You might want to capture the tone of an orator by the use of repetition, or by the use of short sentences, or even non-sentences. You might want to engage the audience by the use of the first-person plural as in 'Let us go on …' or by the use of the second person as in 'You must be aware that …'. You might want to use questions and rhetorical questions such as 'Did you know that …?' or 'Surely you know that …?' Don't be afraid to address your audience as you would do in a real speech. The ending of your speech is also important. Finish on a high note, or a persuasive note, certainly a note appropriate to the task set. There are examples of speeches in units 6 and 12.

Discursive/argumentative speeches

We have been treating speeches as imaginative writing, as we did with letters and magazine articles. Sometimes, however, you will find a speech being asked for in the discursive/argumentative section of the examination. An example of a question asking for a speech of this nature is given in the task below.

Autobiography

When we compiled our list of imaginative topics at the start of this unit we did not include autobiography, or writing about your own life. This was because your own life is real; it does not come out of your imagination! In that respect it might best be described as personal writing. However, autobiography will probably appear in your examination paper under narrative/descriptive/imaginative writing and so it is appropriate to discuss it here. As with biography the key factor in good autobiography writing is **tone**.

Tone

As with biography, people want to read autobiography to find out information about the writer's life, personality and relationships. The tone should therefore be knowledgeable and sometimes confidential. As with biography, include anecdotes or reflections which draw the reader into your piece of writing.

18 Exemplars of good imaginative writing

As with narrative and descriptive writing, it is impossible to give many examples of good practice in one book, but the purpose of this chapter is to try to bring together some of the main points made in the last chapter about imaginative writing. We will not have space to cover all the genres discussed in the last chapter, but we will look at some of them to reinforce points made about writing in a particular genre.

Diary

The three short extracts that follow are from perhaps the most famous diary ever written. Anne Frank's family hid in an attic in Amsterdam to avoid capture by their oppressors during the Second World War. Anne, aged 13, kept a diary of the time spent in the attic, or annexe.

Task

Write a short commentary on these diary extracts, picking out the features of good diary writing which we established as being **content** and **tone**.

The 'Secret Annexe' is an ideal hiding-place. Although it leans to one side and is damp, you'd never find such a comfortable hiding-place anywhere in Amsterdam; no, perhaps not even in the whole of Holland.

The right door leads to our 'Secret Annexe'. No one would ever guess that there would be so many rooms hidden behind that plain grey door. There's a little step in front of the door and then you are inside.

And as for us, we are fortunate. Yes, we are luckier than millions of people. It is quiet and safe here ... We are even so selfish as to talk about 'after the war', brighten up at the thought of having new clothes and new shoes ...

Anne Frank *Diary of a Young Girl*

Sample commentary

The tone is confidential. The reader is being invited to share not just life events of the writer, but also her thoughts and opinions. The reader is forced to imagine what it must be like to live in fear of one's life in cramped conditions. At the same time something of the personality of the writer comes through. She is grateful for what she has and her liveliness is apparent even in these short extracts.

Script

The extract below comes from Arthur Miller's play *A View from the Bridge*. Eddie and Beatrice, a married couple, have been arguing a lot lately because Catherine has fallen in love with Rodolpho, whom Eddie strongly dislikes. Catherine is Eddie's niece, and Eddie and Beatrice have looked after her since she was a little girl.

Task

Write a short commentary on the extract, picking out features of good script writing, which we established as being **plot**, **character**, **setting** and **theme**, where theme could involve conflict.

EDDIE: You used to be different, Beatrice. You had a whole different way.

BEATRICE: I'm no different.

EDDIE: You didn't used to jump me all the time about everything. The last year or two I come in the house I don't know what's gonna hit me. It's a shootin' gallery in here and I'm the pigeon.

BEATRICE: Okay, okay.

EDDIE: Don't tell me okay, okay. I'm tellin' you the truth. A wife is supposed to believe the husband. If I tell you that guy ain't right [for Catherine] don't tell me he is right. ... And I don't like you sayin' I don't want her marryin' anybody. I broke my back paying for her stenography lessons so she could go out and meet a better class of people. Would I do that if I didn't want her to get married? Sometimes you talk like I was a crazy man or sump'm.

BEATRICE: But she likes him.

EDDIE: Beatrice, she's a baby, how is she gonna know what she likes?

BEATRICE: Well, you kept her a baby, you wouldn't let her go out. I told you a hundred times.

(Pause.)

EDDIE: All right. Let her go out, then.

BEATRICE: She doesn't wanna go out now. It's too late, Eddie.

(Pause.)

EDDIE: Suppose I told her to go out. Suppose I –

BEATRICE: They're going to get married next week, Eddie.

Arthur Miller *A View from the Bridge*

Sample commentary

There is clearly conflict in the plot. The conflict has been going on for some time: 'The last year or two'. The character of Eddie is developed to show his possessiveness towards Catherine, a reluctance to let her grow up, a pride in the sacrifices he made for her education and his fear of letting her have a boyfriend. Eddie thinks that wives should listen to their husbands and perhaps he thinks the husband should be the boss in his home. The plot is tense and poignant when Eddie decides to reverse his previous decision about Catherine's social life; he is willing to let her go out now, but it is too late. Eddie is the victim of his own possessiveness and this is brought home to him when he is told that Catherine is to be married soon. Conflict is further shown here in that Beatrice knows about the wedding but Eddie does not. Thus Catherine and Beatrice have been plotting behind Eddie's back. There is obvious dramatic tension in this short extract, establishing the expectation of further conflict and even suffering, of things about to go badly wrong.

Biography

The biography writer is a long-time friend of the writer Graham Greene.

Task

Write a short commentary on this biography extract, picking out features of good biography writing, which we established as being **content** and **tone**.

Many years later, during one of my visits to [Greene's home in] Antibes, we went out shopping one morning to buy something for supper when a lady came into the shop where we were waiting to be served and, noticing two smoked trout in Graham's shopping basket, asked him where she could obtain them. Graham immediately left me in charge of the purchases and accompanied the lady to the shop where he had bought the trout.

Leopoldo Duran *Graham Greene, Friend and Brother*

Sample commentary

The writer relates a simple anecdote about the man whose biography he is writing. He knows that readers will be curious to have inside information, to read something not otherwise known. The tone is therefore anecdotal and confidential, as if the writer is talking directly to the reader and revealing something of his subject's private life and personality. The content is simple and easy to read, a little piece of information for those interested enough to read a biography of a particular famous person.

Autobiography

The passage below is an extract from Nelson Mandela's autobiography *Long Walk to Freedom*.

Task

Write a short commentary on the passage, picking out features of good autobiography writing, which we established as being related to **tone**.

I was no more than five when I became a herd-boy, looking after sheep and calves in the fields. I discovered the almost mystical attachment that the Xhosa people have for cattle, not only as a source of food and wealth, but as a blessing from God and a source of happiness. It was in the fields that I learned how to knock birds out of the sky with a slingshot, to gather wild honey and fruits and edible roots, to drink warm, sweet milk straight from the udder of a cow, to swim in the clear, cold streams, and to catch fish with twine and sharpened bits of wire.

Nelson Mandela *Long Walk to Freedom*

Sample commentary

The writer is a famous person and, although much would be known by the reader of his adult life, it is refreshing to read of his childhood. The writing has a confidential tone as if taking the reader back in time. The reader is drawn into the beliefs and practices of the Xhosa people. The writer shares the Xhosa gratitude for cattle in his happy and uninhibited drinking from the cow's udder. By identifying himself with a particular way of life, the writer draws the reader into an appreciation of that way of life.

Exam tip

If you choose to write imaginatively in a particular literary genre, keep that genre in the forefront of your mind throughout your time spent writing so that you adhere to its conventions.

(19) Discursive and argumentative writing

Discursive or argumentative writing involves discussing, or arguing around, a particular topic which may be either prescribed by the examination question or left to your choice. The task of discursive writing is closely linked to that of argumentative writing. The main difference is that in discursive writing you are asked to discuss, which usually means providing points both for and against, whereas in argumentative writing you are asked to argue a case, which usually involves only points for or points against a particular opinion. In both discursive and argumentative writing you might be expected to try to persuade the reader that your point of view is correct. The extent to which you are expected to be persuasive will be determined largely by the wording of the examination question, although the need to be persuasive might be implied or optional rather than stated. Discursive writing will generally be more balanced than argumentative writing, in that opposing views of the same case might be asked for. Good discursive and argumentative writing share some characteristics which are listed below.

Characteristics of discursive and argumentative writing

Each type of writing involves:

- taking several lines of argument and developing them
- presenting lines of argument in an ordered fashion
- giving evidence to support the lines of argument
- linking coherently each line of argument.

There are basically two differences between discursive and argumentative writing:

- Discursive writing requires providing points for and against.
- Argumentative writing requires providing points either for or against.

Task

Below is a list of topics for discursive and argumentative writing. Write each of them down and say whether you think it is discursive or argumentative. Note at this stage that all of these topics are emphatically either discursive or argumentative; the reality of examination questions is that some topics on a question paper will be more measured or even vague in their wording. However, dealing with these straightforward topics will help you to focus on the difference between discursive and argumentative writing and become comfortable with the skills required by each.

1 The advantages and disadvantages of school uniform.
2 Smoking: a menace in society.

Sample response

Topics **1**, **4** and **5** are discursive. Topics **2**, **3** and **6** are argumentative.

Topics **1** and **4** are obviously discursive in that they are asking for two opposing sets of points. Topic **5** is less obviously discursive, but close inspection shows that it invites the reader to give the advantages of the Internet as well as the disadvantages which could lead to a call for its censorship.

Topic **2** must be argumentative as it would be impossible, surely, to find any socially acceptable reasons for describing smoking as a good thing. In topic **6**, even a writer sympathetic to boxing would not be right to include a pro-boxing line of argument because of the strong and one-sided vocabulary of the question itself. Topic **3** is clearly asking the writer to produce arguments all pointing in the same direction, namely towards a good education.

Task

Make up six essay titles of your own, three which are discursive and three which are argumentative.

Now, let's go back to the list of common characteristics and deal with each point in turn.

Taking and developing several lines of argument

Let's think about the topic 'Capital Punishment'. Although this could be either discursive (for *and* against) or argumentative (either for *or* against) let's imagine that this is a discursive topic. In other words, we're looking for several, say two or three, points in favour of it and two or three points against it.

Task

Write down two or three points for capital punishment and two or three points against it.

Sample response

For
It acts as a deterrent and discourages would-be offenders.
It provides revenge for the victim's family and for society.
The punishment fits the crime; serious actions – serious consequences.

Against
It offends the sanctity of life. Life is sacred.
Miscarriages of justice happen where the wrong person is put to death.

Each of these points would need to be developed in your piece of writing but they provide the skeleton outline.

Presenting lines of argument in an ordered fashion

Whether your piece of writing is discursive or argumentative, having assembled your points, you must then order them. You have a choice of two ways: either start with what for you is the most powerful point, move on to the next most powerful point and so on, or start with what for you is the least powerful point, move on to the next most powerful and up to the most powerful. If your essay is discursive you must also decide whether you personally are for or against. You must still come up with the points for and against, but your own personal view will determine whether you start with points for or points against. The better way to structure a discursive essay is to deal with your own viewpoints second. So if you are *for* the topic, your section plan should be like this: introduction, points against, points for, conclusion. If you are *against* the topic, your section plan should be like this: introduction, points for, points against, conclusion.

Task

For the discursive topic 'For and Against School Uniform':

1 Write down two or three points for school uniform.
2 Write down two or three points against school uniform.
3 Order your points (either most important to least or vice versa).
4 Decide whether you are for or against.
5 Draw up your section plan.

Giving evidence to support your argument

Discursive or argumentative writing which merely states points without developing them is weak. You must develop points made by offering evidence to support them. This will obviously depend on the topic chosen. But in the case of the capital punishment essay you could give evidence to show that capital punishment is a deterrent. Evidence would be to compare murder rates of countries with the death penalty with murder rates in countries without it. Where miscarriages of justice are concerned it might be possible to give evidence of someone put to death who was later found to have been innocent.

Task

Write down evidence from your own knowledge which could be used in the argument for school uniform. Next do the same for the argument against school uniform.

Linking each line of argument coherently

We have already established the need to cluster points, whether points for and points against in a discursive essay, or just for or against in an argumentative essay. We have also established the need then to put the points in order. Only then can writing begin. It is also important to link points for and points against and to show when your writing is moving from for to against, or from against to for; in other words to show a change in direction in your discussion.

> ### Task
>
> Divide the following words and phrases into two groups, those which link and those which show a change of direction: **a** *similarly*, **b** *another point*, **c** *nevertheless*, **d** *likewise*, **e** *furthermore*, **f** *however*, **g** *in addition*, **h** *conversely*, **i** *in the same way*, **j** *on the other hand*.

Sample response

> Links are **a**, **b**, **d**, **e**, **g** and **i**. Changes of direction are **c**, **f**, **h** and **j**.

Argumentative essays

Although this unit may seem to be concentrating on discursive writing, it is by understanding the techniques of discursive writing that the techniques for argumentative writing fall into place. However, we have yet to deal with the persuasive nature of many argumentative writing topics.

> ### Task
>
> As head girl or boy of your school, write to the school principal asking for an improvement in some area which is causing concern among fellow students. Remember to be both persuasive and respectful.

How would you tackle this topic? You would establish your area of need, for example the school library. You would make a list of points, in this case points which would improve the library facilities. These are all *for* points, for example more cash for books which need to be replaced, more cash for new titles altogether, new furniture (explaining what is wrong with the old furniture) and some way of ensuring that silence is observed in the library. Next you would order your points in the way shown earlier in this unit. Now you are ready to begin writing. It is important to observe the appropriate tone, one which you imagine a student would use to a school principal. Respectful expressions such as 'I feel that', 'I hope that you will', 'May I point out that' are clearly more appropriate than 'It's absolutely outrageous', 'What kind of place do you think you're running anyway?' or 'I demand that something is done now'.

The persuasive nature of other topics might involve more emphatic language. This is where close reading of the topic and an understanding, as ever, of audience are required if you are to do well in argumentative writing.

Discursive essays may also be required to be persuasive. This depends on the topic set and the way in which you decide to approach it but persuasive language belongs more comfortably with argumentative writing.

Argumentative writing also enables the personality of the writer to shine through in a way which isn't always possible with discursive writing. For example, in argumentative writing you may be able to use a wheedling tone or a humorous tone to advantage, depending of course on the topic. You can be comically persuasive or use a dry sense of humour to persuade the reader that you are correct. There might be more scope for figures of speech, especially those with a personal touch, for example rhetorical questions.

Introductions and conclusions

Whether your piece of writing is discursive or argumentative, it will need to have an introduction and a conclusion. Each of these paragraphs will probably be short. Although there is probably less scope for eye-catching openings in discursive and argumentative writing than there is in narrative, descriptive or imaginative types, that is no excuse to make your opening dull. For example, you might begin with a short sentence or with a question.

Here are some possible openings for the essay. 'School Uniform: For and Against'.

- School uniform: a necessity or an outmoded dress code?
- School uniform is a hotly debated issue.

It would not be a good idea to begin:

- I have been asked to write a discursive essay on school uniform.

Your piece of writing needs a conclusion to show that your arguments have been fully developed and considered. In the case of discursive writing, the concluding paragraph gives you an opportunity to show your own views and opinions. In the case of argumentative writing, you have a chance to round off your line of argument with a final appeal to the reader whom you are trying to persuade to your point of view or to give a final comment in a chosen style, for example humour.

Task

Write a discursive essay entitled:

- Capital Punishment: For and Against *or* • School Uniform: For and Against.

Task

Write an essay in which you try to persuade other students to take up a hobby you are interested in.

Exam tip

Before beginning your discursive or argumentative writing, always take time to work out a logical paragraph plan as outlined in this unit.

20 Exemplars of good discursive and argumentative writing

In this unit we will examine two pieces of discursive writing and one piece of argumentative writing produced by students at AS level.

Task

Look back at the guidelines established in the last unit about discursive and argumentative writing. Use these guidelines to write a commentary on the following piece of writing.

Topic: For and against school uniform

This subject is a controversial one and in some parts of the world court cases have been instigated over whether or not school students should be forced to wear uniform. What are the pros and cons? What price do we pay for school uniform by taking away that person's liberty and freedom of choice?

As a high school student, this is a debate in which I find myself often engaged with friends and teachers alike. There are many good points in favour of school uniform, such as the safety aspect. This plays an important part in the debate because it is logical to think that if you can identify the children who attend your school by their uniform, then outsiders sporting track suits and casual wear can be easily identified and if they pose a threat they can be removed. This can be effective in catching and discouraging outsiders from attempting to enter school grounds with the intention to do harm, as has happened in some parts of the world, most recently in Germany.

Another argument in favour of school uniform is that it is very smart looking when there are visitors to the school or when students are visiting places with their school. This helps to build up a good reputation for the school as the visitor or host will have a good impression of smartness and professionalism in the way students present themselves. This can give the impression that even the most rebellious student is neat and tidy. It will also please many mothers and fathers as they see their son or daughter looking smart.

As well as these issues, school uniform also helps to give a sense of identity to the students who wear it, making them feel part of a community and evoking school spirit within them. This helps with morale as many students at high school feel depressed or sad when things are not going their way and trivial things such as a sense of belonging can help make life easier for them, and for their parents when they return home. Also, school uniform helps to cut down on bullying, as people are not picked on for what they wear to school because everyone is equal and wears the same clothes, although many students find a way round this by buying designer shoes, shirts and belts to help make their uniform more individual.

On the other hand, although there are many good points in favour of wearing school uniform, there are also many bad points. One is that school uniform takes away the right of individualism from students by forcing them to wear a piece of clothing which brands them as belonging to a certain school. To say this is acceptable because it promotes safety is not a worthy argument. The real issue as I see it is that liberty has been taken away, the right which we have by living in a democratic country to express ourselves through what we wear.

People can say that a uniform promotes team spirit, such as that which is found in an athletics or sports team, but the fact is that these activities are voluntary and people would not find it acceptable if somebody was forced to join and wear the colours of that particular team. Professional sportspeople who wear a type of uniform get paid and although the law indicates that everyone has a right to education, it does not say that you must be branded like cattle in order to receive it.

Another argument against school uniform is that it takes time and effort to control and monitor people to make sure that they are wearing a uniform. This time could be better spent on correcting behaviour and improving the school as a whole. Surely it doesn't really matter what we wear as long as we are learning.

Many people say that school uniform stops students being bullied because of what they wear, but this is not the case as people will be picked on anyway either for their size, stature or looks. And anyway, what will happen to them when they leave school and find that some people can afford better clothes than they can? In the real world, is there competition? The answer is that there is, and sheltering children from these things just makes it more difficult for them to comprehend and handle when they are older so sheltering them from reality will not do them any good in the long run.

For me, school uniform is not something I hate so much as a thing I should challenge. In reality, we do not all walk about looking the same because we are individuals. From a strictly teenager's point of view, who wants to be dull? Everyone has an urge to rebel against something and for me school uniform is a worthy cause. (800 words)

Sample commentary

The writer has selected points for and points against school uniform and has then ordered them from what for him are the most important down to the least important. He has given links as he moves from point to point and from paragraph to paragraph. When moving from points for to points against, he has shown his change of direction. He has decided that he is against rather than for and has ordered his paragraphs accordingly, to finish with his own personal point of view. He has an introduction and a good conclusion. He has backed up points with evidence.

Task

Look back at the guidelines established in the last unit about discursive and argumentative writing. Use these guidelines to write a commentary on the following piece of writing.

Topic: For and against capital punishment

Capital punishment is one of the most controversial subjects to be discussed today. This controversy is caused by so many people all over the world having so many different views about it. Capital punishment happens when someone is put to death for a crime, for example murder or drug trafficking. Many countries in the world have abolished this form of punishment but there are many countries which use it, including many of the states of America. Many people think capital punishment should be reinstated in Britain, but there are just as many people who think that the criminal system is better the way it is.

One important argument against the death penalty is that sometimes an innocent person is put to death. If capital punishment is used, the authorities must therefore have evidence beyond the shadow of any doubt that they have accused the correct person. Furthermore, capital punishment removes all possibility for a person who has done something seriously wrong to be able to change and to be rehabilitated, or to face up to their past life and repent. In many cases, after capital punishment is abolished, there have been people who committed crimes such as murder, but when they were released after serving their time in prison they did not re-offend but instead they changed and became better people.

Another strong point against capital punishment is that two wrongs do not make a right. Killing a victim, for instance, and then being sentenced to death does not suddenly make everything all right or make things better. A poor, helpless victim's life has been stolen from him, but killing the murderer will not bring the victim back. In addition, some people might argue that it is inhumane and against human rights to hang, execute or electrify a human being in the name of justice. It could be argued that nobody deserves to die in such a horrible way even if his previous actions have been horribly wrong. The counter-argument to this is of course that the criminal by his actions has given up any rights he might have had to humane treatment.

Nevertheless, those who are in favour of the death penalty have many points with which to justify their stance. Most importantly it punishes the criminal by doing to him what he did to others. It acts as a form of revenge for the victim's family by letting them know that the criminal has felt some of the pain he inflicted on another. This is really the only way that people can honestly say that justice has been done. In addition, taking the life of a murderer prevents recidivism, because if the person is no longer alive, then there is no way in which he can commit a crime again.

Furthermore, capital punishment could act as a deterrent to anyone who even thought about committing certain crimes, because he would know that when he was found guilty the death penalty awaited him. Another point in favour of capital punishment is that this method of punishment saves money because instead of the criminal being kept in prison for the rest of his life, he is killed and the money which would have been used to keep him in prison can be used in other, more profitable areas, such as education and hospitals.

After weighing up the arguments for and against capital punishment, I have come to the conclusion that I am for it, and that it is a pity it was abolished in Britain thirty or so years ago. It is a difficult subject to think about, but, on the whole, I feel that more overall can be achieved by societies which retain or reinstate it. (618 words)

Sample commentary

The writer has selected points for and points against the death penalty. She has then categorised these points into what for her are the most important down to the least important. She has given links when moving from point to point and paragraph to paragraph. She has tried to give evidence to support the points she makes. When moving from points against to points for, she has shown the change of direction. She has decided that she is for rather than against capital punishment and has ordered her paragraphs accordingly to finish with her own personal point of view. She has an introduction and a good conclusion.

Task

Look back at the guidelines established in the last unit about discursive and argumentative writing. Use these guidelines to write a commentary on the following piece of writing.

Topic: Write an argumentative essay in which you argue either for or against homework.

I'm the kind of person who will state his opinions about anything he is asked about. One thing which really gets on my nerves is homework.

This essay is part of my English homework. Personally I think that homework is a complete waste of time. Adults seem to have weird brains as they not only think we should do homework but that we should have even more than we already have. I don't know how their brains work, but they're certainly different from mine. After we, school children that is, return home we are asked two questions: 'How was your day?' and the killer question 'Do you have any homework?' What makes these mad people think that after we've returned from a very laborious day at school, we want to go and do more school work is beyond me. When our parents return from work we don't ask them 'How was your day?' and then 'Do you have any more work you could do?' We don't, so they shouldn't either.

There are two main groups of adults: our parents, who like us getting homework, and another group who actually give us homework. This group is, of course, called teachers. Teachers say that homework (a) will help us at the time of our exams and (b) can be fun. I've never once had a piece of homework that was fun but the part about it being helpful I don't completely disagree with. It does get us into the habit of studying but whether it is a boring English essay or a lengthy page of maths equations, no-one really performs to their full potential with homework because they're either listening to the radio or watching TV while doing it.

Homework can be socially divisive. Not everyone has a room of their own to work in at home, with a desk, a desk lamp and a comfortable chair. Some students in my school have to work in the evenings to supplement the family income. They fall further and further behind in their school work because they are unable to keep up with homework. Some students are able to enhance their homework assignments by accessing the Internet from home. This of course depends on the possession of a computer at home. As this is not the case with all students, it seems that homework makes the gap between the 'haves' and the 'have nots' even wider than it would be without homework.

If the government were to abolish homework it would not only make every school child's life easier but also teachers' lives as well. Teachers wouldn't have to put up with unconvincing excuses like 'I've forgotten it' or 'I was at my grandma's house and was unable to do it' or my personal favourite 'I've done it but my dog ate it'. The most popular excuse at my school is 'I've forgotten it'.

I've conducted a survey on homework which consisted of three questions: 'What is your favourite excuse for undone homework?', 'Do you find homework fun?' and 'How long do you spend on homework every night?' For question one, seven out of ten said 'I've forgotten it'. For question two, one out of ten said it could sometimes be fun. For question three, five out of ten said they spend at least two hours a night on homework.

If anyone reading this has the power to get rid of homework, he or she definitely should, as it would make everyone's life easier and all you adults should take heed that one day we will be your age and you will be old and we might just take our revenge. (609 words)

Sample commentary

The writer takes a relatively light-hearted look at this topic. Thus it can be seen that not all discursive and argumentative writing has to be serious and weighty in nature. As the topic was specifically argumentative, that is adopting a standpoint of either for or against, the writer has chosen to write against homework. Therefore all the points he makes are against; there is none of the measured, balanced approach of the discursive essay. The writer has ordered his points giving a paragraph for each. He backs up his claims with evidence. He has a short opening paragraph and a humorous concluding paragraph which neatly rounds off his piece of writing.

More ambiguous topics

These pieces of discursive and argumentative writing have been selected here because they are very clear examples of an obviously stated topic, namely 'for and against' or 'for' or 'against'. However, not all topics in discursive and argumentative writing will be so clearly worded. But if you look behind the wording, you should see either 'for and against', or 'for' only or 'against' only. Look back at what we said in the previous unit if you need clarification.

Exam tip

In discursive and argumentative writing remember to order your points and to link them using one of the methods illustrated in this unit.

㉑ Exam practice in narrative, descriptive and imaginative writing

Write between 600 and 900 words for each composition.

1 Choose *one* of the following settings: a beach, a busy department store or a railway station. Write the opening of a story which establishes the setting you have chosen.

2 Write a drama script which involves conflict between a parent and child. The theme should be fashion *or* homework *or* pocket money.

3 Imagine that you changed places for a day with either one of your parents. Write your diary entry.

4 Write a childhood section of the biography of a famous celebrity from the world of sport *or* music. Your celebrity can be real or imaginary.

5 Write about the family meal that went wrong. You may write humorously if you wish.

6 Write a short story beginning 'It must be years since I saw you!'

7 Imagine that you have just moved to a new neighbourhood and a new school. Write a letter to a friend in your old neighbourhood explaining the difficulties you have had in settling down in your new surroundings.

8 Write the opening of a short story about a character who decides to stop worrying about what other people think.

9 Write a descriptive piece comparing a market at the start of the day as the first customers arrive and its appearance at the end of the day.

10 Write the closing chapter of a novel about a child. The genre can be historical *or* horror *or* mystery.

11 Write a chapter for your own autobiography in which you describe an achievement *or* an embarrassing experience *or* a sad occasion.

12 Think of a colour. Imagine that colour is a room. Describe the room.

13 Write a short story in which the main character has to deal with unpleasant news.

14 Write an article for your school magazine discussing the appeal of a sport you know well, outlining its advantages and explaining what it means for you.

15 There are many days in the year when there are celebrations. Write about a particularly memorable one, describing your thoughts and feelings as well as the celebration itself.

22 Exam practice in discursive and argumentative writing

Write between 600 and 900 words for each composition.

1 The mobile phone: a blessing or a curse?

2 Discuss the ways in which your experience of growing up has influenced your views on bringing up children.

3 'Pop stars are good role models for young people.' Do you agree?

4 The local authorities in your area have decided to sell the town's sports ground to a property developer. Write a letter of protest to your local newspaper.

5 'The older generation has nothing to teach the younger generation.' Discuss.

6 Some people complain that computer games encourage young people to spend time on their own rather than with groups of friends. Do you agree? Write about your views.

7 Choose any problem threatening the global environment on a long-term basis. Discuss the threat presented by this problem and say how you think its effects might be lessened.

8 'Mass media rules!' Discuss ways in which you think the media has brought about significant changes to modern life.

9 The advantages and disadvantages of *either* city life *or* living in the country.

10 Write the speech you would give to a group of young people of your own age who are thinking of enrolling in your school. Try to persuade them that yours is a good school.

11 'Good health is the responsibility of the individual.' What are your views?

12 'Men have much easier lives than women.' Do you agree?

13 Write an article for a school magazine in which you discuss ways in which students can improve their study skills.

14 Write about the ways in which you think your own town/environment could be improved.

15 Write a letter to a friend in which you persuade him/her to take up a particular sport which you yourself enjoy.

Part 2

Advanced Subsidiary Literature in English

Introduction

This part of the book is designed to help you to prepare for your examination in Advanced Subsidiary (AS) Literature in English. Just as in English Language, there are Assessment Objectives that make it clear what skills and knowledge you will be tested on. All of the following Assessment Objectives are tested in each paper.

i Ability to respond to texts in the three main forms (Prose, Poetry and Drama) of different types and from different cultures. (If you are taking the Language and Literature syllabus you respond to texts in two of the three main forms.)

ii Understanding of the ways in which writers' choices of form, structure and language shape meanings.

iii Ability to produce informed, independent opinions and judgements on literary texts.

iv Ability to communicate clearly the knowledge, understanding and insight appropriate to literary study.

The AS Literature in English examination

You will have to sit *two* papers. Each of these carries the same number of marks (50), showing that they are of equal importance, and in each you have to answer two questions in two hours. Remember that Papers 1 and 2 are for the separate Language syllabus; these Literature syllabus papers are called Paper 3 and Paper 4.

Paper 3: Poetry and Prose

In this paper you answer on one poetry text from Section A and one prose text from Section B, with a choice of three texts in each section. There are two alternatives on each text, one an essay question and the other a passage-based question. You have one hour for each answer, two hours for the paper as a whole. Your answers should ideally be between 600 and 800 words.

Paper 4: Drama

As in Paper 3 you answer two questions once again, this time on two plays, with six to choose from. The alternatives are, similarly, either an essay or a passage-based question, to be answered in two hours.

The AS Language and Literature examination

You have to sit two papers, one on composition (a Language paper, see pp. v–vi) and one on literature. The Literature paper is Paper 9 and it is like Papers 3 and 4 combined.

Paper 9: Poetry, Prose and Drama

This paper has three sections and you choose one question from each of *two* of the three. You do not have to study all three genres for this combined exam. You will do poetry and prose, or poetry and drama, or drama and prose. There is a choice of three texts in each section.

Structure of this part of the book

This part of the book is divided into three sections on poetry, prose (with special reference to the novel) and drama. Because the Language part of this book has a great deal of useful information about prose and many exercises on it, you are advised to read the section on 'Passages for comment' in Part 1, and to try some of the tasks set. In this part of the book, the poetry units give advice suitable for those of you who have not studied poetry before, as well as helpful practice for those who are more experienced. The drama section is substantial, with hints and exercises on Shakespeare and other playwrights. Throughout the book sample responses and essays are given to read and discuss with your teacher and classmates. These are not intended as model answers: there is no such thing in this subject, where many different interpretations are possible. They are there to help and stimulate by example. By the time you have finished you will be able to tackle the AS level examination and go on to study A level if you want.

Wider reading and enjoyment

The book is not only intended to help you to pass an examination. It is also intended to be an enjoyable introduction or extension to the world of literature, a world of imaginative insights into the human condition and powerful use of the resources of the language. For this reason there are examples from works other than your set texts and hints for further reading and exploration of this most rewarding area for study.

(23) Introduction to poetry

Responding to poetry and writing about it

This section of the book will help you to express your thoughts and feelings about poetry. The units on this topic are designed to help you to enjoy poetry to the full and to feel more secure about expressing your responses, formulating your own interpretations and supporting your ideas with examples.

Poetry can stretch words to their limit to record unique, direct impressions of experience. A word can achieve its full potential when a skilled poet combines it with other carefully selected words. The elements of a word – its meaning, associations, context, history, sound, even its shape and length – all combine with other words to produce the distinctive qualities of a poem. No wonder that many writers see poetry as the ultimate achievement of any language, the utterance that can never really be translated without losing some of its magic. Read any poem aloud to savour its sounds and rhythms; critical appreciation will follow with practice.

The examination syllabus focuses on a very important Assessment Objective that reminds us that every writer chooses forms, structures and words to shape meanings. Both the writer selecting words and the reader absorbing their effects are important in this process. You are the reader whose close listening and reading, personal experience and enjoyment are most significant for your appreciation. You may find that you observe and give emphasis in a different way from your classmate. Providing that both of you can express your feelings, identify the evidence from the poem you are discussing and argue your case, then neither of you is wrong, necessarily. Both of you are literary critics.

What makes a poem?

> **Task**
>
> Discuss with your group or teacher, if possible, what qualities you think a poem should have in order to be defined as a poem, and make a list.

Sample response

You will probably find some or all of the following on your list:

a Reading a poem out loud can be very exciting/thrilling/funny/sad even if you don't understand all of it completely.

b It is usually 'about' something – a theme; but it doesn't have to tell a story.

c The writer is expressing her/his thoughts on a particular subject so it can be full of humour or emotion such as anger or sadness.

d The meaning can sometimes be difficult at first reading because:
- The words aren't in the usual order.
- Some of them even seem to be missing.
- They appear to be new words not in the dictionary, or don't have their usual meaning.
- The meaning isn't clear, because it is concentrated or ambiguous.

e The language can have lots of figures of speech (such as metaphor and personification) and be very descriptive.

f Sometimes words or phrases or ideas are repeated.

g It is written in lines and the sentences don't reach the end of the page.

h There is a pattern to the way it is laid out (for example in verses, stanzas or groups of lines).

i Sometimes it is very rhythmical and there are rhymes or other sound effects such as alliteration.

Some of the points above can apply to prose or drama as well, of course, but points **a**, **d**, **e**, **f**, **g**, **h** and **i** are probably more typical of poetry. Of all the items on the list, it's probably **d**, with its range of challenges for readers, that worries students the most, especially when they have never studied poetry before or are looking at a poem for the first time. Try not to be too worried about what you see as difficulties of interpretation. Some students spend too much time trying to chase the 'meaning' of a poem and forget about the real words that are the poem. It's important to remember that the poet has made choices to create particular effects, and considering these in detail – their sound, their rhythm, their combination together – often clarifies meaning where it has seemed tricky. The units that follow will explore all the points above and give you practice in writing about them.

Later in this Introduction, the themes of poetry are discussed (**b** and **c** above). Then, unit 24 deals with the language of poetry, its richness and variety, and helps you to interpret lines that are difficult at first, as well as developing your appreciation of images and figures of speech (**d**, **e** and **f**); unit 25 deals with the structures and layout of poems and how they may differ from ordinary speech and prose writing (**g** and **h**); unit 26 discusses rhythm and metre and scansion; unit 27 rhyme and sound effects (**i**). In unit 28 you focus on writing for the exam, with examples of both kinds of examination question. Throughout the units you will have tips about doing well in the exam. The examples used are from the texts on the syllabus now and in the future, as well as others that are especially memorable or appropriate to illustrate particular points.

Look back at the list of qualities that could characterise a poem. How many of them can be seen in the following short poetic text?

> The apparition of these faces in the crowd;
> Petals on a wet, black bough.
>
> Ezra Pound 'In a Station of the Metro'

Sample response

At first there do not seem to be enough qualities to make this into a poem as such. It has only two lines, which are not of the same length, there is no distinctive rhythm or rhyme and there is not even a verb to give action to the situation and point to a theme. [Some students think this is too fragmentary to be classed as a poem and you may have some sympathy with that view.] But it is a very descriptive fragment and it uses two different images – one in each line – to capture the poet's experience of seeing people in a crowded station. [The Metro is the Paris Underground system. If you do not have an underground train system where you live, imagine crowds pouring off a train.] The poem's title is important because it places the poet's observation and allows the reader to conjure up similar experiences. The first image is that the faces are an 'apparition', a word that means appearance, but also 'ghost', suggesting that they do not look like living beings and perhaps are pale and sad. The second image develops the idea by the metaphor of their faces being like petals on a wet black bough: perhaps the poet is suggesting spring when the trees have blooms but no leaves and the weather is still rainy; the petals are white or pale pink and delicate, easily blown away. Both images suggest helplessness and transience: there is nothing substantial or robust in the description at all. So although the poet has only offered us images, they are suggestive ones, haunting even, and the experience of seeing people as vulnerable in the hurly-burly of modern urban life has been communicated in two lines and two evocative images.

The poem is a good example of Imagism. Ezra Pound was one of a group of poets called Imagists who believed that experience was most effectively communicated through images of the senses and this approach is an important element in appreciating *what* a poet is expressing by considering *how* it is expressed. Sense images do not have to be metaphors. The senses are sight, hearing, touch, taste and smell; to these we can add the sense of energy or movement, which is termed **kinetic**.

What is the poem about?

Poets can express thoughts and feelings about anything, so poems can have as their subject matter anything in the world you can think of. There are great poems created about apparently trivial objects like a lock of hair, insects such as a flea or mosquito or growing things such as thistles or mushrooms. Major life dramas such as love, treachery and war do of course also feature. What the poet does with her or his subject matter, and how these ideas are developed, is the poem's theme, or it can be expressed as 'the poet's concerns'. These ideas are not separate from the words they are expressed in: the words *are* the poem.

Your exam syllabus does not set longer narrative poems for study, so all the examples used in this book will be of shorter lyric poems with distinct themes; you will find that length is not necessarily a criterion for excellence.

Themes in poetry

> ### Task
>
> Write down the names of five poems you have studied before and in one or two sentences say what they are about. If possible, with your partner or in a group discuss in more detail how each theme develops as the poem progresses.

It is often easier to summarise the theme of a poem than it is to analyse the poet's methods and the effects of the language used. This poem is about the waste and futility of war, you might say, or the sadness of death, or the passage of time, or how love relationships can be difficult, or how terribly some people in power can make others suffer.

Perhaps the poet gives a different example in each stanza and then concludes by emphasising his point, or uses a little anecdote that illustrates the issue. Or possibly the poet chooses images which are suggestive of her/his thought and doesn't express the thought directly, but we still grasp the gist of the argument.

> ### Task
>
> How would you describe the theme of this poem by William Blake? When you have answered, consider what other elements in the poem could affect the expression of this theme and your appreciation of it.

Infant Sorrow

My mother groan'd! my father wept.
Into the dangerous world I leapt:
Helpless, naked, piping loud:
Like a fiend hid in a cloud.

Struggling in my father's hands,
Striving against my swadling bands.
Bound and weary I thought best
To sulk upon my mother's breast.

Sample response

This poem, one of the *Songs of Experience*, presents a new-born baby uttering its thoughts and feelings, but this infant is very different from the sweet and innocent baby usually imagined being born into a loving, happy family environment. The baby is physically weak but its spirit is already corrupt and aggressive. The poet may be suggesting that children are not born innocent and then corrupted by the world as they grow up. Rather, he suggests, they have an inborn nature which disposes them towards ill temper and sin from the moment they are born into this 'dangerous' world.

What is missing from this response?

This answer interprets the theme of the poem quite successfully, but to focus on theme alone is to neglect other aspects of the poem that influence theme very powerfully. Consider the effect of having the child's voice as the speaking voice of the poem – this creates a powerful impression of a character already formed. Look at the simile 'Like a fiend hid in a cloud' and what it suggests about the devilish and hypocritical potential of the child. The evocative descriptive words 'struggling', 'striving' and the verb 'sulk' are linked in sound as well as meaning, emphasising the child's hostile, resentful attitude and self-conscious behaviour. Similarly the words 'hands' and 'bands' rhyme, suggesting by the implication of their linkage that the hands of the father are restraining rather than lovingly protective. The concise lines, regular rhythm and rhyme give a confident certainty to the meaning and tone of the poem, and are thereby all the more shocking.

'In a Station of the Metro', that little fragmentary poem, showed the importance of style in interpretation. You are reminded similarly by Blake's poem that the way a theme is expressed is vital to its meaning: all the work you do on analysis of style will help you to refine your ideas about theme and you will be able to return to your initial statement about the writer's concerns and make it more subtle and comprehensive.

Exam tip

The words make the poem: its meaning doesn't exist as a separate entity underneath or inside the words like a nut whose shell has to be cracked to find the kernel inside. If you changed some of the words to others with similar meanings but different sounds, the poem would disappear.

Students usually write about a poem's theme and say little about the poet's style and methods. Any close analysis of the language of a poem will enhance the quality of an exam answer.

(24) The language of poetry

This unit will help you to appreciate and deal with some of the poetic uses of language identified in unit 23: first, the figurative language that characterises many poems and expands their imaginative range; second, uses of language that challenge your understanding. The meaning of lines of poetry can sometimes be difficult because the words are new to you, they are not in the usual order or perhaps some are missing, making the utterance ambiguous. It's important to remember that a poet's style is not seeking difficulty for its own sake but striving for freshness of presentation and thought, so that when you study the poem you will be engaged by it and remember it with pleasure as a unique utterance.

Metaphorical language

As you've already seen in unit 23, the language of poetry can be very concentrated. One of the reasons for this intensity of expression is the use of metaphor. Literal language, the language of fixed predictable meaning, is relatively straightforward, but as soon as language becomes figurative (filled with figures of speech) then it becomes highly suggestive and open to imaginative interpretation.

Metaphor is a broad term which encompasses all the comparative figures of speech (simile and personification, for example) rather as the term 'mammal' includes a wide range of animals. (See unit 3 for a more restricted definition of the word 'metaphor'.) It is based, as you already know, on comparison. In the hands of a skilled poet, metaphor extends and enriches meaning, often working at more than one level of comparison and extending through several lines or a whole poem.

Examples

All the examples below are taken from the set anthology, *Touched with Fire* (Cambridge University Press, 1985).

1

In 'Mountain Lion' by D. H. Lawrence the dead lion's face is described as 'bright as frost' (simile) and the rocks where she had her lair as 'blood-orange brilliant rocks' (metaphor) and the green trees in the snow are 'like a Christmas toy' (another simile). These are very visual images and the poem is full of them, making the experience of reading it very evocative. However, the lion is dead and the poet mourns her death through his use of language: frost is cold as well as sharply beautiful, her lair is in rocks the colour of the blood the men have spilled, and the poet, looking out to the strangely empty dream-like world beyond, sees the landscape as reductive and child-like (the Christmas toy, without lasting significance).

2

When Ted Hughes describes the strong, viciously spiked thistles in the poem of the same name he compares them throughout to invading Viking warriors:

> a grasped fistful
> Of splintered weapons and Icelandic frost thrust up
> From the underground stain of a decayed Viking.

These images are visual and tactile too, creating impressions of shape, colour and texture. In the final stanza:

> Then they grow grey, like men.
> Mown down, it is a feud. Their sons appear,
> Stiff with weapons, fighting back over the same ground.

This images the visual decay of thistles into grey-topped thistledown and the difficulty any gardener or farmer would have to try to eradicate them. Like an invading army they will return, renewed and strong like young warriors, to take revenge for earlier efforts to destroy them. The extended metaphor successfully images peoples' attempts to control nature and the spirited defence put up to try to prevent it. What better image is there of the relationship between people and nature than an extended feud which is never over?

3

In 'Afterwards' by Thomas Hardy, a network of striking metaphorical language is used. Here is the first stanza:

> When the Present has latched its postern behind my tremulous stay,
>   And the May month flaps its glad green leaves like wings,
> Delicate-filmed as new-spun silk, will the neighbours say,
>   'He was a man who used to notice such things'?

In the first line, the Present is personified as someone shutting the gate behind Hardy, because he has died. 'Latched its postern' is rather archaic language and was so even at the time Hardy was writing. It reveals that the poet thinks of himself as old, of a previous age, and his death as a quiet slipping away. The gate that closes on his life is a private, old-fashioned side door. The May month in the second line is compared with a butterfly or bird, having 'glad green leaves' on the trees which move in the wind like the creature's wings, and they are like silk, as he says in the third line. Although there are a number of metaphors and similes here, some of the poetic effect and atmosphere are created by words that are not exactly metaphorical, like 'tremulous' which means 'trembling' and suggests the sensitivity or vulnerability of the poet's life, certainly at its close. *He* is tremulous rather than *his stay*, so this is an association between two things rather than a comparison. And the words of the whole stanza have delicate sounds – alliterative and assonant qualities which are highly expressive – as well as rhyme.

4

Philip Larkin's 'Church Going' uses a few well-chosen metaphors. He describes the silence in the church as 'tense, musty, unignorable silence, / Brewed God knows how long.' 'Brewed' is a word used for the making of ale or tea, in which elements are combined and infused over a period of time. The silence in the church has been developed over the centuries, becoming richer and stronger as time goes on, perhaps even becoming stewed as tea does and as the word 'musty' implies. Later, after he pretends to read the lesson, the echoes 'snigger briefly': the disturbance of the silence is personified in 'snigger' as if the echoes are like naughty school children. Both metaphors are somewhat disparaging of the atmosphere of the church and this is appropriate for the poem's structure, which begins rather cynically and ends in more reflective appreciation of what the church stands for.

Task

Look closely at the metaphors in the poems you are studying for the exam, and analyse some of them by writing clearly what things are being compared and what effects these comparisons have.

Neologisms

One difference between most prose and poetry is that poets sometimes create new words (or **neologisms**) to draw attention to the meaning they are conveying. You need to work out what the effect of the new word is in its context. Here are two examples:

1

T. S. Eliot uses a character called Tiresias in his poem 'The Waste Land' (1922) who can predict the future. He says: 'And I Tiresias have foresuffered all'. The word foresuffered does not exist conventionally, but because we know how 'fore' works when added on to the beginning of a word, we can guess that the word means 'foresee and suffer' or 'suffer before it happens'. The tragic situation of one who can foresee all the events of the future is emphasised in the use of this word, making the line of the poem more concentrated and requiring more thought on the part of the reader.

2

Thomas Hardy wrote many poems when his first wife died, remembering the love they had shared in earlier, happier days. In his poem 'The Voice' he imagines hearing her voice as he is out walking by himself and wishes he could see her as she once was, but she is 'ever dissolved to wan wistlessness'. This last word is one coined by Hardy. 'Wist' is an archaic word for 'know' and was old when Hardy was writing too. So 'wistless' means unknowing and 'wistlessness' is the state of not knowing or unconsciousness. All together the word suggests someone who is gone, part of the past, no longer a thinking, feeling person; its sounds are soft, sad and wistful, a word very similar in sound which means 'longing'. In both sound and meaning, therefore, the word chosen by Hardy focuses the sense of loss when the living reflect on the absence of the longed-for dead.

Task

Try to identify some poems in which new words have been created for a particular effect. Your teacher will help you here. You may need a dictionary to help you find the basic building-block words used by the poet.

Unusual syntax and omission of words

An important way in which the language of poetry can differ from the language of prose is in its occasionally unusual syntax; word order can be altered and some words omitted to create an interestingly different effect. (**Syntax** is the arrangement of words into sentences, so that the relationship of each word to the others can be appreciated; each language has its conventions of syntax.) The Pound poem in the last unit was not a complete sentence as it didn't have a finite verb, appropriately for an utterance which records a fleeting impression rather than action.

The following is the first part of an early poem by Sylvia Plath called 'Two Sisters of Persephone' (1956):

> Two girls there are: within the house
> One sits; the other, without.
> Daylong a duet of shade and light
> Plays between these.

Task

Try putting these four lines into syntactically accurate prose and list the changes you have had to make. (You don't need to explain the metaphor about light and shade at this stage.)

Sample response

> There are two girls. One of them sits inside the house, and the other one sits outside. All throughout the day, a duet of light and shade plays between them.
>
> These are the changes that had to be made:
>
> ■ Word order had to be reversed in lines 1 and 2.
>
> ■ 'Within' is an unusual way of saying in or inside.
>
> ■ 'Without' had to be expanded to make it clearer, and so did 'these' in the last line.
>
> ■ We generally say 'light and shade' not 'shade and light', so the more common form was used.

This short example shows clearly that the rearrangement of some words and the omission of others can be very effective. The sample response is prosaic and utterly unmemorable. In the poem, Plath contrasts two ways of living, as illustrated by the two sisters. Beginning with 'Two girls' emphasises this from the outset. By using 'within' and 'without', the contrast is pointed. 'Shade and light' instead of 'light and shade' draws your attention to a familiar phrase and makes it fresh again. Together with the arrangement of the lines and the use of half rhyme (covered in unit 26) an uneasy atmosphere is created and the reader is prepared for the contrasting descriptions which the poet will employ to present her theme, which incidentally moves beyond the domestic into the mythical, as Plath's poetry frequently does.

Here is another example of a poem which uses unusual syntax and omits words to create specific effects. Analyse how Hopkins does this.

> Glory be to God for dappled things –
>   For skies of couple-colour as a brinded cow;
>   For rose-moles all in stipple upon trout that swim;
>   Fresh-firecoal chestnut-falls; finches' wings;
>   Landscape plotted and pieced – fold, fallow, and plough;
>   And all trades, their gear and tackle and trim.
>
> All things counter, original, spare, strange;
>   Whatever is fickle, freckled (who knows how?)
>   With swift, slow; sweet, sour; adazzle, dim;
>   He fathers-forth whose beauty is past change:
>   Praise him.
>
> Gerard Manley Hopkins 'Pied Beauty'

Sample response

Hopkins omits words and writes very concentratedly in this poem praising God's creation. One characteristic method he uses is to create double-barrelled words such as 'couple-colour', 'rose-moles', 'fresh-firecoal' and 'fathers-forth', each of which would require many more words to paraphrase their meaning in prose. The four words 'fresh-firecoal chestnut-falls' delightfully sum up the beauties of autumn when chestnuts fall and fires are made to warm us and to roast the chestnuts. 'Fathers-forth' suggests a loving and enabling parent who cares deeply but is not possessive. Hopkins also uses lists of words whose meaning and sound work together to image the great variety of multicoloured and multi-charactered things and people in the world: 'counter, original, spare, strange ... swift, slow; sweet, sour; adazzle, dim'. He does not need to spell out with unnecessary extra words what he is referring to. The images of the senses (sight, sound, touch, taste, smell and movement are all implied here), together with the sounds of the words, combine to create a picture of a great creation iridescent with change and a great creator whose beauty, in contrast, depends upon his unchanging nature. Hopkins's poetry is rich with similar examples.

Discuss the word order and syntax in some poems you are studying. In almost every one you will find deviations from the 'normal' word order and words omitted. Try to consider the effect these have. A good way to point up the difference is to do as you have done with the Plath stanza earlier in this unit – put the lines into sentences in the usual prose order, adding any words you need to make the meaning clear. The first thing you will notice is how much longer your version is, a reminder that poetry can often be very concentrated compared with prose. You will also notice that the magic has gone.

Repetition and parallelism

Poetic method often includes exact repetition of words and phrases, or whole lines, in order to intensify effects. Parallelism is repetition with some subtle differences. The first example for you to consider is from Tennyson's poem 'Mariana'. Here are the first two stanzas:

> With blackest moss the flower-pots
>   Were thickly crusted, one and all:
> The rusted nails fell from the knots
>   That held the pear to the gable-wall.
> The broken sheds look'd sad and strange:
>   Unlifted was the clinking latch;
>   Weeded and worn the ancient thatch
> Upon the lonely moated grange.
>   She only said, 'My life is dreary,
>   He cometh not,' she said;
>   She said, 'I am aweary, aweary,
>   I would that I were dead!'
>
> Her tears fell with the dews at even;
>   Her tears fell ere the dews were dried;
> She could not look on the sweet heaven,
>   Either at morn or eventide.
> After the flitting of the bats,
>   When thickest dark did trance the sky,
>   She drew her casement-curtain by,
> And glanced athwart the glooming flats.
>   She only said, 'The night is dreary,
>   He cometh not,' she said;
>   She said, 'I am aweary, aweary,
>   I would that I were dead!'

Task

See if you can find examples of exact repetition in these two stanzas. Then look to see if you can find parallelism, where the repeated phrase or construction has a slight variation. Don't include the rhyme at this stage, though it is of course a kind of parallelism.

Sample response

The most obvious repetition is in the final four lines of each stanza where most of the words are the same (and this continues through the poem to the final stanza). Lines 2, 3 and 4 of the final quatrain [four lines] are exactly the same, but in 1 she says 'My life is dreary' and in 2 she says 'The night is dreary'. This pattern is found with 'The day is dreary' used in other stanzas in alternation. The use of a line or lines repeated in this way is typical of certain kinds of poem, such as the ballad, and it is known as a refrain.

   'Her tears fell' is repeated in lines 1 and 2 of the second stanza and there is a mention of the dew, though this is worded slightly differently.

There are other examples of parallelism such as nearly every object being given a descriptive word (an adjective) to qualify it: 'blackest moss', 'rusted nails', 'broken sheds', 'ancient thatch', 'lonely moated grange', 'sweet heaven', 'thickest dark'.

There is a relentless pattern here which is very appropriate for the repetitive, doomed existence of Mariana, waiting for the man who never comes. Her environment is dark and gloomy, and only the 'heaven' (which she cannot face) is 'sweet'. By the final stanza of the whole poem, the refrain's changes reveal a climax of desperation:

> Then, said she, 'I am very dreary,
>   He will not come,' she said;
> She wept, 'I am aweary, aweary,
>   O God, that I were dead!'

We shall now look at an example of a shorter and more modern poem by Stevie Smith that depends equally upon these features. The whole poem is given.

Task

Identify the repetition and parallelism in this poem. What do you notice about the middle stanza?

Not Waving but Drowning

Nobody heard him, the dead man,
But still he lay moaning:
I was much further out than you thought
And not waving but drowning.

Poor chap, he always loved larking
And now he's dead
It must have been too cold for him his heart gave way,
They said.

Oh, no no no, it was too cold always
(Still the dead one lay moaning)
I was much too far out all my life
And not waving but drowning.

Sample response

There is exact repetition in the final lines of stanzas 1 and 3, but parallelism draws attention to subtle differences between 'But still he lay moaning' and 'Still the dead one lay moaning', 'the dead man' and 'the dead one', 'It must have been too cold for him' and 'it was too cold always', and 'I was much further out than you thought' and 'I was much too far out all my life'. Although the poem is relatively short, it builds to an effective climax by repeating ideas with slightly different wording, which draws attention to its variations in meaning. The middle stanza with its emphasis on what people said about him is structured without significant parallelism. The climax of the poem effectively draws attention to the plight of the dead man who people thought was full of fun but who in reality disguised his inability to cope by appearing hearty. The theme is enhanced by the use of parallelism and repetition.

The final example, for you to try on your own, or with your teacher, is a poem by Blake, one of his *Songs of Experience*. Again, it is quoted in full.

Task

Find examples of repetition and parallelism here and try to express their effect. Don't neglect the use of the word 'And' at the beginning of lines – what effect does this have on the pace and atmosphere of the poem?

A Poison Tree

I was angry with my friend:
I told my wrath, my wrath did end.
I was angry with my foe:
I told it not, my wrath did grow.

And I water'd it in fears,
Night & morning with my tears;
And I sunned it with smiles,
And with soft deceitful wiles.

And it grew both day and night,
Till it bore an apple bright;
And my foe beheld it shine,
And he knew that it was mine,

And into my garden stole
When the night had veil'd the pole:
In the morning glad I see
My foe outstretch'd beneath the tree.

Sample response

The poet uses an extended metaphor, hinted at in the title of the poem. His anger is like a seed which is hidden under the ground and nurtured, as a plant is nurtured with sun and rain, by the poet's hypocritical smiles and constant tears. The fruit of his suppressed anger may look attractive and desirable (thus the theft) but in reality it is completely poisonous. His foe is fooled into thinking he has gained something over his enemy, but is caught out, fatally. This horrid little tale of people and their complex relationships has something in common with the Eden myth and may even remind the reader of the poisoned apple in the fairy story Snow White and the Seven Dwarfs.

You will find discussion of regular rhythms and rhymes in units 26 and 27.

Exam tip

By paying close attention to the words in poems – their implications, their sounds and their arrangement – you will gradually become a skilled and responsive literary critic.

(25) Poetic structures

In this unit, you will study the ways in which poetic structures enhance themes, and how the layout of poems differs from prose layout. You will also learn some of the technical vocabulary for discussing the way that lines of poetry are organised.

Theme and structure

The development of a poem's ideas will be made possible by the underpinning structure of the poem as a whole. Where does the poem start, how does it continue and in what way does it reach its conclusion? What relationship do the different sections of the poem have to each other? What effect does this have on the unfolding of the theme of the poem? Always ask these questions about structure, about how the poem is built.

Here are some common poetic structures:

- The poet recounts an experience or tells a little anecdote in the first few sections of the poem and the final stanza or line is a philosophical reflection on the significance of the experience (for example, many of Larkin's poems).
- The poet speaks directly to the reader, adopting the persona of another person and expressing that person's thoughts in character (for example, some of Browning's or Donne's poems).
- The poet expresses many innermost feelings, sharing them with the reader in an intimate way (for example, many of Plath's poems).
- The poet addresses something directly in the second person (*you*), and praises its qualities in an emotional, lyrical way (for example, Keats's *Odes*).
- The poem presents two sides of an argument, sometimes with two different voices, sometimes reaching a conclusion (for example, poems by Marvell or Christina Rossetti).
- The poem is a description – of a person, place or event, moving from a particular experience to generality or from general experience to the particular (many poets).

Task

Take three poems from the poetry you are studying and summarise the structure of each one. Can you add any categories to the list above?

Details of layout

The first part of this book – on AS level English Language – gives many examples of prose layout. Here is another one taken from a short story, 'The Voyage'. You can see by its descriptive quality that it is literary prose, not the language of, say, a newspaper article.

> The Picton boat was due to leave at half past eleven. It was a beautiful night, mild, starry, only when they got out of the cab and started to walk down the Old Wharf that jutted out into the harbour, a faint wind blowing off the water ruffled Fenella's hat, and she put up her hand to keep it on.
>
> Katherine Mansfield 'The Voyage'

Task

Compare the appearance of the piece of prose above, the pages of a novel or short story, or a magazine article, with the following short poem:

> In the village pond
> the full moon is shaken by
> the first falling leaf
>
> James Kirkup 'Haiku'

Sample response

In the *prose* the space on the page is filled with words from left to right; the designer of the book makes the most of the available space on the page, according to the size and format of the book as a whole. Where lines begin or end on the page is irrelevant to the meaning of the sentences written. In a narrow newspaper column, the words have to fit the space too.

In the *poem* the writer has shaped or patterned the words on the page deliberately, making choices for effect. Some of the lines are longer, some are shorter, but none of them uses the whole space.

Exam tip

The poet George Macbeth said, 'A poem is always laid out on the page in a way which has some significance.'

Concrete poems

Poets can sometimes use extreme methods when they lay out a poem on the page, knowing that we will be reading it and assimilating its 'shape'. Here is an example from a poet whose work often deviates from the normal conventions of punctuation and layout. The arrangement of the words symbolises the meaning they express, and thus describe the poem's characters. This sort of poem is known as a concrete poem.

```
                        e
              n   o   r   t
Steve is almost    i   c   h   en  .
David talks Good Sense.
Jane is often v  e   r   y      v  a  g  u  e
Lucy. VERY DENSE.
Catty Cora's fffffull of sssspite.

                       O
Dick is rather         D
                       D.

              a      l
                   n  e
Liz is quite an        G   , but
Alan thinks he's GOD.
```

e e cummings

Task

See if you can find some other examples of poems where the layout is significant in the way it creates shapes or patterns on the page. Try writing a descriptive poem yourself in which you vary the size and layout of the words to give a visual image of the subject of the poem.

End-stopped lines, open lines, enjambment and caesura

The poem that follows shows that a less extreme layout can also be very expressive. It was written by Siegfried Sassoon for Armistice Day, the day when the First World War ended in 1918. You can imagine the poet's intense joy at this experience: he had been an officer in the army and had experienced action himself. You are now going to see whether the arrangement of words into lines in the poem helps to communicate his feelings to you. The poem is structured in two stanzas ('stanza' is an Italian word that means 'room', a place to stop). (Poetic stanzas can be irregular as well as regular.) You will learn some useful technical terms too.

Everyone Sang

Everyone suddenly burst out singing;
And I was filled with such delight
As prisoned birds must find in freedom,
Winging wildly across the white
Orchards and dark-green fields; on—on—and out of sight.

Everyone's voice was suddenly lifted;
And beauty came like the setting sun:
My heart was shaken with tears; and horror
Drifted away ... O, but Everyone
Was a bird; and the song was wordless; the singing will never be done.

The first line expresses a complete thought and is known as an **end-stopped line**. The second line, although it makes sense on its own, needs the third line to complete it and is therefore an **open line**. By the time you get to the end of the fourth line, the meaning is running on into the fifth; 'white' needs 'orchards' to complete the meaning of the phrase. This is known as a run-on line or **enjambment** (from a French word meaning straddling or getting its leg into the next line).

The slight natural pause in the second line after 'filled' and in the third line after 'birds' is known as a **caesura** and most lines of poetry, unless they are very short, have such a pause. Sometimes this is emphasised by a punctuation mark to indicate where you might take a breath if you were reading.

Task

Now look at the second stanza of the poem to see if you can find further examples of end-stopped lines, open lines, enjambment and caesura.

Sample response

Lines 1 and 2 are end-stopped; lines 3–4 and 4–5 are run-on lines (enjambment). There are weak caesuras in lines 1 and 2 and strong ones in lines 3 and 4, with two strong ones in the final line.

Task

Read the whole poem again and try to consider what effect this arrangement of the lines has. Discuss this with a partner or in a group.

Sample response

Each stanza begins more calmly, with the end-stopped lines suggesting that the poet is in control of his thoughts and feelings. But as he continues, it seems that these cannot be contained in end-stopped lines and must burst out into the following ones, culminating in a long emotional line to end each section of the poem, where the caesuras and pauses suggest spurts of emotion. The final words 'on—on—and out of sight' and 'the singing will never be done' give a sense of infinite freedom and joy, and the lengths of these lines compared with the earlier ones enhance this impression.

If the poem was being read out loud to an audience who did not have the text in front of them, the reader would have to be very skilful to create the same effects that you grasp visually.

Exam tip

The shaping and arrangement of lines in a poem reinforce and support its ideas. You could express this in another way: form is essential to meaning.

Verse and stanza

The difference between a verse and a stanza is that a verse is usually the regular unit of structure within a hymn, song or rhymed poem. As these units can also be called stanzas, the term stanza is extremely useful, as it describes both regular and irregular units. (The word 'verse' can also be used to mean poetry in general, for example Kipling's verse means his poetic works.)

Regular verses or stanzas of different lengths have special names as follows:

Number of lines	Name
2	couplet
3	triplet or tercet
4	quatrain
5	quintain
6	sestet
7	septet
8	octave or octet

Larger groupings than this are much more unusual, and might even be called a verse paragraph if there are no breaks.

The sonnet

Poets sometimes follow a traditional pattern in the structures they adopt, and there are many such traditional forms. The one you are most likely to encounter at this stage is the sonnet, a fourteen-line poem with particular variations of rhyme, rhythm and structure. The sonnet is derived from two main varieties: the Petrarchan (or Italian) and the Shakespearean (or Elizabethan). Many poets have adjusted the strict rhyme scheme of the Petrarchan to suit themselves, but usually they follow one of two structures. The first one is an octave (eight lines) followed by a sestet (six lines) which generally groups the ideas or reflections into these two sets of lines. This can be seen in the following sonnet by Shelley:

> I met a traveller from an antique land
> Who said: Two vast and trunkless legs of stone
> Stand in the desert. Near them, on the sand,
> Half sunk, a shattered visage lies, whose frown,
> And wrinkled lip, and sneer of cold command
> Tell that its sculptor well those passions read
> Which yet survive (stamped on these lifeless things)
> The hand that mocked them and the heart that fed:
> And on the pedestal these words appear:
> 'My name is Ozymandias, king of kings:
> Look on my works, ye Mighty, and despair!'
> Nothing beside remains. Round the decay
> Of that colossal wreck, boundless and bare
> The lone and level sands stretch far away.

Percy Bysshe Shelley 'Ozymandias'

Here the first eight lines describe the situation and appearance of the ruined statue, stressing the pride and tyranny of the former ruler. The final six lines articulate the ambitious words on the statue's pedestal, emphasising the ultimate ruin of his former glory, the decay of his grandeur, in a barren landscape, empty of 'works' or achievements. The brevity and focus of the sonnet form here are particularly effective in their comment on the vanity of human ambition.

The second form that sonnets take is the Shakespearean division of three sets of four lines followed by a final couplet which clinches the main idea of the poem. Here is an example:

> Let me not to the marriage of true minds
> Admit impediments, love is not love
> Which alters when it alteration finds,
> Or bends with the remover to remove.
> O no, it is an ever-fixèd mark
> That looks on tempest and is never shaken;
> It is the star to every wand'ring bark,
> Whose worth's unknown, although his height be taken.
> Love's not Time's fool, though rosy lips and cheeks
> Within his bending sickle's compass come,
> Love alters not with his brief hours and weeks,
> But bears it out even to the edge of doom:
>> If this be error and upon me proved,
>> I never writ, nor no man ever loved.

Shakespeare 'Sonnet 116'

The first four lines assert the permanent and reliable quality of love between true minds; the second group of four lines forms an extended metaphor suggesting that love is like a star which is used by seafarers to guide their way, even in tempests at sea, representing life's vicissitudes. The final quatrain claims that even the passage of time does not alter love, and Time is here personified traditionally as an old man with a sickle. So firmly does the poet believe what he has written that he sums up in the final couplet by staking his reputation as a writer and experience as a lover to confirm what he has said. This is typical of the Shakespearean sonnet: the three quatrains are self-contained but are all variations on a theme, often using metaphor to extend and amplify the thought, and the final couplet confirms the theme strongly. Once again the brevity and self-contained perfection of the sonnet form are very effective for expressing the poet's thought.

You will study closer analysis of the rhythmical and rhyming patterns of poems such as these in units 26 and 27.

Exam tip

Never forget that the poet's choice of form, structure and language shapes meaning.

26 Scansion

The analysis of poems into stanzas, lines and pauses is part of a process called scansion. This includes rhythm and rhyme and their effects, which follow in the next part of the unit. Your work here will help you to appreciate the way that word sounds affect meaning.

Rhythm

'Rhythm' comes from an ancient Greek word meaning 'flow'. Nothing could be more familiar to us: all around us, natural and human-made rhythms – repeated and regular – give movement and shape to our lives. The seasons follow each other in a regular pattern; night and day alternate in regular succession; inside our bodies, our hearts and lungs work rhythmically. Clocks strike, car engines tick over and music throbs, all switching between one state and another (tick-tock-tick-tock, dark-light-dark-light and so on).

Task

If possible, discuss with a partner or your group some other examples of rhythms at work in our lives.

Syllables

We dance and sing and make music, creating our own rhythms in an obvious sense, but our language too has its own rhythmical patterns, flowing in an undulating or wave-like arrangement of stronger and weaker elements. Individual words have their own rhythms, depending on how many syllables they have. A syllable is one sound and each word we utter is made up of one or more syllables:

red know find	Each has one syllable.
better pencil movement	Each has two syllables.
poetry computer advising	Each has three syllables.

In each of these words some of the syllables are stressed, or emphasised, when you say them out loud and some are not stressed. It is the pattern created by the alternation of the stressed and unstressed syllables which creates the rhythmical effect of words, and, in turn, the sentences or lines of poetry that they form. (You may come across the words 'strong' or 'weak' used instead of 'stressed' or 'unstressed'.)

Marking stressed syllables

If you are analysing rhythm and want to show that a syllable is emphasised or stressed, use a mark / or – on top of the syllable. If the sound is not stressed, the accepted notation is a ˘ or × shape. Later, when you become more experienced, you won't need to use these: you'll be able to glance at a poem, speak it in your head and hear at once what the pattern of rhythm is.

The rhythms of poetry are easiest to see when the lines have a regular pattern, and this is your next area for study. Later you'll analyse some less regular lines and what is known as syllabic verse. The name for the organisation of rhythms into regular and recurring patterns such as you find in poetry is **metre**.

Metre

'Metre' means measure and you already use it to measure length (centimetre) and distance (kilometre). (In the USA it is spelt *meter*.)

In poetry, metre is the measurement of an arrangement of rhythms, and it has its own terminology which is traditional and common to many languages. When you analyse the pattern of stressed and unstressed syllables in a line of poetry, you are identifying the characteristic metre, especially if it's regular. This is part of a process known as scansion, one aspect of which you are familiar with already – line division. Another aspect of scansion to consider is the rhyme scheme, which you will study in unit 27.

How to scan a regular line of poetry

Identify the syllables in each word and decide whether they are stressed or unstressed, marking them on top with a – or ˘ as you go. Use your common sense about the sound of the word, then read it aloud, exaggerating the whole line slightly to identify the beat. If two or three syllables recur in a pattern, this forms a metrical unit of rhythm and is known as a **foot** (the plural is feet).

Count the number of feet in the line, marking the divisions between the feet with a vertical line. Marking syllable divisions with a line when you start is helpful but this won't be necessary when you become more experienced. Similarly, you will soon be able to count the number of feet without using the line divisions, or even marking the stresses, though this will take a little more practice.

Here are some examples for you to try; I've done the first line for you as a guide and marked the syllables (but not the feet) in each line.

> Wi̅ll/o̐ws whi̅t/e̐n, a̅s/pe̐ns qu̅i/ve̐r,
> Litt/le bree/zes dusk and shi/ver
> Thro' the wave that runs for e/ver
> By the is/land in the ri/ver

Tennyson 'The Lady of Shallott'

In the stanza above, the recurring pattern or foot is – ˘, repeated four times in each line. This pattern is called a **trochee** (the *ch* pronounced like a *k*) or you can call it a trochaic foot. It has a falling rhythm – try reading it out to yourself and listening to the regular rhythms of each line and the way it dies away.

Task

Divide the following verses into syllables and mark those which are stressed and those which are unstressed. Remember they are all regular patterns.

1
The Curfew tolls the knell of parting day,
The lowing herd wind slowly o'er the lea,
The ploughman homeward plods his weary way,
And leaves the world to darkness and to me.
Gray 'Elegy Written in a Country Churchyard'

2
The Assyrian came down like the wolf on the fold,
And his cohorts were gleaming in purple and gold;
And the sheen of their spears was like stars on the sea,
When the blue wave rolls nightly on deep Galilee.
Byron 'The Destruction of Sennacherib'

3
Perishing gloomily,
Spurred by contumely,   **contumely** harsh treatment
Cold inhumanity,
Burning insanity,
Hood 'The Bridge of Sighs'

1

This foot (˘ −) is known as an **iambus** or you can call it an iambic foot. It has a rising rhythm.

2

This is another rising rhythm, but the pattern here of two unstressed syllables followed by a stressed one (˘ ˘ −) is called an **anapaest** (or **anapaestic** foot).

3

The pattern here is known as a **dactyl** (− ˘ ˘) and these are dactylic feet. It has a falling rhythm which seems to suit very well the meaning of the poem's lines here: doomed and melancholy.

A useful verse

More than 200 years ago, the poet Samuel Taylor Coleridge wrote a little verse for his son to teach him the basic feet which you've just been working out. Here it is; I've marked the stresses for you.

> − ˘ − ˘ − ˘ −
> Trochee trips from long to short;
> From long to short in solemn sort
> − − − − − −
> Slow spondee stalks; strong foot! yet ill able
> − ˘ ˘ − ˘ ˘ − ˘ ˘
> Ever to come up with dactyl trisyllable.
> ˘ − ˘ − ˘ −
> Iambics march from short to long;
> ˘ ˘ − ˘ ˘ − ˘ ˘ − ˘ ˘ −
> With a leap and a bound the swift anapaests throng.

The **spondee** mentioned here is an occasional foot with two stressed syllables; obviously you couldn't have a whole poem made up of them. (Why not?)

If you count the number of feet in the extracts you've analysed, you'll find the following: in your examples there are four feet in the Tennyson, five feet in the Gray and Byron and two in the Hood. Here are the technical names for this analysis:

1 foot = monometer

2 feet = dimeter

3 feet = trimeter

4 feet = tetrameter

5 feet = pentameter

6 feet = hexameter

Longer lines of seven, eight and nine feet are sometimes, but rarely, found. Now you know the correct terminology to describe the metre of a particular regular line: dactylic tetrameter or iambic pentameter, for example.

Iambic monometer is extremely rare, but an example follows:

Thus I
Passe by,
And die:

This is the first stanza from 'Upon His Departure Hence' by Robert Herrick. Most lines of poetry are longer than this, though these spare, depressive lines are very effective for the poet's wretched mood.

The most common regular meter in English poetry is iambic pentameter, which has been used by every great traditional poet in English. Those parts of Shakespeare's plays that are in verse are in iambic pentameter, which is known as blank verse when it has no rhyme at the end of each line. You'll see more examples of his language in units 35 to 40 on drama.

In this unit you've moved quickly from the rhythms of individual words to their measurable flow in regular lines of poetry. The terminology you've learned applies usefully to many older poems, though you will find little irregularities within basically regular pieces.

Exam tip

Knowing the technical vocabulary is helpful and interesting, but your knowledge must always be directed towards appreciation of the effects of what you have observed. It is the means to an end, not an end in itself.

Variations in the pattern

If you speak lines of poetry out loud and listen to their sound, the natural, conversational rhythms of the words being used to express particular thoughts are obvious. These may not fit a perfectly regular pattern and you'd have to distort the natural pronunciation and stress of the words to force them into one. If every foot and every line in poetry were perfectly regular, or exactly like all the others, it would be precise in a mathematical sort of way, but it would be monotonous and inflexible.

Exam tip

Some of the most effective lines of poetry contain skilful variations which emphasise important words. The reader's attention is caught because a potentially smooth rhythm has been disrupted.

Now that you know the basic metres, you will be in a position to appreciate variations and feel their effects. Even in lines you consider to be basically regular, there are some small deviations from the basic pattern where the meaning or natural pronunciation demands it.

In unit 25 you looked at a poem by Siegfried Sassoon from the point of view of its layout in lines and stanzas. Now look again at the first stanza of the poem and try scanning it.

> Everyone suddenly burst out singing;
> And I was filled with such delight
> As prisoned birds must find in freedom,
> Winging wildly across the white
> Orchards and dark-green fields; on—on—and out of sight.

Sample response

- Line 1: The first two feet are dactyls, followed by two trochees (four feet, so it is a tetrameter).

- Line 2: This is a regular iambic tetrameter.

- Line 3: This is iambic, but the last foot has an extra unstressed syllable (the 'dom' of 'freedom'). [This pattern is known technically as an amphibrach and may occur in this way at the end of a line.]

- Line 4: This has two trochaic feet followed by two iambic ones.

- Line 5: This is an unusually long line, with six feet instead of four. It also has an unusual pattern of stresses too, which throws particular emphasis on certain words:

Orchards	and dark	green fields;	on—on	and out	of sight
trochee	iambus	spondee	spondee	iambus	iambus

Study tip

It's important to realise that where the stresses come may be a matter of opinion, not scientific fact; you might have disagreed with this analysis of line 5 of the Sassoon poem. The word 'green' could be unstressed or stressed, for example: if unstressed, that would have been another iambic foot. If both 'green' and 'fields' are emphasised, it draws attention to their similar sound and lengthens the phrase effectively. Look at the way in which the meaning of the final line is also enhanced by its length: 'on—on—and out of sight'.

Task

Analyse the second stanza of this poem by Sassoon. You will find it printed in full in unit 25. Discuss your analysis with a classmate or your teacher.

The next example is a poem written in basically iambic pentameter with many skilful and effective irregularities. These enhance the poet's emotional state as well as emphasising particularly important words. The poet is Sir Thomas Wyatt, who was writing in the 1530s and 1540s, and the subject is his rejection by women, one in particular, who used to love him. You will note that the passage of centuries has not affected certain basic human themes, though more recent feminist critics might have something to say about his attitudes. The spelling has been modernised and you are given the meaning of words now out of date.

Task

Scan this poem and see where the stressed syllables are.

They flee from me, that sometime did me seek	**sometime** once
With naked foot, stalking in my chamber.	
I have seen them gentle, tame, and meek,	
That now are wild, and do not remember	
That sometime they put themselves in danger	
To take bread at my hand; and now they range	
Busily seeking with a continual change.	
Thanked be fortune it hath been otherwise	
Twenty times better; but once, in special,	
In thin array, after a pleasant guise,	**array** clothing
When her loose gown from her shoulders did fall,	**guise** masked ball
And she me caught in her armes long and small,	
Therewith all sweetly did me kiss	
And softly said, 'Dear heart, how like you this?'	
It was no dream; I lay broad waking:	
But all is turned, through my gentleness,	
Into a strange fashion of forsaking;	
And I have leave to go of her goodness,	
And she also to use newfangledness.	**newfangledness**
But since that I so kindly am served,	fondness for new things
I would fain know what she hath deserved.	

The rhythms of this are complex and subtle. Your scansion will show some regular lines and others where variations occur. Here are three examples, though you probably found more than this.

Sample response

> 1   They flee from me, that sometime did me seek
>   With naked foot, stalking in my chamber.

Line 1 is regular iambic pentameter, establishing an overall pattern at the beginning. Line 2 begins within the pattern, with the first two feet iambic. But the word 'stalking' upsets this pattern, emphasising the strong determined movement referred to (and emphasising the animal images used).

2   And she me caught in her armes long and small

At the time of writing the word 'armes' would have two syllables, not one as 'arms' does today. Imagine this line made regular:

> She caught me in her armes long and small.

The line as written by Wyatt has a completely different emphasis: the phrase 'she me caught' with its three stresses focuses powerfully on the action and creates a pause after the word 'caught' (the caesura) before the delicate description of her long slender arms.

3   It was no dream; I lay broad waking:

The line begins regularly enough, but after the caesura pause ('dream') there are four stressed syllables: I, lay, broad, wak-(ing). [Even if you decide that 'I' should be unstressed, there are still three together.]

   The poet is reminding himself that he is wide awake, not daydreaming or asleep; these experiences were real and in sharp contrast to his present state of dejection because he has been forsaken. The stressed syllables draw attention to this.

Syllabic verse

You may have noticed that all the examples of basically regular poetry here were written centuries ago. Of course there are more recent examples, but it's certainly true that modern and contemporary poets don't use those traditional forms as consistently as their predecessors. More modern poets may have written regular poems in which the regularity is achieved only in the number of syllables per line: this is known as syllabic verse. You might well find it easier to scan this more recent verse that doesn't fit the traditional metrical patterns. You count the syllables *whether they are stressed or not* and see whether each line has the same number.

Task

Look in an anthology and see if you can find any poems that don't seem to fit a traditional metrical form. If it's obviously a more modern piece, try counting the syllables. If it appears to have no regular structure at all, is not syllabic and has no rhyme, then it is probably free verse (see below).

Task

Try counting the syllables in the following and you'll see how easy it is to scan this kind of poetry:

> Dusk softens round the leaf and cools the West.
> Rhythmical fragrances, wind, grass and leaves,
> Fly in and out on scented cadences.
> I go into the bedroom of the world,
> Discovering the long night of my life.

Douglas Dunn 'A Summer Night'

Sample response

Each line has ten syllables.

The following poem is complete. Its title, 'Metaphors', is a reference to a figure of speech with which you are familiar, and the poem is a kind of riddle. If you count the syllables here, as well as the number of lines used, you will perhaps be able to guess what the answer to this riddle is.

> I'm a riddle in nine syllables,
> An elephant, a ponderous house,
> A melon strolling on two tendrils.
> O red fruit, ivory, fine timbers!
> This loaf's big with its yeasty rising.
> Money's new minted in this fat purse.
> I'm a means, a stage, a cow in calf.
> I've eaten a bag of green apples,
> Boarded the train there's no getting off.

The poet is Sylvia Plath, and she is writing a poem about pregnancy. The nine syllables and nine lines are particularly appropriate in this case, suggesting in their form the length of time her physical being is affected and combining well with some very descriptive metaphors.

Haiku

Haiku is a kind of syllabic verse that is great fun to write yourself. It was originally a Japanese verse form consisting of 17 syllables altogether in three lines of five, seven and five syllables. Because it's so short it can only express one idea, feeling or image, but this can be very effective: it is like a snapshot in words. The poem used at the beginning of unit 25 is a haiku.

   Provided that you can count syllables, it isn't difficult to write a haiku of your own. A class were given a list of subjects and here are three of the results, for the titles 'Exams', 'Holidays' and 'My Favourite Word':

Exams are coming	5 syllables
Revision and timed essays	7 syllables
O please let me pass!	5 syllables

Sand between the toes
The shock of the tumbling waves
Time sleeps on the beach

My favourite word
Is onomatopoeia
But how to spell it?

Try writing your own haiku on one of the following subjects: food, memory, rain.

Free verse

At first sight, free verse has no apparent regularity in its form, but it is in fact designed cunningly in the cadences and breath groups of the speaking voice. It is given shape by the use of repetition, parallelism, enjambment (run-on lines) and pauses, and is as carefully designed as regular iambic pentameters. This is an example from D. H. Lawrence, who wrote many free verse poems in contemplation of animals.

Identify examples of repetition, parallelism, enjambment and pauses in the poem and discuss their effect.

> Climbing through the January snow, into the Lobo canyon
> Dark grow the spruce-trees, blue is the balsam, water sounds
>   still unfrozen, and the trail is still evident.
>
> Men!
> Two men!
> Men! The only animal in the world to fear!
>
> They hesitate.
> We hesitate.
> They have a gun.
> We have no gun.
>
> Then we all advance, to meet.
>
> Two Mexicans, strangers, emerging out of the dark and snow
>   and inwardness of the Lobo valley.
> What are you doing here on this vanishing trail?
>
> D. H. Lawrence 'Mountain Lion'

Sample response

The word 'men' is repeated three times in one- and two-word sentences with exclamation marks to emphasise their destructiveness. The third stanza uses parallelism in 'They hesitate. / We hesitate.' and 'They have a gun. / We have no gun.' Both parties are uncertain, but only one group has a weapon. Enjambments are used as part of the natural description at the beginning and end of the extract, lending an emphatic quality to the words 'sounds' and 'still' in the first section and 'snow and inwardness' in the last. Additionally, the first lines of the first and fifth stanzas do not contain a finite verb, giving a sense that the actions of 'climbing' and 'emerging' are still continuing, also helped by the enjambment. If read aloud, the pauses between lines give a dramatic significance to the encounter being described, and the final line of the extract is a direct question, which also lends dramatic emphasis.

Pace

The word 'pace' is used to denote the speed at which a verse moves. In some poems, the pace is regular and steady and in others there is a perceptible speeding up or slowing down. This affects the meaning of the poem, and its atmosphere. In the Lawrence poem above, for example, the section where the poet and his companions meet the strangers is slowed by the short lines and brief repetitive sentences. The Byron poem 'The Destruction of Sennacherib' quoted on page 134 has a swift flowing pace which drives through the poem, aptly mirroring the movement of fighting troops.

Exam tip

Always try to identify the effects of layout, rhythm and pace in the poems you are analysing, relating them as closely as possible to the development of the poet's thoughts and observations.

27 Rhyme and sound effects

When people are asked what gives poetry its special quality, nine out of ten will mention *rhyme* first. This is not only because you remember the nursery rhymes and poems of your childhood; it's also because you know instinctively that sounds are an integral part of the meaning of words in poems.

Rhyme is the agreement in sound between words or syllables. These words rhyme: *night, sight, fight*; so do these: *flying, dying, implying*.

This echoing of sounds can give pleasure to the hearer and is probably associated with the pleasure we have in music. Even tiny children love rhyme: their delight in nursery rhymes such as 'Humpty Dumpty' is largely because the words 'go together' in sound – and of course the rhythms are usually very regular too.

Rhyme also helps to structure or shape poetry, organising the verse, binding it together and intensifying the meaning, because words that rhyme are more noticeable than words that don't rhyme. This is an effect similar to a random visual pattern where you would notice a repeated motif immediately.

Some poets never use rhyme, but it is the commonest and oldest form of metrical device, even so. Your analysis of metre or scansion will therefore often include consideration of rhyme. It is usually thought of as occurring at the ends of lines of poetry, but it can also occur within lines, in which case it is known as **internal rhyme**.

How to indicate a rhyme scheme

The accepted method of indicating a rhyme scheme is to use small letters of the alphabet to denote the rhyming sounds at the ends of lines. Remember, it's the sounds not the spellings of the words which are important; you'll need to say the words over to yourself to see if they rhyme. After all, English spelling being what it is, *cough* rhymes with *off*!

Here is a pair of rhyming couplets:

A mighty creature is the germ,	a
Though smaller than the pachyderm.	a
His customary dwelling place	b
Is deep within the human race.	b

Ogden Nash

If you were to use the terminology you already know, together with this new information, you might say something like this:

The regular iambic tetrameter together with the rhyming couplets aabb create a comic effect here. The pairing of 'germ' with 'pachyderm' (elephant) is particularly incongruous.

Although accurate, it wouldn't be very helpful just to say 'This poem rhymes aabb' without any analytical comment.

Now try these two stanzas from 'The Rime of the Ancient Mariner' by Coleridge. Mark the metre (it's a regular one) and indicate the rhyme by underlining rhyming words and putting a, b, c and so on.

> And now there came both mist and snow,
> And it grew wondrous cold:
> And ice, mast-high, came floating by,
> As green as emerald.
>
> And through the drifts the snowy clifts
> Did send a dismal sheen:
> Nor shapes of men nor beasts we ken—
> The ice was all between.

Did you notice the internal rhyme in line 3 of the first stanza and lines 1 and 3 of the second? You still say 'it rhymes abcb' but also 'there are internal rhymes in lines 1 and 3'. The rhythmical and rhyming effects are very obvious in these two stanzas; say them out loud to hear what a thrilling effect they have.

Different rhyme schemes

Look at the following poems or extracts from poems and mark the rhyme scheme at the side, using the alphabetical notation you've learnt:

1 My mother groan'd! my father wept.
   Into the dangerous world I leapt :
   Helpless, naked, piping loud;
   Like a fiend hid in a cloud.

   Struggling in my father's hands,
   Striving against my swadling bands.
   Bound and weary I thought best
   To sulk upon my mother's breast.
                    William Blake 'Infant Sorrow'

2 Only a man harrowing clods
      In a slow silent walk
   With an old horse that stumbles and nods
      Half asleep as they stalk.
        Thomas Hardy 'In Time of "The Breaking of Nations"'

3 Side by side, their faces blurred,
   The earl and countess lie in stone,
   Their proper habits vaguely shown
   As jointed armour, stiffened pleat,
   And that faint hint of the absurd –
   The little dogs under their feet.
              Philip Larkin 'An Arundel Tomb'

4 These, in the day when heaven was falling,
   The hour when earth's foundations fled,
Followed their mercenary calling
   And took their wages and are dead.

Their shoulders held the sky suspended;
   They stood, and earth's foundations stay;
What God abandoned, these defended,
   And saved the sum of things for pay.

A. E. Housman 'Epitaph on an army of Mercenaries'

5 What passing-bells for these who die as cattle?
   Only the monstrous anger of the guns.
   Only the stuttering rifles' rapid rattle
Can patter out their hasty orisons.
No mockeries now for them; no prayers nor bells,
   Nor any voice of mourning save the choirs,—
The shrill, demented choirs of wailing shells;
   And bugles calling for them from sad shires.

What candles may be held to speed them all?
   Not in the hands of boys, but in their eyes
Shall shine the holy glimmers of good-byes.
   The pallor of girls' brows shall be their pall;
Their flowers the tenderness of patient minds,
And each slow dusk a drawing-down of blinds.

Wilfred Owen 'Anthem for Doomed Youth'

Sample response

> Some of these rhyme schemes are simple and others are more complex in the way that the rhyming sounds are interwoven:
>
> **1** aabb
> **2** abab
> **3** abbcac
> **4** abab (with the a rhymes feminine and the b rhymes masculine)
> **5** ababcdcd; effegg

The final example's rhyme scheme is typical of the sonnet form in which the poem is written (the sonnet is discussed in unit 25).

Some useful definitions

- **masculine rhyme** a rhyme on one syllable only, as used by Blake, Hardy and Larkin above.
- **feminine rhyme** a rhyme on two syllables, as Housman uses on 'calling' and 'falling' and 'suspended' and 'defended'.

- **ear rhyme** a true rhyme when spoken aloud, but looks as if it shouldn't be by its spelling. 'Choir' and 'shire' in Owen's poem are like this (as are the words *cough* and *off* mentioned earlier).
- **eye rhyme** looks as if it should rhyme from the spelling but doesn't – there are no examples of this in the poems above, but the words *rough* and *cough* would be eye rhymes.

Half-rhyme or pararhyme

Half-rhyme is widely used in modern and contemporary poetry. Wilfred Owen, whose sonnet you have just analysed for full rhyme, used half-rhyme extensively in other poems he wrote. Half-rhyme and pararhyme are the most common names but there are others such as near, approximate and slant rhyme.

Half-rhyme repeats the final consonant sound in words without the vowel sound corresponding. Where the use of a full rhyme may give an impression of confidence and completeness, a half-rhyme can help to create a sense of unease or disturbance.

The effect of half-rhyme

The poem you looked at part of earlier, 'An Arundel Tomb', has full rhymes throughout, until its very final lines, where the poet uses a half-rhyme in conclusion:

Time has transfigured them into	a
Untruth. The stone fidelity	b
They hardly meant has come to be	b
Their final blazon, and to prove	c (half-rhyme)
Our almost-instinct almost true:	a
What will survive of us is love.	c (half-rhyme)

Sometimes the last line of this poem is taken out of its context and quoted to prove a point (an optimistic point about human nature) but it can't be read in such a way. The poet's use of the two 'almosts' in the penultimate (second to last) line warn the reader that the statement is being subtly qualified and this is enhanced by the poet's use of the half-rhymes on 'prove' and 'love'. You'll notice that the half-rhyme here takes the form of an eye-rhyme; in the following stanzas (the beginning of 'Miners' by Wilfred Owen) the half-rhymes are mostly not eye rhymes.

Task

Mark the words which half-rhyme at the ends of the lines:

> There was a whispering in my hearth,
> A sigh of the coal,
> Grown wistful of a former earth
> It might recall.

> I listened for a tale of leaves
>   And smothered ferns;
> Frond-forests; and the low, sly lives
>   Before the fawns.

Sample response

The half-rhyme here runs abab, as it does throughout this poem about the hardships suffered by miners early in the twentieth century. The wistful, melancholy tone of the poem depends on the skilful use of pararhyme.

Task

Read the rest of both these poems: they are widely anthologised.

Task

Here is the middle stanza of a poem by Elizabeth Jennings called 'The Enemies', where the mysterious, disturbing quality of the invasion is enhanced by the use of loose half-rhymes. You might not notice them unless you look closely.

Mark them in the usual way (underline and a, b, c and so on).

> Now in the morning all the town is filled
> With stories of the swift and dark invasion;
> The women say that not one stranger told
> A reason for his coming. The intrusion
> Was not for devastation:
> Peace is apparent still on hearth and field.

Sample response

The pattern of half-rhymes runs ababba.

Other effects of sound

Rhyme is only one of several features of language in poetry which use the sounds of words to influence or reflect their meaning. Among these features are alliteration, assonance, consonance and onomatopoeia.

Alliteration

Alliteration is the repetition of consonant sounds especially at the beginning of words; poets have used it for centuries. In Old English verse (before the Norman invasion) alliteration was an essential part of the metrical scheme of poems and even more important than rhyme. It is still used widely for particular effects. A modem poet, Ezra Pound, whose poem 'In a Station of the Metro' you have already studied, wrote a version of an Old English poem called 'The Seafarer' and he included all the alliteration from the original; you can appreciate its flavour without having to learn the old language. Here's part of it: the letters which alliterate are underlined.

> <u>M</u>ay I, for <u>m</u>y own <u>s</u>elf, <u>s</u>ong's truth reckon,
> Journey's jargon, <u>h</u>ow I in <u>h</u>arsh days
> <u>H</u>ardship endured oft.
> <u>B</u>itter <u>b</u>reast-cares have I a<u>b</u>ided, ...

The first lines of James Elroy Flecker's poem 'The Old Ships' alliterates evocatively:

> I have seen old ships sail like swans asleep ...

Alliteration can also be an essential ingredient of the fun in comic verse or tongue-twisters such as 'Peter Piper picked a peck of pickled pepper' or 'She sells sea shells on the sea shore'.

Assonance

Assonance is the repetition of vowel sounds within words that have different consonants. There is assonance in the long *o* sound in the following words: *home, road, bone, foe.*

Consonance

Consonance has identical consonants but different vowels, such as *slip* and *slop, creak* and *croak*. The kind of half-rhyme used by Wilfred Owen in 'Miners' is largely a kind of consonance.

Onomatopoeia

There are a number of words whose sound seems to imitate their meaning, so that the sound reflects the sense of the word. That is the definition of onomatopoeia, or echoism as it is sometimes called. English is a very onomatopoeic language and perfectly suited to poetry.

The effect of individual sounds

There's more to analysing the effect of these sound patterns than just underlining the ones which are the same as each other. The speech sound itself which is being repeated may well have a particular effect, and you should try to identify this:

- *k, g, ch, qu, st, ts* These can be hard, violent sounds, noisy and harsh: try saying *crag, clock, biggest, stick*; *t* and *d* can have a similar effect.
- *m, n, ng* These are humming, singing, musical sounds which can also have a gently sinister effect: *humming, moaning, murmuring*.
- *f, w* These sound soft and light: *flow, fly, winnow, furrow*.

You could continue in this vein: *z* sounds harsh and *sh* sounds soothing, long vowels sound slower and more peaceful, while short ones give the impression of quick movement.

You may feel that such close examination of English sounds is slightly ridiculous. Certainly, if you've never really considered the sounds of our words, some of the claims made above may seem far-fetched. A few years ago, however, a columnist in a Sunday newspaper had a competition to find the ten most beautiful words in the language, with a prize for the winner with the most persuasive list of ten. What was interesting about the results (and the columnist published all his favourite entries as well as the winning one) was the number of words which all or nearly all the entrants had included; out of the hundreds of thousands of possibilities, some recurred again and again. They were all words whose sound reflected and intensified their meaning: words like *cool, moon, velvet, softness* and *mellow*. So it seems that some words have a powerful effect when meaning and sound coincide. What would your ten words be?

Task

Review what you've learned in this unit and units 25 and 26, then read and enjoy the sounds and rhythms of the following lines, the choric song from Tennyson's poem 'The Lotus Eaters':

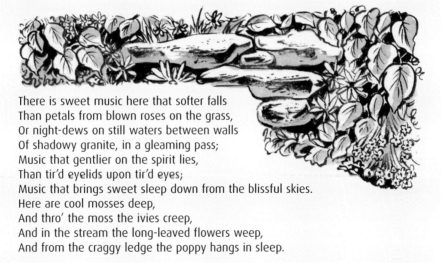

There is sweet music here that softer falls
Than petals from blown roses on the grass,
Or night-dews on still waters between walls
Of shadowy granite, in a gleaming pass;
Music that gentlier on the spirit lies,
Than tir'd eyelids upon tir'd eyes;
Music that brings sweet sleep down from the blissful skies.
Here are cool mosses deep,
And thro' the moss the ivies creep,
And in the stream the long-leaved flowers weep,
And from the craggy ledge the poppy hangs in sleep.

Exam tip

Under exam conditions you do not have time for extensive comment on rhythms, rhymes and sound effects. But a few well-chosen examples will enhance your work immensely.

28 Writing on poetry for the exam

You have a choice between two kinds of questions in the exam: the critical essay on your set text and the close critical commentary on a poem taken from it. In this unit, you will get some guidelines on both alternatives, so that you feel confident about answering either type under exam conditions. You may be studying a particular poet, whose work has characteristic features that you have discussed as part of your preparation for the exam. You may be using an anthology, a collection of poems, some of which have ideas, or themes, in common. In either case, you have the advantage that you will have studied the poems before the exam takes place – it is not an unseen poetry paper – and so you will be writing from a position of strength.

Studying an anthology

An anthology is a collection of poems that will not be by the same writer or even necessarily on the same topics. However, there will be some links between them and it is these that the question setter will exploit.

Studying an individual poet

The work of an individual poet will vary, but there will be some concerns that the writer constantly returns to, and you will be able to find these once you know the whole work well. Additionally there will be characteristic features of style that you come to identify as typical of your particular poet.

Study techniques

Whether you are studying an anthology or a collection by one poet, the techniques described below will be helpful.

Begin with individual poems

It is best to read, discuss and analyse individual poems first so that you appreciate each one before you embark on attempting to find links between them.

Once you have studied and enjoyed a range of poems, you will begin to see that they have thematic or stylistic links. For example, your anthology may contain a number of poems about an aspect of nature or which use the natural environment as a background; there may be poems about childhood, death, time or age; or even something as apparently mundane as using the telephone. Your poet may always use regular verse forms and rhyme, together with physical symbols of states of mind, as Blake does; or characteristically comical–serious, laconic perceptions such as those of Stevie Smith.

Create headings

List the poems that could be used if there is a question on a particular topic. In the anthology *Touched with Fire* (section A), for example, you could begin your list as follows:

Nature
Tall Nettles
Thistles
Mushrooms
Afterwards

Death
Elegy Written in a Country Churchyard
Cold in the Earth
Felix Randal
Afterwards

What you will notice at once is that the poem 'Afterwards' appears in both lists, because it is about the death of the poet but also uses much natural description. 'Mountain Lion' is also about death, but the death of a lovely wild creature. 'The Wild Swans at Coole' uses beautiful natural description but is about the passage of time and an individual ageing and realising with regret that he has lost his capacity for passion. Your list will therefore be much longer than the number of individual poems because some will appear twice or more. If you are studying an anthology, you should be creating a matrix of topics in this way, so that you will be prepared for any question in the exam. Usually you are asked to discuss two or three poems that are linked by topic, and you will have plenty to choose from. If your set text is a selection of one writer's work, you will find one of the delights of studying a particular poet is that as you become familiar with the individual poems you gradually begin to form a sense of the themes and style that characterise her/his work.

Task

If you are studying an anthology, create a list or matrix of poem topics. Be prepared to find a poem that doesn't seem to fit the mould as well as one or two that appear in two or three lists. In the case of an individual poet, try to divide the poems into topics and also identify recurrent features of style.

Poetry essay

Task

Several poems in your selection concern death. Referring to two poems, discuss how they explore this subject.

The sample below is a full and carefully structured essay, in which the poems are discussed individually and a personal response given by the writer.

Sample essay

The two poems I have chosen are both by Thomas Hardy: one about the death of his first wife and the second imagining his own death. The first is very poignant as it involves the sadness of a real death and fond memories of a loved one; the second poem is about a deceased man who was very observant and appreciative of the beauties of the world around him, but it is not so sad because it is hypothetical: the poet is imagining what people will say when he dies, so his death obviously hasn't happened yet.

'The Voice' is about the ghost of the poet's lost love, whom he follows out into the rainy meadows. He hears her voice calling him and remembers when they first met years before. Now he is alone and haunted by what sounds like her voice calling him, but it could just be the north wind in the thorn trees.

The poem is simply structured in four stanzas, the first expressing how much the poet misses her. She seems to be calling him and saying she is the same as she was when they first met, 'when our day was fair'. In the second stanza, the most colourful and lively, the poet remembers his love in her 'air-blue gown' waiting for him when they were going out together in town. The third stanza contrasts with this warm picture of the past, though, because he begins to doubt that it really is her voice: 'is it only the breeze …?' The final line of this stanza is heart-rending in the way it questions if she will be 'heard no more again far or near'. The last stanza creates an image of the poet stumbling along on a chilly autumn day, desperately following what might be the voice of the ghost, 'the woman calling'.

The images created by Hardy are not metaphorical ones, but images of the senses: the sound of the woman calling, the sound of the wind in the trees, the visual image of her dress so vividly remembered, the old man 'faltering forward', the leaves falling all around him. Much of the effectiveness of the poem comes from the sounds he creates through alliteration ('faltering', 'forward' and 'falling', for example) and the complex and very evocative rhyme scheme, which culminates in the final stanza. In the first two stanzas, lines 1 and 3 have a three-syllable rhyme: 'call to me', 'all to me'; 'view you then', 'knew you then', and this has an almost jaunty air. But the three syllables of 'listlessness' and 'wistlessness' in the next stanza sound wretchedly long drawn out and sad. By the time the last stanza is reached the whole rhythm has changed and the lines are shorter, as the rhymes are: 'forward', 'norward', 'falling', 'calling'. The poet's sense of loss is inescapable.

'Afterwards', on the other hand, expresses the poet's own sense of what has been important to him in his life. He wonders if his neighbours will recognise after his death all the sights and sounds of nature he would have appreciated when he was alive. In the first stanza it is the new leaves of spring, in the second the hawk at dusk, in the third the hedgehog going across the lawn and in the fourth the night sky in winter. These seem to mirror the passage of the seasons too. The final image is the bell tolling for his funeral.

Because he is speculating, the poem contains several questions about how he will be remembered. Sadly the answer to the poet's questions is probably 'No': ultimately, few people recognise your real interests and concerns after you have died (or even when you are alive). Only he really knew what he observed in nature and cared about: perhaps a person who was very close to him would have some insight, but certainly not his neighbours.

The language used by Hardy is very delicate and expressive, showing his sensitivity: 'Delicate-filmed as new-spun silk' (a simile); 'an eyelid's soundless blink', 'mothy and warm / When the hedgehog travels furtively'. His diction is often archaic ('postern' and 'bell of quittance'), which suits a man who imagines slipping away from his own life. He uses many double adjectives such as 'new-spun', 'wind-warped' and 'full-starred', and this gives a richly descriptive impression of the natural beauty he is celebrating. The last line of each stanza is in direct speech: what he imagines the neighbours will say about him: 'He was one who had an eye for such mysteries'.

By imagining the reaction to his own death in this poem, Hardy certainly succeeds in conveying his love of nature, so its final effect is much more positive than 'The Voice'. 'Afterwards' is full of the beauties of the natural world which will continue to exist after he has gone, so I do not find it so depressing, although ironically it is a sadder poem than when he wrote it, because Hardy is dead now. 'The Voice' reminds you that loved ones may die and leave you desperately searching for them, straining to hear a sound of their voice in the wind or catch a glimpse of them in your memory, but to no avail.

Poetry analysis

Task

Comment closely on the following poem:

London

I wander thro' each charter'd street,
Near where the charter'd Thames does flow,
And mark in every face I meet
Marks of weakness, marks of woe.

In every cry of every Man,
In every Infant's cry of fear,
In every voice, in every ban,
The mind-forg'd manacles I hear.

How the Chimney-sweeper's cry
Every black'ning Church appals;
And the hapless soldier's sigh
Runs in blood down Palace walls.

But most thro' midnight streets I hear
How the youthful Harlot's curse
Blasts the new born Infant's tear,
And blights with plagues the Marriage hearse.

William Blake

Sample response

Blake is highly critical of London and the wretched lives that Londoners lead, but he is also critical of institutions such as the church, the monarchy and especially marriage, which take away people's freedom. His emphasis on the innocent suffering is enhanced by two references to small children.

The poem is structured in four stanzas. The first imagines the poet walking through streets filled with unhappy people; their lack of freedom is the subject of the next stanza. The sacrifices of those who give their lives for others' comfort – such as chimney sweeps and soldiers – are emphasised in the third stanza, but the final stanza is the climax of the poem, with its exploration of the trade of the 'Harlot' and her new-born infant.

The diction of the poem is deceptively simple, but some repeated words give emphasis to their meaning. The word 'charter'd' (having a royal charter) is repeated in the first stanza, and it has an ironic tone: it makes no difference to the lives of the inhabitants that the city is recognised and honoured with a royal charter, the poet stills 'marks' or notices in their faces 'marks' (signs) of weakness and misery. The pun on 'marks', as well as the use of the first person, shows the poet's close involvement with the people he observes. He also repeats 'in every' four times, making the universal wretchedness inescapable. Grown-ups and children are equally affected by fear. The word 'ban' and the metaphor 'mind-forg'd manacles' suggest that people themselves are to blame for the chains that bind them and make them fearful. The word 'cry' is also repeated three times, for the Man, the Infant and the Chimney-sweeper, again emphasising a universal misery. The soldier sighs as his blood runs down 'Palace walls', a vivid criticism of the monarchy who wage wars without a thought for those who do the fighting. The Harlot does not cry though, she curses and 'Blasts' her new-born infant, perhaps because its presence, rather than bringing joy, makes carrying on with her business difficult.

The final line, the climax of the poem, is concentrated in its meaning and uses metaphor to express its paradoxical conclusions. Marriage is blighted with plagues by the Harlot because she is selling sex for money, often to married men. The plagues are both physical and metaphorical: the physical diseases she has will be passed on to the man and also to his wife, but the man's recourse to harlots suggests that the marriage is corrupted. However, that is not the end of the final line: the marriage that Blake imagines being cursed and made rotten is itself deathly, a 'hearse' carrying the coffin of love. The 'mind-forg'd manacles' have invented marriage to restrict and confine men and women, and to kill love; marriage is rotten in itself and made more so by the presence of prostitutes who 'sell' love on the streets. The 'charter'd streets' of the first line have become 'midnight streets' by the last stanza, revealing all the vice and limitation of the lives of the city. Blake's use of a regular stanza form and an abab rhyme both add to the emphatic effect of the poem and the tone gathers momentum up to the final, terrible lines, where the new-born are blasted and the married are blighted, the rhyme on 'curse' and 'hearse' drawing the words together in meaning as in sound.

Both these sample essays make reference to theme, structure, language, tone and rhythmical patterns and always try to relate the poet's methods and the effects created. Both show a personal response to the poems chosen.

Check list

Take care that in your preparation for the exam, and in the exam itself where appropriate, you refer to the following in whatever order suits your topic and your essay plan:

- Subject and situation: identify these very briefly
- Theme: obviously important, but relate it to style as you go
- Structure and verse form
- Language: figures of speech, images of the senses
- Diction: the kinds of words used
- Rhythm, rhyme, pace and other sound effects such as alliteration and assonance
- Atmosphere
- Tone: the speaking voice of the poem, which may be sad, angry, excited, wistful and so on.

Exam tip

Make sure that your answer relates theme and style throughout, and that you use examples to support the points you make. You will not have time to say everything and the examiner does not expect you to!

29 Studying a novel

The second section of Paper 3 is devoted to prose works. This section of the book will help you to answer the questions on your prose set texts, which are likely to be novels, as this is a literature examination. A helpful starting point would be to revise units 1–12 on 'Passages for comment' in the Language part of the book to remind you of how to look closely at the language of prose and some of its distinctive features.

Approaching a novel

Every novel is unique, but for each one there will be a writer, of a particular gender and age, who lived or is living at a particular time and in a particular place. This individual has ideas and attitudes to life which will be expressed in the novel because she or he wrote it. For each novel there is a reader too – you – with your own facts of biography and preference. The text itself has a narrator (or narrators) to tell the story, a setting or settings, and characters. The novel is written in language which is structured into sentences, paragraphs and (probably) chapters. The interaction between these elements creates an incomparable experience for the reader, an experience that might last over several days or weeks, depending on the length of the novel and how much time you have to read. Unlike many poems, which can easily be read at one sitting, a novel becomes part of the very fabric of your daily life as you snatch a couple of chapters on the train or before going to sleep. Sometimes you are fortunate enough to have time to read the whole thing without interruption, for example when on holiday or recovering from an illness. These units are designed to help you to express in words your experience of reading and enjoying a novel as well as developing a critical framework for appreciating any other work of prose that you read.

In this unit you will look at narrators and settings and briefly at whether a particular novel is more concerned with concrete description or the creation of consciousness. In unit 30 you will examine some openings of novels and what they show. Other units discuss structure, characterisation, answering a passage question and doing an essay on a novel in the exam.

Narrative and telling stories

The telling of stories is as old as human society. In the past many stories were not recorded in writing but spoken, passed down from one generation to the next (the oral tradition). Everyone loves stories and much of our conversation consists of telling other people about our experiences: what happened, who said what and to whom and how we felt about it. We listen avidly to others' accounts of their doings. Beyond our own domestic and social world we tune in to the news stories of the world, the public narratives. We also create narratives within our own minds, rehearsing conversations, imagining events and dreaming, by day and night.

If possible tell a partner the story of one of your dreams, or an event which happened over the weekend. Discuss the potential this has for a short story.

The narrator

Every narrative has at least one narrator: the person who tells the story. In most everyday situations the narrator is easy to spot: she or he is a reporter being her/himself in an easily defined context. But in a work of prose fiction the writer chooses a narrator to present her/his story in a way that will be effective. This may involve writing in her/his own voice or it may mean adopting the voice of someone else – a character in the story – or a mixture of both. So any writer may begin as narrator by using her/his own voice, then introduce a person to tell the story, a story in which there are characters who also have their own voices and who may tell part of the story, or write a letter or diary. This is known as **multiple narration**.

In the novel *Wuthering Heights*, by Emily Brontë, the novelist does not speak in her own voice at all, but uses two very different narrators to tell the story. Within their telling of the story further characters speak, write letters and contribute their own points of view. This may sound complicated but it is very effective in presenting different views of the same events (and in that sense much closer to our own experience).

First-person narrative

When a character tells the story in the first person (*I*) this is known as first-person narrative. The *I* who speaks in a novel, short story or poem can be known as the **persona**. You can say that the writer adopts the persona of that particular character; so, for example, in *Wuthering Heights*, Emily Brontë adopts the persona first of Mr Lockwood, then of Nelly Dean. Later, when another character writes a letter or tells a substantial part of the story, another persona is being used.

The word 'persona' comes from a Latin word meaning mask; the writer's own identity is hidden by the mask of the chosen narrator.

Name some novels written in the first person. Identify who the *I* of the story is. Can you find a story where the *I* changes and becomes another person?

Omniscient narrator

Not all stories are told in the first person. Sometimes the narrator's viewpoint is that of the writer her or himself; if the writer moves from character to character freely, knowing everybody's thoughts and feelings and showing that she/he has all the information about what has happened and is going to happen, then obviously the narrative isn't restricted to one person's point of view. It is told in the third person (*he, she, it* or *they*) and may range widely, seeing all the different parts of the narrative with equal clarity. This kind of storyteller is known as an omniscient narrator because she/he knows everything. The word 'omniscient' – all-knowing – is often used to describe God and in a sense this kind of storyteller is God-like; after all, a character can be born or married or killed at a stroke of a writer's pen! This is probably the commonest approach for a writer to adopt and it has been used successfully for centuries.

Task

What are the advantages and disadvantages of:

    a the first-person narrative method?
    b the omniscient narrator?

Sample response

When a writer creates a character who tells a story, the reader is able to understand and appreciate the innermost thoughts and feelings of that person, often noticing their flaws and idiosyncrasies, as well as the narrowness of their vision of the world. Perhaps what they say is unreliable, and the reader is given the opportunity by the writer to spot this, which creates many interesting ironic effects. The omniscient narrator style, in contrast, gives the possibility of many different perspectives, and comments across a range of characters and situations.

Task

Here are two short paragraphs, one from *North and South* by Elizabeth Gaskell and one from *The Great Gatsby* by F. Scott Fitzgerald. Read them and see if more than one point of view is being given. In extract 1 try to identify any moments where the narrator seems to know more than the character does, and is letting the reader know about it. In the second extract the narrator of the story, Nick Carraway, is describing his first encounter with Gatsby, who is fifty feet away looking at the stars. Try to identify any moments where the writer is trying to overcome the disadvantage of having a first-person narrator.

1
Margaret opened the door and went in with the straight, fearless, dignified presence habitual to her. She felt no awkwardness; she had too much the habits of society for that. Here was a person come on business to her father; and, as he was one who had shown himself obliging, she was disposed to treat him with a full measure of civility. Mr Thornton was a good deal more surprised and discomfited than she. Instead of a quiet middle-aged clergyman, – a young lady came forward with frank dignity, – a young lady of a different type to most of those he was in the habit of seeing.
2
I decided to call to him. Miss Baker had mentioned him at dinner, and that would do for an introduction. But I didn't call to him, for he gave a sudden intimation that he was content to be alone – he stretched out his arms toward the dark water in a curious way, and, far as I was from him, I could have sworn he was trembling.

Sample response

1

First of all there are two characters and we are shown the thoughts of both of them. (This would be impossible if Margaret were telling the story in the first person – how would she know that Mr Thornton was not used to seeing young women like her?) The narrator seems more interested in Margaret than Mr Thornton, at least at this point in the story. Some of what Gaskell writes shows Margaret's own thoughts and consciousness of herself, but there are moments when Gaskell gives the reader more about Margaret than the character knows herself: is she aware, for example that she is straight, fearless and dignified, and that this is 'habitual to her'? Probably not. She does know that she feels no awkwardness, and that she wants 'to treat him with a full measure of civility', but then 'frank dignity' seems to be the writer again, making sure that we know clearly how Margaret is behaving. It is possible, therefore, for the writer to use the omniscient narrator method and still get close to the innermost thoughts of a character.

2

Nick's character seems from this short passage to be friendly but also tactful. His description of Gatsby shows him to be sensitive and observant. It is central to the novel that the main character, Gatsby, who is not the narrator, is watched and described by someone, the narrator Nick, who is observant, otherwise how would the reader find out about him? However, Fitzgerald makes sure that the disadvantage of the single viewpoint is lessened by adding in some observation for us that goes further than Nick's viewpoint. Would it be possible to see someone trembling if they were fifty feet away, and in the dark? I think not, but the reader accepts this additional detail from the author and gains their first impression of a lonely, but romantic and passionate man, trembling in the dark.

Mixed narrative

A writer can enjoy the benefits of both kinds of narrative approach by adopting an essentially third-person structure and then having lengthy passages within it where a character or characters tell part of their story in the first person. A striking example of this method is *A Grain of Wheat* by Ngugi wa Thiong'o, where there seem to be two omniscient voices: one who has much political knowledge and one who is like a storyteller in the oral tradition. But all the main characters also tell their own stories in the first person, creating a patchwork of intimate voices, offering distinctive points of view.

Exam tip

Whether a writer uses a first-person, third-person or mixed narrative approach, there will always be artistry in its handling so that particular effects can be achieved.

Background and setting

The novelist chooses to set a novel in a particular society at a specific time, which may not be contemporaneous with the novelist's own life. It may be in the far or not so distant past, or even, in the case of a science fiction work, set in the future. As part of your preparation for the exam, make notes on the novel you are studying:

- Where and when is it set?
- What kind of society is depicted?
- Is there more than one setting/society?
- What effect does this have on the narrative/creation of characters?
- Is the setting a background for the action, or does it assume greater importance in the structure of the novel as a whole?

An example of a novel where setting is particularly important is *North and South* by Elizabeth Gaskell, where the distinctive geographical settings and cultural oppositions give the novel its title and central concern.

The African settings of *Martha Quest* (Doris Lessing) and *A Grain of Wheat* (Ngugi wa Thiong'o) are essential for an appreciation of the novels' themes and characterisations. The insights into colonial and post-colonial societies depend upon their particular settings.

Concrete creation or stream of consciousness?

Some novels are concrete and realistic in their descriptions of places, attempting to replicate in words the sense impressions of the physical world they focus on, while other works try to create the complex impression of a character's response to that world by giving an impression of the ebb and flow of their consciousness. It is possible to combine the two approaches; this has been particularly evident in more contemporary works of fiction.

Task

The two extracts below are both concerned with a character. Decide which kind of writing each is: concrete and realistic or inwardly responsive. Try rewriting each one in the style of the other.

1

As he entered the shed a pair of startled swallows flew out. A harrow covered in dust and cobwebs occupied most of the floor. Barely able to see in the gloom, breathing an odour of paraffin and wool and tar, he scratched along the walls among picks and spades, odds and ends of piping, loops of wire, cartons of empty bottles, till he came upon a pile of empty feed-sacks, which he dragged into the open, shook clean, and laid out as a bed for himself on the stoep [veranda].

J. M. Coetzee *Life and Times of Michael K*

2

How trifling it all is, how boring it all is, he thought, compared with the other thing – work. Here he sat drumming his fingers on the table-cloth when he might have been – he took a flashing bird's eye view of his work. What a waste of time it all was to be

> sure! Yet, he thought, she is one of my oldest friends. I am by way of being devoted to her. Yet now, at this moment her presence meant absolutely nothing to him: her beauty meant nothing to him; her sitting with her little boy at the window – nothing, nothing. He wished only to be alone and to take up that book.
>
> Virginia Woolf *To the Lighthouse*

Sample response

Extract **1** has concrete and sensory descriptions of the experiences and actions of the main character, presented as external to himself. Extract **2**, also in the third person 'he', is focused internally on the stream of the character's consciousness. If the inner thoughts and feelings of extract 1 were given, it might read as follows:

> Why am I here? he thought. I can't see, I don't know where I'm going and I'm so tired, very tired. What's that terrible smell? If only I could find somewhere to lie down and something to cover myself with, I would lie and sleep, sleep and never get up again.

If the thoughts and feelings of extract 2 were replaced by more concrete images, it might read as follows:

> He sat and drummed his fingers on the red checked table-cloth. He glanced at his wife and son sitting at the window that looked out onto the sea. The old book he was reading was on the table next to his steaming cup of coffee, together with the used crockery, scraps of food and the coffee pot.

Metaphor to express setting

In the following extract a particular setting is used which is neither concrete nor internalised, but expressed with such vivid metaphorical language that the reader is in no doubt of the writer's strength of feeling. It is not directly connected with a character.

> It was a town of red brick, or of brick that would have been red if the smoke and ashes had allowed it; but, as matters stood it was a town of unnatural red and black like the painted face of a savage. It was a town of machinery and tall chimneys, out of which interminable serpents of smoke trailed themselves for ever and ever, and never got uncoiled.
>
> Charles Dickens *Hard Times*

Task

Look closely at the novel you are studying to identify its narrative method/s, approach to setting and distinctive presentation of experience. The next unit will give you further practice, using the openings of novels to do so.

Exam tip

Read your set text thoroughly several times. Once is never enough.

30 The novel: openings and what they show

This unit is going to look at some different openings of novels, how they have been created by their authors, and what effects they produce. You can often guess what sort of work is going to unfold from the first few paragraphs of the narrative. It is really important for the writer to get the opening right, so that you, the reader, are intrigued from the beginning. You long to enter this world, with its distinctive social or natural background, its ideas and characters.

Opening paragraphs from novels

Task

Look closely at each opening below and see if you can formulate a statement about its setting and characters as well as what sort of novel it might turn out to be. The language, as well as the narrator's position, may be helpful clues to you.

1
Okonkwo was well known throughout the nine villages and even beyond. His fame rested on solid personal achievements. As a young man of eighteen he had brought honour to his village by throwing Amalinze the Cat. Amalinze was the great wrestler who for seven years was unbeaten, from Umuofia to Mbaino. He was called the Cat because his back would never touch the earth. It was this man that Okonkwo threw in a fight which the old man agreed was one of the fiercest since the founder of their town engaged a spirit of the wild for seven days and seven nights.

Chinua Achebe *Things Fall Apart*

2
Whether I shall turn out to be the hero of my own life, or whether that station will be held by anybody else, these pages must show. To begin my life with the beginning of my life, I record that I was born (as I have been informed and believe) on a Friday, at twelve o'clock at night. It was remarked that the clock began to strike, and I began to cry, simultaneously

Charles Dickens *David Copperfield*

3
Two elderly women sat knitting on that part of the veranda which was screened from the sun by a golden shower creeper; the tough stems were so thick with flower it was as if the glaring afternoon was dammed against them in a surf of its own light made visible in the dripping, orange-coloured clusters. Inside this coloured barrier was a darkened recess, rough mud walls (the outer walls of the house itself) forming two sides, the third consisting of a bench loaded with painted petrol tins which held pink and white geraniums. The sun splashed liberal gold through the foliage, over the red cement floor, and over the ladies. They had been here since lunchtime, and would

remain until sunset, talking, talking incessantly, their tongues mercifully let off the leash. They were Mrs. Quest and Mrs. Van Rensberg; and Martha Quest, a girl of fifteen, sat on the steps in full sunshine, clumsily twisting herself to keep the glare from her book with her own shadow.

Doris Lessing Martha Quest

4

May in Ayemenem is a hot, brooding month. The days are long and humid. The river shrinks and black crows gorge on bright mangoes in still, dustgreen trees. Red bananas ripen. Jackfruits burst. Dissolute bluebottles hum vacuously in the fruity air. Then they stun themselves against clear windowpanes and die, fatly baffled in the sun.

Arundhati Roy The God of Small Things

5

He speaks in your voice, American, and there's a shine in his eye that's halfway hopeful.
   It's a school day, sure, but he's nowhere near the classroom. He wants to be here instead, standing in the shadow of this old rust-hulk of a structure, and it's hard to blame him – this metropolis of steel and concrete and flaky paint and cropped grass and enormous Chesterfield packs aslant on the scoreboards, a couple of cigarettes jutting from each.

Don DeLillo Underworld

6

The past is a foreign country: they do things differently there.
   When I came upon the diary it was lying at the bottom of a rather battered red cardboard collar-box, in which as a small boy I kept my Eton collars. Someone, probably my mother, had filled it with treasures dating from those days. There were two dry, empty sea-urchins; two rusty magnets, a large one and a small one, which had almost lost their magnetism; some negatives rolled up in a tight coil; some stumps of sealing-wax; a small combination lock with three rows of letters; a twist of very fine whipcord, and one or two ambiguous objects, pieces of things, of which the use was not at once apparent: I could not even tell what they had belonged to. The relics were not exactly dirty nor were they quite clean, they had the patina of age; and as I handled them, for the first time for over fifty years, a recollection of what each had meant to me came back, faint as the magnet's power to draw, but as perceptible. Something came and went between us: the intimate pleasure of recognition, the almost mystical thrill of early ownership – feelings of which, at sixty-odd, I felt ashamed.

L. P. Hartley The Go-Between

7

Rose Pickles knew something bad was going to happen. Something really bad, this time. She itched in her awful woollen bathing suit and watched her brothers and a whole mob of other kids chucking bombies off the end of the jetty in the bronze evening light. Fishing boats were coming in along the breakwater for the night, their diesels throbbing like blood. Back under the Norfolk pines gulls bickered on the grass and fought for the scraps of uneaten lunches that schoolkids had thrown there. The sun was in the sea. She stood up and called.

Tim Winton Cloudstreet

There are only seven examples here, but each one is quite different.

Sample response

1

From the opening words it sounds as if Okonkwo is the hero of this story. He is well known for his bravery and has brought honour to his village. The references to village life and honour, and the names of the people and places, suggest that this is an African story, an impression strengthened by the reference to the 'spirit of the wild' at the end of the paragraph. The fact that the story begins with a fierce fight gives the impression that the narrative will be full of action and excitement, as well as violence. It is a third-person narrative, clearly focused on Okonkwo. The sentence structures have a clarity and simplicity about them which focus on the action.

2

This is a first-person narrative and the 'I' of the story is beginning at the very beginning of his existence. His cry and the striking of the clock at midnight chime together. His first statement is very dramatic, and rather puzzling: how can he not be the hero of his own story? The writer makes it sound as if the boy did some deeds that he was ashamed of at some later stage of his life. He draws attention to the way a small child is reliant on others for details of the first events in his life, and makes the narrative sound as if the main character is now older and looking back on his life story. The sentences are rhythmical and elegant, and they sound portentous when read out loud.

3

This third-person narrative begins with a setting of the scene on a veranda bright with colourful flowers. Before the characters are even introduced, the rich beauty of the flowers and the contrasts between shadow and brightness are emphasised. There are some indications of the setting, such as the mud walls and the petrol tins with geraniums and the red cement floor, which do not sound like England today. (It is in fact set in Africa about fifty years ago.) The two ladies are very talkative: the word 'talking' is repeated, and the word 'incessantly' sounds like a criticism from the narrator. Their tongues have been 'let off the leash': a metaphor which suggests that they are like dogs kept under control most of the time but are now able to run free. This might give the impression that they are normally supposed to keep quiet (perhaps while their husbands do most of the talking – they are both referred to with their husbands' names, not their first names). Martha is introduced right at the end of the paragraph and her age immediately suggests a character who can be sympathised with by a young reader – which of us has not sat as a child trying to amuse ourselves while our elders talk and talk behind us? The writer's use of light and shade images is so extensive that it perhaps suggests that metaphorically Martha's story will be one of striking contrasts. The sentences are long and richly descriptive.

4

This short opening paragraph is extremely descriptive with many adjectives of colour and texture. The combination of this with short sentences and present tense verbs ('is', 'are', 'shrinks', 'gorge', 'hum') creates an immediacy and dramatic impact for a scene in which, as yet, no people have made an appearance. The reader expects an exotic setting (it is India) and the author's voice in the third-person narrative sounds authoritative. However, although the images are exotic and colourful there are also many words that suggest over-ripeness to the point of rottenness ('brooding', 'humid', 'gorge', 'ripen', 'burst', 'fruity') and the flies 'stun themselves' and 'die'.

5

The writer addresses the reader as 'you' and his tone is casual: 'It's a school day, sure', for example. You can almost hear him speaking in an American voice. The prose is in the present tense and the sentences are very varied in their length. At first you wonder what and who he is talking about, but soon you realise that the 'metropolis of steel and concrete and flaky paint and cropped grass and enormous Chesterfield packs aslant on the scoreboards, a couple of cigarettes jutting from each' is a stadium of some kind with cigarette advertising on it. The main character seems to be a young boy who is supposed to be at school but is looking forward to something special. You sense that the boy is going to have a significant experience in this place. The writer's style is contemporary – both informal and poetic – in its descriptions.

6

The 'I' of the story is quite old now – over sixty – and he is looking back on his life. The first sentence of the novel suggests that the past is separate and so distinctly different that it could be like living in another country. But after this rather philosophical opening, the writer uses a number of very physical objects, closely described, to depict the old man's early childhood treasures which he has found in the old box. They include the diary which is clearly the most important object amongst them. As reader, you wonder whether the objects, so carefully described, have a symbolic value – do the magnets represent the magnetism of people, now faded? Or are they the lovingly described evocation of childhood, where every little object collected has its importance for the young person's imagination? The reader expects to return to the past and find out about the diary, and the writer's style and descriptions suggest a past well before the twenty-first century.

7

This is third-person narrative with the narrator very close to the main character Rose, who is, again, a child. From the very first sentence, suspense is created – what is going to happen? 'Something bad' is repeated. The world of childhood experience is captured in the 'awful woollen bathing suit' that she has to wear, and her brothers jumping into the swimming pool (the expression 'chucking bombies' suggesting that this is an Australian setting). But there is also description of the place, not just of the main character's feelings, though the simile 'throbbing like blood' and the gulls bickering on the grass transfer some of her feelings of doom and the atmosphere of children playing into the description of the engines of the fishing boats and the birds on the grass. The writer's style is vivid and you expect all the descriptions to relate to the feelings of the people in the story.

Task

Choose one of the novels whose first paragraph has interested you and read the work. Are your first impressions borne out in the novel as a whole?

Exam tip

Even the smallest section of a novel can give you a sense of the writer's concerns and methods of working. Pay attention to the detail, and the larger picture will emerge clearly.

③① The novel: structure

Make sure you review and practise units 13 and 14 on narrative writing before you begin this unit because your own creative efforts will always help you to appreciate the effects achieved in other writers' work.

A story is not just a series of events; how these are arranged and communicated is very important to the effect of the novel on the reader. The **plot** is the series of events, and they may be complicated in a novel, but telling this story or summarising the narrative is not considered to be an important skill in exams at AS level.

Exam tip
Never tell the story of a novel! You will waste valuable time and gain no marks for doing so.

Chronological arrangement

How the events of the story are arranged is part of the structure of the novel. If you consider the events of your own life, they take place in time and therefore in a particular order. If you try to describe the order in which events actually happened, then you try hard to put first things first and culminate in the final event, as it happened. You might do this if you were describing a car accident to a policeman and trying to be precise. This can be denoted with letters of the alphabet: **a** followed by **b**, **c**, **d**, **e** and so on.

Some novels and short stories are written in this way. At no time is there any irregularity in such works: events happen in the order in which they would occur in real life. If events go from A to Z without deviation, then this may create an atmosphere of regularity and completeness: the story proceeds evenly throughout. Many light novels, intended for whiling away an afternoon in a not very challenging way, are written in such a manner.

But the sorts of novel that are set for study at AS level are often more complex in their structure than this. Every time a writer begins the story in the middle and then goes back to an earlier point in the hero's life, or a character describes a memory of the past in detail, then the chronological pattern is altered and this is bound to have an effect on the reader's understanding and appreciation of the novel as a whole.

Task
If possible, share with a friend an interesting incident that happened to you one weekend. Tell the events in the order in which they actually happened. Then try beginning with the climax of the story and working back to the start. Now see if you can pick an incident from the middle of the story and work backwards to the start and forward to the end. What effect does each method of structuring your story have on your narrative?

You have probably found that some stories are more effective told in one of the suggested ways than others. A dramatic story with tension and a climax may be spoilt if you know the ending first.

Non-chronological arrangement

Order: putting Z first

In the novel *The Unbearable Lightness of Being* by Milan Kundera, the reader is told almost straight away that the central characters, a young couple, are killed in an accident. Everything that follows about their earlier life together is coloured by the reader's knowledge of their untimely deaths. This has a poignant effect on the reader, who can never forget for a moment the fleeting nature of their physical and emotional lives, so vividly portrayed by the writer, but doomed to end early. If you know Shakespeare's *Romeo and Juliet*, you will remember that the Chorus tells us in the first moments of the play that the lovers are 'star-cross'd' and 'take their life', with similar effect. We appreciate the intensity and liveliness of the fated characters much more than we would do if they were to live to an old age and die in their beds.

Changing the order completely

Task

Read the following passages from *The Third Policeman* by Flann O'Brien and work out what the order of the events was, using **a**, **b**, **c** etc. Try to consider the effect of this.

Not everybody knows how I killed old Phillip Mathers, smashing his jaw in with my spade; but first it is better to speak of my friendship with John Divney because it was he who first knocked old Mathers down by giving him a great blow in the neck with a special bicycle-pump which he manufactured himself out of a hollow iron bar. Divney was a strong civil man but he was lazy and idle-minded. He was personally responsible for the whole idea in the first place. It was he who told me to bring my spade. He was the one who gave the orders on the occasion and also the explanations when they were called for.

I was born a long time ago. My father was a strong farmer and my mother owned a public house.

Sample response

Events
a birth
b friendship with Divney
c the idea
d Divney knocked old Mathers down
e smashing the jaw in
f the explanations

But they are arranged in the following order: **e**, **b**, **d**, **b**, **c**, **f**, **a**. The impression created is of a conversation where the ideas are repeated and events do not always come out in the right order. The character speaking sounds as if he takes after his father for strength and has spent much time at his mother's, having many stories to tell of his exploits! If you are studying the play *The Playboy of the Western World* by J. M. Synge you may notice some similarities here.

Frequency: a single event told twice over

In *The Collector* by John Fowles a young woman is kidnapped. The first section of the story is a first-person narrative told by the girl, describing what happens to her. There is a sudden shift in the second section of the novel and the same events are told by the kidnapper, also in the first person. The final section returns to the girl's point of view. This has the effect at first of involving the reader's imagination and empathy with the girl, then creating a profound shock by involving us in the inner life of the kidnapper, enhanced by the use of the first-person narrative twice over. When we return to the girl's viewpoint in the third section, we feel a sense of hopelessness because we know, with the benefit of hindsight into the kidnapper's mind, that she will never escape.

In *Wuthering Heights*, the same narratives are told by different characters, creating a richly complex effect. Different points of view of the same events help in the characterisation of Heathcliff and Catherine as well as Nelly Dean, one of the narrators, with her commonsense view of events. Brontë sometimes delays the second telling of an incident so that our intitial assumptions, based on the first person's account, are challenged. This is particularly used for creating an aggressive image of Heathcliff at first, then making him more sympathetic. It also reminds us that the 'truth' is very difficult to define and depends upon the person telling the story as well as the person listening or reading. Similar effects are created in the modern novel *A Grain of Wheat* by Ngugi.

Exam tip
Ambiguity and the irony that springs from it are among the most significant effects in literature.

Duration of events

Sometimes a novel seems to slow down and at other times speed up. A few years can pass in one sentence. An apparently brief chance meeting can take a whole chapter to describe. Here is a passage from *The Secret Agent* by Joseph Conrad, describing the murder of Mr Verloc, an event which in real time would take only a moment or two.

Task

Look at the pace of the description of this event and try to identify those aspects which slow it down.

He was lying on his back and staring upwards. He saw partly on the ceiling and partly on the wall the moving shadow of an arm with a clenched hand holding a carving knife. It flickered up and down. Its movements were leisurely. They were leisurely enough for Mr Verloc to recognise the limb and the weapon.

They were leisurely enough for him to take in the full meaning of the portent, and to taste the flavour of death rising in his gorge. His wife had gone raving mad – murdering mad. They were leisurely enough for the first paralysing effect of this discovery to pass away before a resolute determination to come out victorious from the ghastly struggle with that armed lunatic. They were leisurely enough for Mr Verloc to elaborate a plan of defence involving a dash behind the table, and the felling of the woman to the ground with a heavy wooden chair. But they were not leisurely enough to allow Mr Verloc the time to move either hand or foot. The knife was already planted in his breast.

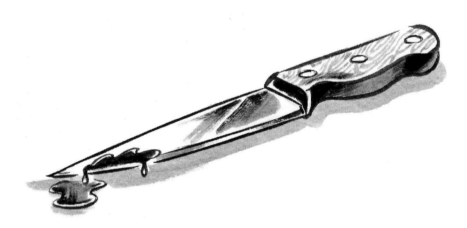

Sample response

Conrad repeats the phrase 'they were leisurely enough' again and again. Ironically the word 'leisurely' itself slows the pace, and the repetitive structure builds suspense until the climax of 'they were not leisurely enough' and then it is too late – the knife is in his breast. Conrad's technique of focusing on Verloc's consciousness slows the events down – one can have many thoughts in just a moment. [Compare this effect with the use of parallelism and repetition in poetry.]

Contrast this with the opening sentence of *A House for Mr Biswas* by V. S. Naipaul, which covers a number of weeks in two brisk sentences:

Ten weeks before he died, Mr Mohun Biswas, a journalist of Sikkim Street, St James, Port of Spain, was sacked. He had been ill for some time.

The connections in a complex narrative

Sometimes the writer will draw attention to the structural links in the story. The following passage, which comes from *Bleak House* by Charles Dickens, reveals the vast and seemingly never-ending material the novelist has at her/his disposal to shape into a novel. The choice will be made to suit her/his theme.

> What connexion can there be, between the place in Lincolnshire, the house in town, the Mercury in powder, and the whereabouts of Jo the outlaw with the broom, who had that distant ray of light upon him when he swept the churchyard-step? What connexion can there have been between many people in the innumerable histories of this world, who, from opposite sides of great gulfs, have, nevertheless, been very curiously brought together?

And the novelist is, of course, doing the bringing together. Victorian novelists, of whom Dickens is one, were very fond of coincidences, not merely to make the plot more engaging, but also to suggest the complex networks of social connections and responsibilities that people try to ignore.

At other times structural links are made by the creation of characters who, placed next to one another, or juxtaposed, bring out the writer's concerns very clearly by contrast. Repetition of image or symbol can also help to create structural links in a novel, and this is discussed in the next unit.

Novel of development

This is a structure where the main character is shown developing through the work, making mistakes and learning until she/he is educated, sometimes morally, into realisation of her/his own shortcomings and sometimes into greater maturity. *Martha Quest* by Doris Lessing is a novel of this kind as are *Great Expectations* by Charles Dickens and *Emma* by Jane Austen. Such novels often show the society in which the novel is set as hostile to the aspirations of the character, though not in the latter case.

Emma is very carefully constructed, with the main character, Emma, making errors of judgement and wrong suppositions which are gradually unfolded and resolved when she learns the truth. Characters are introduced at just the right moments for advancing Emma's progress, and public events such as balls and picnics punctuate the narrative regularly and helpfully for the reader's appreciation of the social setting.

Exam tip

When answering passage questions, make sure that you consider the place of the extract within the novel's structure. Is this one of the many moments when the heroine is faced with her own mistake and has to learn to be more careful? Is this one of the descriptions of the place that regularly punctuate the narrative, drawing attention to a particular theme? Always try to analyse the writer's skill and artistry.

32 The novel: characterisation

Characterisation, or the making of characters, is one of the most important features of any novel and what for many readers makes a novel memorable. It is frequently the subject for examination questions, and your work should reflect your appreciation of both what a character is like and what her/his place is in the ideas and structure of the novel as a whole. You should review units 15 and 16 on descriptive writing as well, to remind yourself of the techniques you learned for bringing characters alive in your own compositions.

Exam tip

At AS level, a description of a character, or character sketch, is not enough; some reference to the role of the character and its contribution to the work as a whole will be essential for a good mark.

In almost every novel a character or set of characters engages the reader's interest from the very outset. In the openings looked at in unit 30 it was clear from most of them that the novel began with a focus on a person. In this unit, you are going to look at some of the techniques used by writers to present a character in the novel as a whole.

In our lives, we meet people and react to their age, gender and appearance, what they do and say, and how they react to us and other people. We know ourselves too, and reflect on our own consciousness, attributes and appearance, though our self-knowledge is likely to be partial and biased. In a novel, the writer selects a narrative method (see unit 29) and then works within this first- or third-person structure to present the appearance, actions and thoughts of characters.

Rounded and flat characters

In creating the world of the novel with its unique and distinctive qualities, the writer has to focus on and delineate the main area of interest and activity. It is rather like a person using a pair of compasses: the point is pressed into the paper and a circle is drawn with the pencil on the other end. The circle and everything inside it represents the focus of the novel, with the point at the centre. Characters close to the centre of the circle may be characterised in full and complex detail, whilst others at the edge of the circle are simply sketched in. Another way of describing this difference is to call the detailed characters 'rounded' because they are apparently three-dimensional and the simple sketches 'flat' characters because they are types: one-dimensional and with perhaps a single feature or mannerism. In some comic novels these features are so exaggerated that you could call such characters caricatures. It would not be wise to dismiss their effectiveness, though, because they might be vital to the plot, or add to the expression of the author's main concerns in the novel, or act as a contrast or parallel to one of the major characters. So the role or function of the character does not necessarily depend on the depth and detail with which it is presented.

Description

The way in which a writer describes a character in a third-person narrative is very revealing, not only of aspects of the character being presented, but also of the writer's attitude to the character.

Task

Look closely at these descriptions. In what ways and how effectively does the writer introduce the character?

1

He was tall and huge, and his bushy eyebrows and wide nose gave him a very severe look. He breathed heavily, and it was said that, when he slept, his wives and children in their out-houses could hear him breathe. When he walked, his heels hardly touched the ground and he seemed to walk on springs, as if he was going to pounce on somebody. And he did pounce on people quite often. He had a slight stammer and whenever he was angry and could not get his words out quickly enough, he would use his fists. He had no patience with unsuccessful men.

Okonkwo in Achebe's Things Fall Apart

2

She had a broad but shapely face, with a pointed chin, severe hazel eyes, a full mouth, clear straight dark brows. Sometimes she would take the mirror to her parents' bedroom, and hold it at an angle to the one at the window, and examine herself, at this double remove, in profile; for this view of herself had a delicacy her full face lacked. With her chin tilted up, her loose blonde hair falling back, her lips carefully parted in an eager expectant look, she possessed a certain beauty. But it seemed to her that her face, her head, were something quite apart from her body; she could see herself only in sections, because of the smallness of the mirror.

Martha in Lessing's Martha Quest

3

John Thompson – tall, a leathery skin that stuck to the bone – did not go to Nairobi, but remained at Githima during the lunch-hour going through the motions of working: that is, he would stand, go to the cabinet by the wall, pull out a file, and return to the table, his face weather-beaten into permanent abstraction, almost as if his mind dwelt on things far away and long ago. His thin hands and light eyes went through each file carefully before returning it to the cabinet. Once or twice he sat up and his finger played with a few creases crowded around the corner of his mouth.

John Thompson in Ngugi's A Grain of Wheat

4

Emma Woodhouse, handsome, clever, and rich, with a comfortable home and happy disposition, seemed to unite some of the best blessings of existence; and had lived nearly twenty-one years in the world with very little to distress or vex her.

Emma in Austen's Emma

Sample response

1

Achebe's presentation concisely depicts some of the most important aspects of Okonkwo. The paragraph gives a very clear description of Okonkwo's distinctive physical features, both of the body – 'tall and huge' – and the face, with its 'bushy eyebrows and wide nose'. The portrait is vivid too in its emphasis on his breathing and the way he walks: both are characteristic and somehow larger and more significant than the average (and the way he walks will later be important when he is in disguise). His impatience and aggressiveness are also skilfully expressed, but there is something slightly contradictory in the way that he can both pounce and stammer: a contradiction which is to prove central to Achebe's portrayal of his hero. He is not simply a strong and simple man; his innermost thoughts and emotional reactions will be given to us. The paragraph as a whole combines key features of his appearance with characteristic behaviour and action and suggests something of the writer's approach to his character: scrupulous, objective and clear-sighted.

2

Martha's face is described in detail, and at times she sounds like the heroine of a light romance, with her 'full mouth' and 'loose blonde hair falling back'. But Lessing offers hints of a much more interesting heroine: the contrasting pointed chin and severe eyes suggest someone sharper and more critically intelligent. Her desire to see herself in the mirror more fully and her careful adoption of a particular facial expression and pose are typical of an insecure adolescent. However, the dislocation of her head from her body in the description also images the contradictions of Martha. Just as the whole being is never resolved satisfactorily in the mirror here, neither is Martha's situation in the novel as a whole. Lessing's prose is thus symbolic and alternates between more objective description and close narrative focus on Martha's thoughts and feelings ('It seemed to her...').

3

The physical description here is concise but very vivid: 'tall, a leathery skin that stuck to the bone'. It sounds sinister and unpleasant, showing, rather than just telling, at an early stage of the novel, John Thompson's hard character. 'Leathery' and 'weather-beaten' remind the reader that he is a white man who has spent some time in the harsh African climate. His 'thin hands and light eyes' also sound disturbing: 'thin' and 'light' are both words showing lack of depth and substance. His actions suggest that he is distracted, his thoughts far away, going through the motions of working. The creases at the corners of his mouth are 'crowded' there as if lines have gathered as a result of his scheming, rather than because of smiling or some warmer human activity. Ngugi's prose is sharply descriptive and succinct; it is without sympathy. At no time here does he try to express the inner thoughts of Thompson.

4

Emma and her situation are described in five adjectives: 'handsome', 'clever', 'rich', 'comfortable' and 'happy'. These are strong words which have no shadow of ambiguity about them. Combine these with her youth, and Emma has everything one could wish for! But Austen's prose always reveals a very careful choice of words: in 'seemed to unite some of the best blessings of existence', 'seemed' strikes a warning note, and this is confirmed when the reader is told she had lived to this point 'with very little to distress or vex her'. Austen suggests here that perhaps never having had to face distress or vexation is not the best way to become mature. Always having had looks, brains and money might not be the best way of developing as a person. Moreover, are these the 'best blessings' of existence? There is nothing here of those virtues which could be called 'blessings', such as kindness, unselfishness, sympathy and so on. In this brief paragraph, Austen establishes herself as an omniscient narrator who is clear-sighted and who may be critical. Later in the novel she does present Emma's own thoughts and feelings, but it is clear that these are often restricted by Emma's limitations, which Austen makes the reader aware of through the irony of two different points of view: Emma's and her creator's.

Association of character with setting or symbol

Another way in which characters can be presented is by associating them with a particular setting or symbol, a physical representation of an idea or quality. In *Great Expectations*, Miss Havisham is always associated with a dark room full of dust, cobwebs and images of the past; the bleakness of Heathcliff's character in *Wuthering Heights* is emphasised by association with the moors and their wild weather, his relationship with Catherine like the rocks beneath the earth. *The Great Gatsby* contrasts the house of Tom and Daisy Buchanan with that of Jay Gatsby: the former old and well-established, part of the wealth of a dynasty; the latter new and built to impress, with a library containing books whose pages have not even been cut and a cupboard full of beautiful but unworn imported silk shirts. In Hardy's *Tess of the D'Urbervilles*, the phases of Tess's life are enhanced by the different natural settings in which they take place. In *Martha Quest*, the dress that Martha makes for the dance symbolises her independence from her parents and her rejection of her mother in particular. In George Eliot's *Middlemarch*, the symbols of mirror and window represent respectively the ego (the personality focused on itself) and the more altruistic and outward-looking escape from self.

Parallels and contrasts

Minor characters can contribute to the plot or enhance the themes of a novel by providing reinforcement of the qualities of a major character, or, conversely, throwing their characteristics into clear relief by the contrast they provide. In *Emma*, Miss Bates may be trivial, loquacious and boring, but, by contrasting her with the shallow, pretentious Mrs Elton, Austen is able to show her open, sincere and unmalicious nature. Equally, Mrs Elton's interfering and spiteful nature does contrast unfavourably with Emma's interventions: Emma may be presumptuous but she learns from her mistakes and gains sense and judgement as the novel progresses, unlike Mrs Elton. A further novel by Austen is built upon the contrast between two sisters, Eleanor and Marianne: *Sense and Sensibility*.

In *Things Fall Apart*, the thematic importance of the Ibo tribe and the changes that are threatening its established society are enhanced by the contrast between Okonkwo and Unoka: the man of action and the poet who loves music and flute-playing. Without Unoka, Ibo life would be more one-dimensional in its presentation and Okonkwo's characterisation would be less sharply focused as a result.

In Charlotte Brontë's *Jane Eyre*, the contrasting characters of Rochester and St John Rivers help to present the ambiguous nature of Jane Eyre: the struggle within her nature between passion and control. Some literary critics argue that Brontë is more successful in her creation of Jane than of these two male characters, who are criticised as unconvincing and two-dimensional. However, if you realise their structural function in the novel as contrasting with each other and intensifying Jane's nature (the novel's main concern), then they could be seen as more successful.

Task

If possible, discuss the characters of the novel you are studying with a fellow student. How many are created in depth? Are they paralleled/contrasted with another character in any way? Can you identify any symbols or settings that are associated with them?

Exam tip

Enjoying a novel thoroughly can sometimes lead you into thinking of the characters as real people. It's important to remember that they are being employed by the writer for particular effects in the novel as a whole. Remembering this will give your exam essays extra credit.

33 The novel: writing on prose passages for the exam

For each set text that you study, there are two alternative exam questions: one is an essay on an aspect of the novel such as its characterisation or main concerns; the other is an extract from the work, which you have to analyse in detail.

Prose analysis

In this unit, you are going to work on the skills of prose analysis so that you feel confident about tackling the passage questions on your novel and any other prose work that you study in the future.

You have already covered analysis of poetry for the exam. Many of the lessons learned there are just as useful here.

Points in common with poetry

a You are familiar with the work, whether poem or passage of prose, because you have studied the set text. So you are able to establish the subject, situation and background straight away.

b You will still need to work through the set prose text carefully to make sure you are clear about the sense of the words. As you do this, consider the structure carefully – in a poem, you will be guided by the stanza divisions; in prose, although it is an extract from a larger whole, the examiner who sets the paper takes great care to choose a passage which has a clear, complete structure of its own.

c You will be able to identify the main concerns (or themes) of the set passage, just as you do in poetry criticism. You know the themes of the novel as a whole, but not all of them will be evident in the passage. Read carefully and don't make assumptions.

d Prose writers use imagery and figures of speech just as poets do, so you will be able to identify metaphor, hyperbole and so on in your prose extract, discussing its meaning and effect in a similar way. Equally, identifying any noteworthy diction is important whether you are scrutinising a poem or a piece of prose.

e The writer's tone is an important feature of any piece of writing, whether in prose or poetic form. If you find this a difficult aspect of analysis, you might find it helpful to think of tone of voice if it were read aloud and what you are able to deduce from this.

f Finally, the atmosphere created in the prose passage is just as worthy of discussion as it may be in a poem.

New skills to develop

a When writing on a poem, you know you need to discuss its form: its distinctive rhythms, metrical scheme, rhyme and use of sound effects such as alliteration, assonance and onomatopoeia. When analysing a prose passage, you will need to look at its division into paragraphs and sentences. Don't assume that prose doesn't have any rhythms of its own. In the passages that follow, you will see that prose writers also vary their sentences, use parallels and contrasts, and build to climactic moments.

b Prose writers also use longer passages of description and reflection than poets tend to do and you will need to observe and comment on the effect of these.

c Dialogue is widely used in the novel. When you come to the section of the book on drama, there is a unit which includes discussion of dialogue, because plays work only with visual effects and words spoken by characters. Dialogue in the novel is supported and contextualised by description, commentary and reflection. A character's thoughts in a play will need to be expressed in some kind of soliloquy or aside, but in the novel they can be explored fully by the narrator, whether the narrative is in the first or third person.

Passages for comment

> ### Task
>
> Using the skills described above, analyse each passage in some detail.
>
>
>
> **1**
> Paul had never risen from his little bed. He lay there, listening to the noises in the street, quite tranquilly; not caring much how the time went, but watching it and watching everything about him with observing eyes.

When the sunbeams struck into his room through the rustling blinds, and quivered on the opposite wall like golden water, he knew that evening was coming on, and that the sky was red and beautiful. As the reflection died away, and a gloom went creeping up the wall, he watched it deepen, deepen, deepen, into night. Then he thought how the long streets were dotted with lamps, and how the peaceful stars were shining over head. His fancy had a strange tendency to wander to the river, which he knew was flowing through the great city; and now he thought how black it was, and how deep it would look, reflecting the hosts of stars—and more than all, how steadily it rolled away to meet the sea.

As it grew later in the night, and footsteps in the street became so rare that he could hear them coming, count them as they passed, and lose them in the hollow distance, he would lie and watch the many-coloured ring about the candle, and wait patiently for day. His only trouble was, the swift and rapid river. He felt forced, sometimes, to try to stop it—to stem it with his childish hands—or choke its way with sand—and when he saw it coming on, resistless, he cried out! But a word from Florence, who was always at his side, restored him to himself; and leaning his poor head upon her breast, he told Floy of his dream, and smiled.

Charles Dickens Dombey and Son

2

But the rain when later it fell, did not break into violence. It drizzled continuously, varying neither in speed nor in volume. The country, it seemed, was going to plunge into one of those stinging drizzles that went on endlessly. On such days the sun never said good morning, or else good night. Without a watch, you could never guess the time.

At his mother's hut in Thabai, Karanja crammed a few clothes into a bag.

'You'll not let me make you a cup of tea?' his mother asked again. She sat on a stool near the fireplace; her right leg bent at the knee, resting on a hearthstone. She was bowed double, leaning forward, so that her chin and hands rested on the bent knee. Wairimu was wizened, with hollow eyes and protruding jaws. Her eyes now watched the silent movements of her son at the door.

'No,' Karanja said, after a pause, as if words and speech cost him pain.

'It is raining outside. A cup of hot tea will warm you inside – since you say you'll not stay here for the night.'

'I've already said I don't want tea – or anything,' he said, his voice raised with obvious irritation. The irritation was directed less at Wairimu than at the bag he handled, the smoke-ridden hut, the drizzle outside, at the life and things in general.

Ngugi A Grain of Wheat

3

I do not have the run of the house as before. The Governor's wife is still frightened of me; she's afraid I will have another fit, and she doesn't want any of her best teacups broken; you would think she never heard anyone scream before. So I do not dust these days, or carry in the tea tray or empty the chamber pots or make up the beds. Instead I am set to work in the back kitchen, cleaning the pots and pans in the scullery, or else I work in the laundry. I do not mind that so much as I always liked doing the laundry, it is hard work and roughens the hands, but I like the clean smell afterwards.

I help the regular laundress, old Clarrie, who is part coloured and used to be a slave once, before they did away with it here. She is not afraid of me, she doesn't mind me or care what I may have done, even if I killed a gentleman; she only nods, as if to say, So that's one less of them. She says I am a steady worker and pull my share and don't waste the soap, and I know the treatment of fine linen, I have the way of it, and also

---

how to get out the stains, even from the blonde lace, which is not easy to come by; and a good clear starcher too, and can be trusted not to burn the things in ironing, and that is enough for her.

At noon we go into the kitchen and Cook gives us what is left over, from the larder; at the very least some bread and cheese and meat broth but usually something more, as Clarrie is a favourite of hers and is known to have a temper if crossed, and the Governor's wife swears by her, especially for laces and ruffles, and says she is a treasure and has no equal, and would be annoyed to lose her, so she is not stinted; and because I am with her, neither am I.

Margaret Atwood *Alias Grace*

Sample responses

1

The passage, which is narrated in the third person, focuses on Paul, who is lying in bed ill, in a house which is in a city (there is mention of streets and lamps) but also near to a great river. (In fact it is set in London and the river is the Thames.) The paragraphs trace through a day and into the evening and night as Paul lies there watching and listening to the sights and sounds, apparently not sleeping. At the end of the passage, there is a reference to telling Florence, or 'Floy' as he calls her, about his dream of the river, though to the reader it seems like a waking dream.

Dickens is closely attuned to the boy's observations, thoughts and feelings throughout the passage and uses language successfully to create the world of someone very ill. He lies 'quite tranquilly' during the day and at night waits 'patiently' for daybreak. Some of his observations are gentle, beautiful ones, such as the sunbeams and the peaceful stars. Dickens uses onomatopoeic words to describe the effect of the sunbeams which came into Paul's room 'through the rustling blinds and quivered on the opposite wall'. They are 'like golden water' and the simile of water is in contrast to the inexorable dark river described later in the passage. But as night falls, the beauty falls away and as 'a gloom went creeping up the wall, he watched it deepen, deepen, deepen, into night'. The repetitive structure here emphasises the night fears which afflict him. Although he tries to think of the light sources, the lamps and the 'peaceful stars', his mind keeps returning to the 'resistless' dark deep river flowing towards the sea. Although Florence is described as being always at his side, Dickens so effectively evokes Paul's half-conscious state that we are barely aware of Florence and her devotion.

Dickens uses sympathetic words such as 'his little bed' and 'his poor head' to encourage the reader's identification with the sick child, but his description of the deep black river and its relentless flowing towards the sea suggests that the child's death is inevitable and the river symbolises this. The passage has a very sad atmosphere and the reader is moved by the child's imminent death.

The sentence structures are long and cumulative, building effectively with their repetitions a sense of the boy's reflective and compulsive thoughts: 'Then he thought how the long streets ... how the peaceful stars ... now he thought how black it was ... how deep ... how steadily ...'. The sentences flow rhythmically and relentlessly like the river, until one sentence near the end, whose rhythms are choppy and desperate: 'He felt forced, sometimes, to try to stop it – to stem it with his childish hands – or choke its way with sand – and when he saw it coming on, resistless, he cried out!' Dickens's use of varied sentence structures is particularly striking, and not just in this novel.

2

This third-person narrative deals with Karanja packing up and leaving his mother's house. It begins and ends with a description of the weather and the setting and in the central section gives the conversation between Karanja and his mother.

Although Wairimu is described, it is clear that the narrator is closer to the character of Karanja as his thoughts and feelings are given to the reader while hers are not. The descriptions of Wairimu are external ones: 'She was bowed double, leaning forward ... Her eyes now watched the silent movements of her son.' Karanja's feelings are closely observed and conveyed to the reader: 'as if words and speech cost him pain', 'his voice raised with obvious irritation ... at the life and things in general'.

Ngugi uses pathetic fallacy to enhance the feelings of Karanja, so that the dull, wretched weather reflects his own mood. The personification of the sun in the first paragraph − 'the sun never said good morning, or else good night' − effectively suggests the way in which mood can be created by the weather, or weather chime in with mood. [**Pathetic fallacy** is the term used to describe the literary presentation of inanimate objects in nature as possessing human feelings. Here the writer uses it to link state of mind and weather.]

The dialogue is brief and concerns an everyday matter − having a cup of tea. If this were a play, the two characters would have only a brief interchange. But because it is a novel, the writer is able to explore and expand on the feelings of one of the characters in particular and use the setting of the 'smoke-ridden hut, the drizzle outside' to give depth to those feelings.

Ngugi's style is precise and his sentences brief and elegant. It is easy to picture the scene and to appreciate the feelings of Karanja, but there is no attempt to draw sympathy for him here − this is the human condition, and we have to just get on with it.

3

This is a first-person narrative, told by a girl who is clearly a maid in the house of the Governor, although it is his wife who dominates the domestic scene. Amidst all the domestic talk of chamber pots, laundry and food, there is a reference to the first-person narrator having had a fit at some point and also having 'killed a gentleman', which contrast strongly with the domestic context; neither is elaborated on here. The passage is structured in three paragraphs: the first gives details of the work the narrator now has to do in the light of her earlier accident (dropping something because of a fit); the second introduces Clarrie and the girl's work with the laundry, but also informs the reader of the killing; and the third describes the food they eat and the position of Clarrie in the household.

The maidservant tells her story in long but simply constructed sentences, with many references to everyday household objects. This gives the impression of someone quite simple speaking directly to the reader, an impression further enhanced by the use of the present tense throughout, and the unemotional tone. There is little reflection on her feelings and thoughts. She likes doing the laundry because of the 'clean smell', she can see that Clarrie 'is not afraid' of her, she knows that she has 'the way of' fine linen, but these observations are expressed without pride or strength of feeling.

There is no dialogue in the passage, though there is much indirect speech: what Clarrie says about her, what the Governor's wife says about Clarrie, and by implication feels about her (the narrator). This has the effect of creating an atmosphere of gossip in the household and a strong sense of hierarchy, with the narrator reporting it all matter-of-factly, if a little breathlessly, to the reader.

The last passage is the only one written in first-person narrative and the writer has skilfully created a character by use of language focused on the everyday, without much reflection or emotion.

Exam tip

Attention to the detail of language, form and tone is essential in writing critical analysis of prose extracts. Always substantiate your ideas with brief supporting quotations.

34 Writing an exam essay on prose

Revise unit 19 on Discursive and argumentative writing. Remind yourself of the steps you need to undertake to plan and write a clear discursive essay. Essays on literature can be discursive or argumentative but are generally discursive, considering more than one side of the argument and supporting the points they make by close reference to the text in question.

Task

When you have reviewed that unit, read the following essay, written by an AS level student under exam conditions. You do not need to have studied the novel *Things Fall Apart* to appreciate the essay, as its argument is very clearly structured. It introduces the topic, discusses one side of the proposition and then the other, coming to a thoughtful and balanced conclusion at the end. Its use of connectives between paragraphs is particularly helpful, because the reader is in no doubt as to the direction the essay is taking.

Sample essay

'Women can be seen as both superior and inferior to men in *Things Fall Apart*.'
In the light of this statement, discuss your view of the position of women in the novel.

It is true that the presentation of women in Things Fall Apart is an apparently contrasting one. One view of them is that they are supreme; while another is that they are really outsiders in the society. The novel explores these two perspectives of women.

Without question, the society is intrinsically patriarchal. This is evidenced throughout in many ways, with many of the important ceremonies being 'for men'.

Ibo women have no say in village matters such as legislation, village councils and war. The running of the village is done by men. Meetings in the town square are conducted by men as well. Unsurprisingly, at the highest level of the Ibo judiciary system – the *egwugwu* – it is the titled and influential men like Okonkwo behind the masks. Women are generally uninvolved. At the *egwugwu*-judging ceremony, for example, the man's wife is not even there to present her case. Her brothers-in-law represent her. This indicates the lack of a woman's case in political society.

Ibo women are also treated as inferior to men; moreover, their inferiority is accepted by both men and women. For example, all Ibo society accepts wife-beating as an allowed practice. In addition, women are bargained off to suitors with a suitable dowry which is negotiated by men. The bride is involved only in the role of serving. In general the women seem to be outsiders in a lot of aspects of village life: socially they are considered inferior, politically they are not present. The roles they do play in the village are domestic ones – cooking, cleaning and looking after children.

Even in agriculture there is a ready distinction between men and women. Okonkwo asserts that plants like coco-yam and beans are what women and children grow – 'Yam was a man's plant'. The importance of yams as a subsistence product is evidenced by the New Yam Festival, so women are inferior in this respect.

Religiously too there is evidence of male and female distinction. The spirits that appeared for Ezudu's funeral are entirely men – 'The most dreaded of all [the spirits] ... he was always alone.' The *egwugwu* are entirely male. In families, as we can see from Okonkwo, it is always the man who can set up a shrine to his own personal god. From all this we may draw the conclusion that women were inferior to men, outsiders in their life.

Perhaps the most important and direct representation of Ibo women as inferior societal outsiders is the recurrence of the term *agbala* throughout the novel. *Agbala* is defined very early on as a derogatory term for a titleless man, but we also find out that it means 'woman'. The equation of a woman to a titleless man, in a society where title is a judge of a man's individual worth, can hardly be a clearer indication of where women stand in Ibo society.

However, the novel does not give only a one-sided presentation of women. Women do play an important part in Ibo society.

Clearly in terms of religion there is male domination in the areas of worship, judicial ceremony and gods. However, we are introduced to two figures that assert a female role in this area – Ani and Chielo. Ani is the earth goddess representing fertility and abundance. The whole of Ibo society, including men, respect her highly, as evidenced by the incidents of the week of peace, in which one of the village elders expresses great disapproval at Okonkwo's careless disregard for the rule against wife-beating. This incident shows two things: one, that to displease Ani would incur her wrath and was considered a genuine threat to the village's well-being; and two, that there were existing limitations on the practice of wife-beating. The latter is reinforced later with the men's verdict as *egwugwu* that 'it is not bravery when a man fights a woman'. The society is collectively aware that women do have a place. We can see this also by the appropriation of titles by women, for example the eldest wife in the household.

Chielo too is a prominent figure. She is a respected and feared priestess – the Oracle. The Oracle features prominently in male decisions regarding war, for example the Oracle was consulted over the issue of the Ibo woman killed by another clan. The Ibo respect the Oracle's words and choose the peaceful solution, believing she is the voice of Agbala, a goddess. We can see here that *agbala* is not just a derogatory name for a man but a significant religious – and female – symbol.

In short, we can see two apparently conflicting presentations of women – one that perceives women as inferior outsiders in most of Ibo society, and one that reveres their status as superior. But the two are not so much conflicting as logically complementary. The statement 'mother is supreme' indicates the reverential status of women in the context of their roles in society as mothers, a role of unparalleled importance since children will grow up to take their places in the clan. This creates a new perception of how women – and men – are presented in the novel: both occupy their respective spheres. The ceremony may be for men, but women have their day too, when they take over the job of collectively cooking for the whole village. Their contributions to religion and society are of fertility (Ani) and peace (Oracle). Since we can see throughout the novel that the Ibo society is heavily agricultural, as well as typically gentle, diplomatic and peaceful, the importance of these two contributions cannot be underestimated.

This complementary duality is also supported in the structure of the novel by the fact that the ones who fail – Okonkwo and Unoka – see males as superior, whilst the successful character Obierika understands the importance of both sexes throughout.

Comment on the essay

The writer refers knowledgeably to the text and supports her argument with a few well-chosen direct quotations. It is not an open book exam, so the examiner does not expect lengthy quotations. This essay is a substantial achievement and would gain a high mark.

Exam tip

Know your set text really well, answer the question and structure your argument clearly, illustrating it as appropriate.

(35) Studying a play

Plays are written to be performed by actors and watched by an audience, and this is the single most important difference between drama and the other literary forms. When you read a novel or poem, it is usually a solitary activity (though of course either form can be dramatised). The units on plays are intended to help you to get to grips with the dramatic form and the kinds of effects writers can achieve when they write for an audience in the theatre. The plays you are studying for the examination are theatrical pieces rather than writing for television or radio. If you have seen your set play only on video or in a cinema version, you should try to imagine how it could be staged for live performance. The word 'staging' means the whole process of realising a dramatic work for performance.

Exam questions on drama

Your exam questions will be either an essay on an aspect of the play such as themes, characterisation or the methods used by the playwright to express these, or an extract from your set play for close critical comment.

What to expect at a play

The experience

Full-length plays take between one and four hours and are usually watched at one sitting. They are enthralling: going to the theatre is a great experience and always exciting, even if you are seeing a familiar play newly directed and performed by a different cast. This helps to account for the way enthusiasts go to see the same Shakespeare play again and again over the years. They want to experience yet another, different interpretation and see a fresh actor give new life to a familiar role.

The plot of the play and its structure

The experience of watching all at one sitting means that the work usually has a kind of dynamic, rhythmical movement; change is activated, surprising and complicating events occur and expectancy and uncertainty are generated in the audience as they watch. There are peaks and troughs of excitement, climaxes and quieter moments. The audience may feel some satisfaction when a final resolution is reached. A strong and often complicated plot is a common feature of good drama, because it must entertain and engage the audience from start to finish. Even *Waiting for Godot,* the modern classic once criticised because nothing happens and nobody does anything, depends upon the audience's expectation that there will be a plot, and their reaction to finding that there isn't much of one. Some contemporary drama has indeed tried to move away from the strongly plotted form and offer inconclusive, open-ended conclusions, but every drama, including *Waiting for Godot*, has its moments of climax and excitement, and endings do not have to have a wedding or a death to bring a play successfully to a close. Every play will, however, have an expressive structure by which the playwright shapes the dynamic process, communicating and exploring the major issues of the play.

The characters

Characters are often used to engage the sympathies and involvement of the audience; or they may represent ideas that the playwright would like the audience to think about. In the latter case the characters need not be sympathetic or likeable: indeed some dramatists have made characters deliberately unlikeable so that the audience concentrates on the ideas and not the human sympathies. Characters speak (in verse or prose) and at times they are silent. They do things and they react to each other. As in prose writing, they may have qualities or actions which are paralleled or contrasted with one another to highlight particular themes. Their motivation is the mainspring of the play's plot.

   When you are reading the play, rather than watching a performance, you need to try to imagine the action. What about the characters who are not speaking, for example? What might their reaction be to the events going on? To use an extreme example, in the last scene of Shakespeare's *King Lear*, the King's three daughters all lie dead on the stage in front of him, and this is the physical context for all the speakers.

The setting

When you use the word 'setting' to discuss a novel, it means the time(s) and place(s) in which the action of the novel is set. The meaning of 'setting' in drama is more specifically focused on the environment in which the actors perform.

   Whether a play is performed in a traditional theatrical space with a stage set and curtains, or in the middle of a room without scenery, or even read in class, it has a setting to its action and this will be established by the playwright, either by stage directions which give instructions or, like Shakespeare's plays, in the language spoken by characters. The setting could be a dining room or a forest, a temple or a castle, an island, a bedroom or the deck of a ship. There may be special effects of lighting or music, or spectacular ones such as thunder and lightning. The playwright will make a choice of setting for the particular effect she/he is aiming at. When you are reading a play alone in your room, you have to use your imagination to envisage the setting, and when you are writing in the exam, you mustn't forget that the text you are discussing is a play, meant for performance, not a text like a novel.

The issues

Drama is a very effective medium for the exploration of domestic, social, political and philosophical issues in an intense, highly charged atmosphere. Everything will be settled after a couple of hours – what Shakespeare calls 'the two hours traffic of our stage', so it has to be presented concisely. It is worth considering why a writer, especially a contemporary one, has chosen to write a play rather than a novel, since both could theoretically engage with the same themes. A play's impact will be vivid, immediate and powerful; its main concerns will be conveyed directly by the actions and reactions of a group of characters and there is no quiet or reflective description as there can be in a novel. There is no omniscient narrator guiding the reader's observation, nor is there the single focus of a first-person narrator. This can make conflict on the stage particularly aggressive, love scenes extraordinarily tender and death especially poignant. Humour will make an audience laugh out loud in a way that few respond to even a very amusing novel.

Accepted forms

Plays, particularly those of Shakespeare or of an earlier age, are often categorised as comedy, tragedy, history, farce, and so on. They are at times given a historical category, such as Restoration comedy. These categories are helpful in a general way, but are only a guideline, since every tragedy has its humorous moments, just as every comedy has more poignant ones; many historical dramas are tragic, and many farces are satirical. Be prepared to redefine the plays you are studying, and keep an open mind.

Task

What sort of play are you studying? Write down where and when the action takes place, and then say whether you think it is a drama of domestic or personal issues; an analytical, perhaps critical, comment on a particular kind of society; a play of moral dilemmas; a play of political insights; a play of philosophical questioning; or perhaps all of these! Decide which kind of issue dominates.

Sample response

Domestic issues

The Glass Menagerie by Tennessee Williams is set in the southern United States in the era of the Depression between the two world wars. This play has only four characters, three of whom are in the same family. The main character, who addresses the audience in soliloquy and tells the story as narrator, leaves the family and escapes its confines at the end of the play, but still feels the guilt and sadness of leaving his crippled sister behind. Through a small number of closely entwined characters, Williams explores escapism and the fragility of the human personality with poignant effect. Even though this centres on a family and their relationships, the social setting is important for appreciating the family's lack of money. The mother Amanda, superbly characterised by Williams, is less annoying when you understand her concern for making ends meet and for the future of her crippled daughter. Shakespeare's plays have family dramas at their very heart: In *The Comedy of Errors*, the two Antipholus brothers, separated after birth, are like the two halves of a divided personality; in *Macbeth*, the relationship between the Macbeths is central to the development of the play and its exploration of ambition and conscience. In *The Playboy of the Western World*, the mainspring of the plot is Christy's claim that he has killed his father.

Plays of ideas

Top Girls and *Serious Money*, by Caryl Churchill, are clearly plays of ideas, with a number of characters who are not particularly engaging to the audience's sympathies, but who represent the working out of some subtle and even paradoxical thoughts on a particular subject: in these two cases, feminism and monetarism. Women are shown to have been humiliated by men through the centuries in *Top Girls*, but now that in the twentieth century they have achieved supremacy in the office environment, it is at the expense of their finer feelings: they have perhaps become as unpleasant and oppressive as the men who dominated them previously. In spite of the serious issues raised by the playwright, these are at times highly amusing and witty plays. Shakespeare's plays have strong themes underpinning the action, but the characters are also well developed and explored.

Plays of social analysis

J. M. Synge's *The Playboy of the Western World* is a comedy which caused riots in the theatre when it was first performed because its unsentimental depiction of Irish peasants and its use of extreme language offended many conventional people, although the language is also unusually expressive. [Plays are often controversial at the time they are first performed, particularly when they are sharply analytical of particular social groups and their behaviour. For this reason, you should always place a play in its historical and social context as part of your initial preparation for the exam, although you will never have direct questions about those aspects.]

Wycherley's *The Country Wife* is typical of Restoration comedy in its witty exposé of sexual hypocrisy. The plot is complicated, the characters largely types, but the verbal wit and the farcical action are very appealing. The audience laugh, but they appreciate the serious point even as they enjoy the social comment. The fact that a play is a comedy does not prevent it from exploring serious and even profound ideas.

Exam tip

Take care that you do not seek to categorise a play too simply. When you study any of the examples given above you will find that a domestic drama can be socially perceptive; that a social satire can contain serious themes; that a comedy can have very poignant moments.

In units 36 to 38 you will look firstly at common themes, then at how plays are structured and the effect this can have on the concerns of the playwright, and finally at some aspects of characterisation.

(36) Studying the themes of plays

Plays can explore ideas very vividly; in essay questions, when you are asked about the playwright's **concerns**, **issues** or **themes**, you are being asked to discuss the ideas of the work being studied. If you are asked to focus on the writer's **methods**, then the emphasis is on style and structure. If the word **effects** is central to what is asked for in the question, then you are considering how the reader might respond to the playwright's methods of dealing with her/his themes.

Here are some common concerns explored by playwrights.

The family drama

Almost everyone belongs to a family and has parents and probably brothers and/or sisters. If you are a mature student you may be married or have children of your own. This basic domestic and social situation is one of the great universal experiences that forms the basis for most Shakespearean and other dramas.

Exam tip
'Universal' means that everyone can share the experience. Remember this if the word occurs in an examination question.

Task
If possible, in a group, share the details of your family and where you come in it. For example are you the middle one of three children, as I am? Or are you the older brother of two? Do you have only one parent? Are you an only child? More importantly, how do you feel about it? Do you think your younger sister is the favourite of your father? Does your father or mother tell you what to do? In the marriages you have observed, is there a dominant partner?

Variations on these issues arise in every play written by Shakespeare, and are often central in other dramas, such as Synge's *The Playboy of the Western World* or Wycherley's *The Country Wife*. In *The Glass Menagerie*, by Tennessee Williams, a mother and her two children are the close focus of an intense drama. In *Macbeth*, the two central characters affect each other's behaviour profoundly, as married couples often do, though the outcome is not usually as tragic. A similar theme is handled very differently in *The Comedy of Errors*, where Antipholus reacts strongly to his wife's nagging and bickers with her continually, but in this case to the delighted amusement of the audience.

Many of Shakespeare's plays have two different brothers, one of whom seems good and the other evil. This is significant in, amongst others, *Hamlet* (old Hamlet and Claudius), *The Tempest* (Prospero and Antonio), *Much Ado about Nothing* (Don

Pedro and Don John) and *As You Like It* (Duke Senior and Duke Frederick). In *The Comedy of Errors*, the two brothers are both likeable, but have very different personalities, even if they share the same name!

By contrast, twins in Shakespeare are sometimes shown as very close (such as Viola and Sebastian in *Twelfth Night*, or the two brothers Dromio in *The Comedy of Errors*). Father and child relationships are explored too, with only a few mother–son relationships depicted. Fathers are often shown as domineering and manipulative with their children, with mothers often absent from the family scene. Polonius, Shylock, old Capulet, Prospero and many other fathers reveal an authoritarian streak and Hamlet's father gives him an impossible task to do from beyond the grave. In *The Glass Menagerie*, written some four hundred years later, the father is absent and the mother has to struggle to bring the children up without him. The brother and sister, Tom and Laura, are very close and when Tom leaves the family at the end of the play he is haunted by guilt because he has abandoned her. The two sisters Marlene and Joyce in Caryl Churchill's *Top Girls*, apparently opposites, share an intense relationship and are bound by a family secret which is revealed at the end of the play.

These close relationships – both loving and hostile – are a reminder to the audience/reader of the complexities of close human relationships common across the centuries. Each playwright's handling of them shows that even in the best families there may be discordant, dangerous elements. But Shakespeare's use of balanced characterisations also reveals in the playwright a love of patterns, of parallels and contrasts which illuminate each other by being placed next to one another (**juxtaposition**), and this reminds us that his plays are both poetry and drama. Tennessee Williams also speaks of having a poet's love of symbols.

Task

Look closely at the pairing of characters in the play you are studying, whether related by family or by function in the drama. They may seem at first to be opposites, but when you study them more closely they may be more ambiguous, with parallels as well as contrasts.

Love

Love is a favourite theme of comedies, which often end in marriages and pairings, but it is also significant in tragedy. Shakespeare's *Antony and Cleopatra* and *Romeo and Juliet* are both love tragedies. 'The course of true love never did run smooth' as one of the characters says in *A Midsummer Night's Dream*, and most audiences expect these complications in a play. But in Shakespeare's plays love is also imaged as a kind of madness, and can make people behave in bizarre and unlikely ways. The transformation of Bottom the Weaver into an ass in the *Dream* is a dramatic way of suggesting that love can transform us, even make fools of us, and that we can fall in love with the most unlikely others, as Titania, Queen of the Fairies, does with Bottom. The way in which the women fall for Christy Mahon in *The Playboy of the Western World* is central to the effect of that play, as is the schoolgirl passion for the gentleman caller Jim that Laura has nurtured within herself in *The Glass Menagerie*.

Gender debates

Gender debates fill Shakespeare's comedies, with the battle of the sexes raging in *The Taming of the Shrew* and *Much Ado about Nothing*, and cross-dressing in *Twelfth Night* and *As You Like It* reminding the audience of the complexities of sexuality. But the vulnerability of both sexes is evident throughout his tragedies too, with women's honour underpinning men's reputation in *Othello* and *Hamlet*. Honour and reputation are similarly key themes in *The Country Wife* and all Restoration comedy. They give rise to much comic business, but the theme is shrewdly handled by the playwright. The feminist issue is paramount in *Top Girls* by Caryl Churchill, with the first scene establishing the theme strongly.

Power and authority

So far the themes mentioned have been familial or personal ones. But much drama is also concerned with power and authority and with the nature of society and the way it is governed. Even in a domestic drama such as *The Glass Menagerie*, the social pressures of the time are a powerful background to the action, and society's expectations of conventional behaviour drive Amanda's actions and behaviour towards her children. In *Top Girls*, Churchill's focus depends upon the patriarchal societies that women have had to endure throughout history. Arthur Miller's play *The Crucible* reveals the powerful grip of a ruling group who rule by fear and will not allow individual freedom of thought and speech.

All of Shakespeare's history plays and most of his tragedies are close examinations of politics and power, and the ambitions of those who would seek to aggrandise themselves: nobles wanting to become kings, kings wanting to dominate or wage war, politicians wanting to manipulate or blame others. This may lead to violence, and there are many examples in all the plays of exiles or murders of kings and princes to satisfy the ambitions of those who want to rule themselves. If there are such disturbances in society, then order will give way to chaos, and peace may slide into war. Shakespeare uses images of breakdown in nature and the wider environment to mirror and intensify this chaos, so you see conflict erupting on a large scale. Under such circumstances some followers will be treacherous, others loyal – another area of great interest to the playwright. Interestingly, Shakespeare often shows that a person's mind is like a kingdom which can lose its control and become disordered. Similarly the image of madness which characterises his depiction of love can also be shown as vital to his depiction of tragic characters such as King Lear and Ophelia. In *King Lear* the disorder in the king's mind is mirrored in the breakdown of society in his kingdom, and is given metaphorical emphasis by the huge storm.

Task

Who wields authority in the play that you are studying? Who has power and in what way do they use it? Who shows her/himself to be loyal and who acts treacherously in their own self-interest? What social pressures are shown to impinge upon the lives of the characters? Make a list of your answers to these questions and discuss them with a classmate.

If you are studying *Macbeth*, consider what suggestions there are in the text that the king's death is disruptive of society and nature as a whole. Your answer to this will help you to understand what happens when Caesar is assassinated in *Julius Caesar*. In *Top Girls*, how many women reach the top in a business environment and with what effect?

Surface and substance

One of the great themes of Shakespearean and Restoration drama is the contrast between the way things appear to be and what they really are: appearance and reality, as students love to call this theme. Perhaps it is not surprising that men and women of the theatre are obsessed with the deceitfulness of surfaces. For whatever reason, this dichotomy (or split) between being and seeming runs through the characters, the situations and the language of all of Shakespeare's plays, and of the plays of the Restoration period such as *The Country Wife*. Characters disguise themselves, pretend to be what they are not, act or put on a show and behave hypocritically. Apparently noble characters are revealed to have flaws, fools are shown to be wiser than clever people, and even the evil can sometimes have redeeming features. 'Don't judge at face value' seems to be a central theme of all of Shakespeare's work, and it is highly ironic that he should use that most artificial of media – the theatre – to persuade us to think more deeply about what appears before our eyes. The hypocrisy of society is, similarly, a matter for satirical exposure in Restoration and other comedy.

Mistaken identity is a variation on this theme. In *The Comedy of Errors*, the fact that there are two pairs of identical twins, the Antipholus brothers and their servants the Dromio brothers, allows Shakespeare to create a chaotic world of mistaken identity which is hilarious for the audience but confusing for the characters, who are forced to face the issues of their own nature and identity before all is resolved. We have already discussed how Margery Pinchwife's disguise as a boy brings out the lustful intentions of Horner in *The Country Wife*.

Exam tip

A playwright's use of the contrast between appearance and the reality beneath is by no means simplistic: sometimes good characters are forced to disguise themselves in order to survive in a hostile world.

Task

Make a list of the dominant ideas or themes in the play that you are studying. As you develop your skills of analysis, you will be able to identify the means by which the playwright explores these themes: through the play's structure and action, through characterisation, and through language and tone.

(37) Studying play structures

Linear structure

How a play is put together will have a significant effect on the audience's response to its main concerns. All plays will have action and may enact a kind of linear process. The beginning gives the background and prepares the potential for conflict, or shows the pressures which come from certain characters' motivations. Then the central section can reveal complications developing, a counter-force operating and conflict coming out into the open. Finally an ending is reached, often after many climaxes in the action. There may be a different state of affairs by the end, the world of the play may have altered, the balance of power is different, or perhaps someone has changed. There may be a resolution, a denouement or unravelling. In some plays, deaths end the action, in others, marriage or other kinds of union. This linear structure of exposition, development, complication and denouement is very dynamic and uses climaxes effectively.

In some contemporary plays the situation may seem to have gone nowhere and returned to where it began, but in fact there is always more process than first appears. Godot has not arrived, true, but the audience is now fully acquainted with the two tramps and has experienced their personalities and obsessions, as well as gaining insight into the playwright's view of existence (in Beckett's *Waiting for Godot*).

Shakespeare's plays are divided into five acts, each of which has a number of scenes, some brief – a mere ten or twenty lines – and some lengthy, with several hundred (which can themselves be divided into shorter units, although nominally one scene). More contemporary drama may have only two or three acts. The act and scene are units of the structure that the playwright uses to present and develop her/his themes.

Plot

All plays have a plot or story, though some are simpler than others. The story of a Shakespeare play is always complex, with many characters and a number of stories going on at the same time and interweaving one with the other. The secondary plots are known as **sub-plots**. The main plot of a Shakespeare play never follows through scene after scene without a break, but is constantly interspersed with the sub, secondary or parallel plots. The effect is of a rich weave of different threads, all moving onward, interacting and intersecting unstoppably.

Shakespeare's plots are not original in the sense that they use known stories by other writers, often combined. However, these stories always have a different emphasis and meaning when Shakespeare modifies or adds to them. Originality of plot was not particularly prized in his day and his audiences would have appreciated a new slant on an old story.

The complexity of the plot of some plays means that sometimes students believe they are doing something worthwhile when they tell the story of a play.

Unfortunately at this level, telling the story doesn't get you any marks – you are expected to know it as the baseline from which you develop your critical insights into other features of the work.

Exam tip

Get to know the story really well but never tell it in the exam: this wastes time and gains no marks. After all, the examiner already knows it.

Exposition

All plays, of whatever era, have an exposition from which the audience will gain essential information about the world of the play, its themes and the characters in it. The playwright always has the challenge of making the exposition interesting because it could be boring if the first characters on the stage just repeated the details of the story up to that point in a long-winded or list-like way. This may be done through swift sequences at the beginning sketching in the important aspects of the situation or, at the least, giving the audience hints. An exposition will usually suggest or reveal something that will cause a complication or complications: these will be developed from the original situation, right through the central section of the play.

Shakespearean exposition

If you read or see a play by Shakespeare, you are given your background information in the first scene or two; and the causes from which the unfolding effects will eventually be revealed. Here are four of Shakespeare's expositions as an example:

1 A storm at sea created by a magician brings a group of courtiers onto an island. You are then told the story of how the magician came to be there and why the tempest was essential to his plans through the device of his telling his daughter the story of the past (Prospero in *The Tempest*).

2 An old man from Syracuse has been found in the hostile neighbouring state of Ephesus. Under the law he must either be put to death or pay the fine of 1,000 marks. He tells the sad story of the break-up of his family in a shipwreck and his more recent search for one of his twin sons (Aegeon in *The Comedy of Errors*).

3 A young man has been made to work as a servant and denied his inheritance by his older brother, who hates him and tries to get him killed in a wrestling match (Orlando in *As You Like It*).

4 Three witches meet in a storm and agree that they will meet Macbeth. When the scene changes, the King is being given a report of a bloody battle which has been going on, in which his follower, the noble Macbeth, has fought bravely. The Thane of Cawdor has behaved treacherously, so the King announces that he is to be put to death and Macbeth is to receive his title.

Look back at each of the examples given and see if you can identify the action within each exposition that sets the play in motion, rather than simply filling in the background knowledge. You will need your teacher's help here for plays you are not familiar with.

Sample response

Each of these events has far-reaching consequences in its respective play.

- In **1** the storm brings the characters onto Prospero's island, so that he can deal with those who treated him badly in the past, including his brother.

- In **2** the quest for a thousand marks and the quest for a young man who is one of twins will set in motion the comedy and complication of the plots of the play.

- In **3** a wrestling match is arranged, at which Orlando will triumph, fall in love with Rosalind and thereafter be forced to go and seek his fortune

- In **4** the witches know Macbeth and are seeking him out just as he is promoted for his bravery; his latent ambition will be encouraged by his promotion and by the witches' promises of grandeur.

More examples of exposition

Beginning the play near the end of the story

This is often just before the crisis happens or as a memory of what has happened before. In Sophocles' great tragedy *Oedipus Rex*, the King has already murdered his father and married his mother long before the action of the play starts. When he demands the truth out of the old shepherd, we, and Oedipus, discover the essential facts and the crisis breaks. In *The Crucible* (Arthur Miller), John Proctor's affair with Abigail is over and she has been dismissed from the household, but the consequences of that relationship are still to unravel as the play progresses. In *The Comedy of Errors*, the rupture of the family, the splitting up of the twins and the loss of the mother have all taken place before Antipholus of Syracuse arrives in Ephesus at the beginning of the play.

Introduction of a major character

She or he often has unresolved problems, or an aim which is, as yet, unrealised. Christy in *The Playboy of the Western World* is an example of the former and Horner in *The Country Wife* the latter.

Memory plays

At the beginning of Tennessee Williams's *The Glass Menagerie*, Tom has already left home and is reflecting on the past. He tells the audience it is a 'memory play' and guides their responses and sympathies into the first scene.

Fighting talk

The exposition of *The Alchemist* by Ben Jonson is a fierce quarrel between the three collaborators in which the situation of the play is very naturally exposed for the audience, who wonder how long it will be before their plans are discovered or their quarrel breaks out afresh. The opening of *Romeo and Juliet* is a quarrel between the household servants of Montague and Capulet, from which the situation of the 'two households both alike in dignity' is revealed to the audience.

Thematic prologue

Top Girls has as its first act a surrealistic scene set in a restaurant which is completely timeless since all the female characters in it come from down the centuries to celebrate the promotion at the office of the twentieth-century woman Marlene. They give a historical context to this triumph. Their conversations are witty and celebratory, but the whole scene is undercut by the disturbing stories of misery, domination and suffering at the hands of men which emerge during the evening. In this way the scene is set with a feminist agenda, the dominant theme that will affect the rest of the play.

Task

How do the openings of the plays you are studying prepare the audience for the action?

Action

The central action of a play is often forged by a chain of cause and effect, which the audience can believe and be involved in.

Sometimes one of the characters is a driving force who makes things happen, for example Shakespeare's Richard III or Norman in Alan Ayckbourn's *The Norman Conquests* or Horner in Wycherley's *The Country Wife*.

Perhaps the hero has to face obstacles before his goals can be reached, and these struggles may be mental, something within her/his own nature, rather than physical or contextual. Shakespeare's tragic heroes are often in this category. Tom in *The Glass Menagerie* has to overcome the grind of daily life which holds him back from breaking free and becoming a writer, yet ironically when he does this he is plagued by guilty memories of the past. Christy Mahon in *The Playboy of the Western World* 'kills' his father twice before he can earn any respect or devotion from those around him. In *Top Girls*, this pattern is ironically reversed for Marlene, who is shown as successful from the outset. The play gradually reveals her inner life and secrets. In Harold Pinter's play *Betrayal*, the action runs backwards so that the final scene is the first in chronological time, making the adulterous relationship which is its subject both more poignant and more pointless. The climax of the play is the first meeting of the lovers, not the last.

The action can also generate tension which the playwright sustains by withholding information from the audience or keeping them in suspense. The tension can rise and fall through the central section of the play, but its general trend is upwards.

Task

Look at how Arthur Miller builds up tension in the following sequence from *A View from the Bridge*, where Eddie Carbone, with his wife Beatrice, is waiting for his niece Catherine to come home after being out at the cinema with one of the illegal immigrants they are giving a home to. Show how the dialogue develops the relationship between Eddie and Beatrice and exposes the tensions between them. (You will find another example from this play in unit 18.)

EDDIE: It's after eight.

BEATRICE: Well, it's a long show at the Paramount.

EDDIE: They must've seen every picture in Brooklyn by now. He's supposed to stay in the house when he ain't working. He ain't supposed to go advertising himself.

BEATRICE: Well, that's his trouble, what do you care? If they pick him up they pick him up, that's all. Come in the house.

EDDIE: What happened to the stenography? I don't see her practise no more.

BEATRICE: She'll get back to it. She's excited, Eddie.

EDDIE: She tell you anything?

BEATRICE: (*Comes to him, now the subject is opened*) What's the matter with you? He's a nice kid, what do you want from him?

EDDIE: That's a nice kid? He gives me the heeby-jeebies.

BEATRICE: (*smiling*) Ah, go on, you're just jealous.

EDDIE: Of *him*? Boy, you don't think much of me.

BEATRICE:	I don't understand you. What's so terrible about him?
EDDIE:	You mean it's all right with you? That's gonna be her husband?
BEATRICE:	Why? He's a nice fella, hard workin', he's a good-lookin' fella.

Sample response

The pattern of the dialogue here is one of aggression (Eddie) followed by peace-making justifications of Catherine's behaviour (Beatrice). This creates tension since the couple are in disagreement and there is an underlying sense that there is more to the disagreement than at first appears. Eddie keeps changing the ground for his objections: first it is just that they are late, so late they could have seen every film that was on; second he takes issue with the fact that Rodolpho, the immigrant, is out at all – he should be hiding at home, in Eddie's opinion. Then it is Catherine's lack of study – she is not practising her shorthand skills any more. Gradually the objections begin to focus in on the boy she is spending time with – Eddie does not like him, he does not think he is good enough for his beloved niece, and by the time the end of this extract is reached he is coming directly to the point: 'That's gonna be her husband?' The position of Beatrice is interesting: she knows what Eddie is getting at but tries to keep the peace at first and make justifications for Catherine's behaviour which she sees as natural. When she says affectionately, 'She's excited, Eddie', his immediate response is suspicion: 'She tell you anything?' And her response to her husband is also affectionate: when she says, 'go on, you're just jealous', Miller makes it clear that she is 'smiling'. But this disjunction between them is part of a wider pattern of distrust and suspicion in the play, which will end tragically. Here, suspense is created as the audience waits to see what will happen when Catherine does finally come home from the movies.

Resolution

In a comedy, the resolution often results in marriages and pairings, the unravelling of the complications in a happy ending. The French word *dénouement*, or untying, is often used for this stage. In *The Comedy of Errors*, the resolution includes some wonderful surprises which in the theatre can have the audience applauding spontaneously. In a tragedy deaths will occur but there may be a sense ultimately of a new beginning. In more contemporary drama, the final scene may be much more open-ended than those in earlier plays, with endings that suggest further complication or even a return to the status quo of the very beginning of the play.

Task

If possible, discuss with your teacher or group the ending of the plays you are studying. How satisfied are you that the ending resolves the issues raised by the play?

Symmetric structures

The dynamic linear structure discussed above is not the only way in which playwrights handle their material. Although the action is driving onward, another kind of network operates simultaneously in plays through parallels and contrasts of scene and character; by means of image patterns in the language which recur and develop their ideas through repetition and elaboration; and through symbols used by playwrights to focus important themes. These networks are known as symmetric structures.

Imagery

Imagery is one of the most important symmetric structures used in Shakespeare's plays, and is also employed by other playwrights.

You will remember from the poetry units that imagery is the word used for metaphorical language. Shakespeare's work is rich in imagery. Here are some notable examples of evocative metaphors and similes:

1   It seems she hangs upon the cheek of night
    As a rich jewel in an Ethiop's ear
                                    Romeo and Juliet

2   ... my age is as a lusty winter,
    Frosty, but kindly.
                                    As You Like It

3   Why strew'st thou sugar on that bottled spider
    Whose deadly web ensnareth thee about?
                                    Richard III

4   ...my desire,
    More sharp than filed steel, did spur me forth;
                                    Twelfth Night

5   ... Here lay Duncan,
    His silver skin laced with his golden blood;
                                    Macbeth

Task

Look carefully at the comparisons suggested here and what effects they have.

Sample response for extract 5

> By comparing Duncan's dead skin with silver, Macbeth gives an image of pallor but also of something precious. His blood, normally red, is imaged as gold, more precious than an ordinary mortal's because he is the king, even though dead. The word 'laced' gives a visual image of the tracery of blood on his skin, but lace is also a word associated with the clothing of the nobility. So the imagery given by Shakespeare to the guilty Macbeth is very visual in its effect, but also reveals Macbeth's awareness of the precious majesty of Duncan: the murderer is in no doubt of the enormity of his crime, and this is revealed through the imagery.

These individual images are very effective in themselves at stirring our imaginations. However, Shakespeare also uses imagery in repeated patterns. The first of the images here, from *Romeo and Juliet*, is part of a whole network of images of light and darkness in that play which, taken together, point strikingly to the intensity of the lovers' passion and the tragedy of their demise. Old Adam comparing himself to winter in the second example, from *As You Like It*, is appropriate for a play which uses the seasons throughout as counterpoint to the human activity. Richard III is constantly compared to a spider with webs of deceit and extraordinary venom in the play of that name. Filed steel features in *Twelfth Night* literally as the swords with which people fight, and metaphorically to represent the pangs of unrequited love. *Macbeth* is notable for image patterns of blood, from the first bloody man in Act 1 Scene 2 throughout its horrible murders to the final decapitation of the central character.

Other more recent playwrights use similar techniques. Wycherley uses recurring images in *The Country Wife*: of disease, particularly sexually transmitted disease, to highlight the themes of sexual honour and promiscuity; of money and property to point the transactional nature of many relationships, particularly marriage; and of food, as an image of sensuous pleasure akin to sexual delight. In *The Glass Menagerie*, Williams employs a number of images that suggest the past, a time when Amanda was a desirable unmarried girl or when the family were together, before their father left them.

Task

Discuss whether the play you are studying has recurring patterns of images. What are they? Try to use a library to find books on Shakespeare's imagery or use search facilities on the internet to identify literature websites that allow you to find instances of a word representing an image in a play. (For Shakespeare, you could try darkness or blood in *Macbeth*, madness in *The Comedy of Errors* and *Twelfth Night*, corruption in *Hamlet* or storm in *King Lear*).

Parallels and contrasts

Parallel scenes are another effective symmetric device used for emphasis. A playwright may use a great variety of types of character and dramatic effect; however, there may also be parallel scenes which, set against one another, have an intensifying effect on the drama and point the contrasts that also exist. In every case the play's themes are emphasised too. Such situations may also give rise to dramatic irony, where the audience knows something that particular characters are unaware of.

In Churchill's *Top Girls*, scenes at the office and at Joyce's house are strongly contrasted: one is urban and affluent, the other rural and poor. The scenes have very different tones and language, emphasising the lack of cohesion in women's roles in society and the difficulty the sisters have in communicating with each other.

There are parallel scenes in *The Glass Menagerie*, where Amanda is trying to sell magazine subscriptions over the telephone. In these one-sided conversations, the audience will laugh at the way Amanda tries so hard and so irritatingly, and will appreciate the unseen and unheard person's responses to her. But the serious point that the family is in financial difficulty makes each parallel sequence poignant.

In *Romeo and Juliet*, there are two scenes (Act 2 Scene 5 and Act 3 Scene 2) when the Nurse brings news to Juliet: in one she brings the happy news of Romeo's arrangement to meet and marry her and in the other, the terrible news that Romeo has been responsible for the death of Juliet's cousin Tybalt. In each case the structure of the sequence is the same: the Nurse doesn't come out with her news directly and Juliet is desperate for it. The effect is to create comedy in one and tragic suspense in the other, but in both the Nurse's middle-aged slowness and commonsense approach to life contrast sharply with Juliet's vivid and impulsive youth. The contrast of youth and age is one of Shakespeare's great themes, nowhere more obvious than in the juxtaposition (or placing next to one another) of these two parallel scenes.

In *As You Like It* Duke Frederick is seen at the court in Act 1 surrounded by his lords; when you meet his exiled brother Duke Senior for the first time in the forest of Arden at the beginning of Act 2 their situations seem completely different. Duke Senior is shivering under a tree by a stream! But Duke Senior is attended by his lords too; he has a court jester, a minstrel and several attendants who behave in an orderly and civilised way and who have retained their courteous manners (the word 'courteous' as you can see comes from the same root as 'courtly'.) This parallel/contrast is an example of the way in which the court is contrasted with the forest, yet retains some elements which are similar, avoiding a simplistic contrast.

Contrasts and parallels of character are discussed in unit 38.

Exam tip

When you are writing on an extract from your set play, consider its place in the development of the play as a whole: not only its place in the unfolding of the plot and the intensifying of the drama, but also its relationship with any parallel scenes.

Task

Try to identify parallels and contrasts within your set play or any others that you have read or seen. What effect does this juxtaposition of scenes have?

Symbols

The theatre is a visual medium and playwrights often use physical symbols as structural devices. They are symmetric rather than linear and may represent ideas or develop characterisation, proving a constant physical reminder to the audience of what they stand for.

The Glass Menagerie is itself symbolic of the fragile world inhabited by Laura Wingfield, with the unicorn perhaps representative of Laura's uniqueness. When Jim breaks the unicorn, it suggests the rupture of all her romantic dreams of him, nurtured since high school. The old victrola represents the father of the family, and Laura's constant playing of it reveals her nostalgia for the time when he still lived with them. Williams at first intended the play to have 'legends', or key ideas and phrases, projected at the side of the stage to focus the audience's attention on the ideas of the play as they developed; in practice, however, this has rarely been incorporated into productions of the play. The result of this has been to emphasise the naturalism of the play and to diminish its symbolic and representative qualities.

In Caryl Churchill's *Serious Money* the telephone represents the world of speedy communications and insider dealing. It rings incessantly, and characters pass information and gossip very quickly to each other and to the audience.

In *Othello* the handkerchief is the physical 'proof' that Othello thinks he needs to show that Desdemona is unfaithful. In fact, the way he impresses the story of the handkerchief upon her shows his domination of her and determination that she should be what he wants her to be (or has decided she is).

Task

Look closely at the play you are studying and see whether any of the symmetric structures described above are used by the playwright to enhance theme or characterisation.

Exam tip

Awareness of a play's structure and a willingness to try to discuss it are characteristic of higher-quality answers.

(38) Characters in drama

The characters in a play, whether by Shakespeare or Synge, Williams or Wycherley, are often very memorable; it is not surprising that students relate immediately to them, especially if they have seen the play on stage or in a video version. As in the novel, the people who inhabit the action can be the natural focus of any reader or audience when they first encounter that work.

Exam tip
Many exam questions focus on character, so you need to be well prepared for this topic. However, at AS level they will not simply ask for descriptions of characters; there will always be a particular focus and you will need to direct your material carefully to that.

This unit will give you some guidelines on studying play characters with the exam questions in mind.

Created in words

Characters in a play are not real people; they are created first and foremost by language and imagery. But because actors interpret them, they seem real to a reader or audience, and you are bound to respond to them with feeling. It's just important to make sure that you can identify the reasons for your interpretation or your powerful response by quoting the words and images that have influenced you, especially if you are answering a passage question or an essay on characterisation. The word 'characterisation' means *making* a character and it reminds you that the writer has chosen words and tones to create a particular effect. What impressions are created of the characters described here, and of the people describing them?

1   O, she doth teach the torches to burn bright!

Romeo of Juliet

2   ... how lovely and sweet and pretty she is ...
    ... in the eyes of others – strangers – she's terribly shy and lives in a
    world of her own and those things make her seem a little peculiar.

Amanda and Tom of Laura in *The Glass Menagerie*

3   I am determined to prove a villain ...

Richard III of himself

4   Yet do I fear thy nature;
    It is too full o' th' milk of human kindness ...

Lady Macbeth of Macbeth

5 She has no beauty but her youth; no attraction but her modesty; wholesome, homely and housewifely; that's all.

Pinchwife of Margery in The Country Wife

6 My wife is shrewish when I keep not hours

Antipholus of Ephesus of his wife Adriana in The Comedy of Errors

These examples show how the use of language, spoken by characters but obviously created by the playwright, help in the making of character. Characters may say things about themselves in a soliloquy, as in **3**, or they may make comment on others, as in the other examples. Of course what we say of others is a significant comment on ourselves and, in a play, characters' gossip about others or direct comment to their faces illuminates both the speaker and the person spoken of. Romeo's passion as well as Juliet's beauty are expressed in the imagery and tone of **1**, just as the relationship of the Macbeths and their relative toughness is seen in **4**, though that is Lady Macbeth's viewpoint of course. Later she is shown not to be as hard-hearted as she boasts here and her unconscious mind rebels against her, as you see vividly in the sleepwalking scene. In **2** Amanda describes her daughter with characteristic exaggeration and optimism. Tom loves his sister no less, but is much more realistic about her personality. Richard III's determination 'to prove a villain' does show his evil nature, but it also shows his love of play-acting and self-conscious assuming of roles for himself. Ironically, Pinchwife's description of his wife Margery tells us nothing of her fresh, attractive beauty: this is the deliberately misleading description of a jealous husband who wants to deter hopeful suitors. Antipholus's remark in **6** reveals a sociable man who likes to enjoy himself, but whose wife gets cross with him when he is late home. This is one of the recurrent comic situations in the play, as well as a source of more serious analysis of what marriage entails for its participants.

Exam tip

Look closely and critically at what characters say of themselves and what they say about each other in the play you are studying. What effect does this have in the overall structure of the play?

Characters in action

There are few stage directions in a Shakespeare play. But those that do exist, together with the words given to each character, contain enough clues for the director or the attentive reader to visualise the actions and gestures that the characters will perform. 'Actions speak louder than words', as the old saying has it, and certainly the way Iago behaves towards Othello gives us a very different view from the hypocritical words he speaks to him with apparent sincerity. Other dramatists give quite full stage directions, even describing the appearance and manner of the characters when they first appear. George Bernard Shaw, for example, often gives very lengthy descriptions of characters, more in the manner of a novelist. Tennessee Williams, in *The Glass Menagerie*, gives much description as well as commentary on the action, and many hints about tone and emotional quality for the actors playing the parts.

Television in particular has made audiences used to very naturalistic acting; in the theatre, stronger projection and more exaggerated gestures and actions are necessary to communicate to the whole audience, even those in the back rows of the theatre.

Task

Take a scene from the play you are studying and note the stage directions. Then look at the dialogue and consider what prompts it offers to the action. How does this action illuminate the characterisation (and indeed the themes) in the scene? The first example is from Scene 4 of *The Glass Menagerie*; the second is from Act 1 Scene 2 of *King Lear*.

Extract 1

(*... Tom blows on his coffee, glancing sidewise at his mother. She clears her throat. Tom clears his. He starts to rise. Sinks back down again, scratches his head, clears his throat again. Amanda coughs. Tom raises his cup in both hands to blow on it, his eyes staring over the rim of it at his mother for several moments. Then he slowly sets the cup down and awkwardly and hesitantly rises from the chair.*)

TOM (*hoarsely*): Mother. I – I apologize, Mother. (*Amanda draws a quick shuddering breath. Her face works grotesquely. She breaks into childlike tears.*) I'm sorry for what I said, for everything that I said; I didn't mean it.

AMANDA (*sobbingly*): My devotion has made me a witch and so I make myself hateful to my children!

TOM: *No*, you *don't*.

AMANDA: I worry so much, don't sleep, it makes me nervous!

TOM (*gently*): I understand that.

AMANDA: I've had to put up a solitary battle all these years. But you're my right-hand tower! Don't fall down, don't fail!

TOM: (*gently*): I try, Mother.

Extract 2

GLOUCESTER: Edmund, how now! What news?

EDMUND: So please your lordship, none. (*Putting up the letter.*)

GLOUCESTER: Why so earnestly seek you to put up that letter?

EDMUND: I know no news, my lord.

GLOUCESTER: What paper were you reading?

EDMUND: Nothing my lord.

GLOUCESTER: No? What needed then that terrible dispatch of it into your pocket? The quality of nothing hath not such need to hide itself.

Sample response

1

Williams gives a great deal of information through his stage directions about action, gesture and tone of voice. There are many adverbs offering modifiers to the way characters should speak the lines ('hoarsely', 'grotesquely', 'sobbingly', for example). The two characters have had a row the previous night and Tom feels regretful about his anger towards his mother. His apology is genuine, and he shows understanding of his mother's anxieties. The word 'gently' is used twice to suggest his tone of voice. Tom is the main character of the drama and the narrator as well: the audience are well disposed towards him and he must remain a sympathetic character, so his anger is felt to be understandable because Amanda is very irritating, but he is a loving son, so he apologises to her afterwards. The audience will sympathise on both occasions. Amanda's concern for the family and attempt to lean on Tom are both very clear in this encounter, and an audience can see her point of view too. But ironically she will try to lean on him once too often, and he will be driven away to seek his independence by his feelings of captivity within this needy family circle. Here the coffee drinking and the gestures with the cup are eloquent in showing the awkwardness of the encounter; a little later in the scene Amanda will, characteristically, be nagging Tom again – about his coffee drinking, so the props are used skilfully by Williams in the scene to give symbolic representation of the emotions and issues between Tom and Amanda.

2

Edmund is trying his best to get his brother, whom he hates, into serious trouble. He wants his father to see the letter, but he wants to appear decent and loyal to both his brother and father, unwilling to cause trouble. You can imagine him reading the letter and pretending to hide it ostentatiously. It will appear very stagey and exaggerated in production. Yet it makes clear dramatically what Edmund is doing and is only a physically represented image of what brothers and sisters do all the time: jockey for position with their parents. The sly, treacherous nature of Edmund is made clear through his actions as well as his words. His old father's rather ponderously authoritarian approach is at this point perhaps slightly humorous, particularly as Edmund has just gained the audience's sympathy in an earlier soliloquy. These audience attitudes to the two characters will develop and change as the play proceeds. Although this is a short sequence, its use of the word 'nothing' and 'the quality of nothing' parallels the previous scene where Cordelia said 'Nothing' to her father and prompted his terrible rage. Thus Shakespeare illuminates action and theme as well as character in a very short dialogue. In this play the plots involving Lear and his daughters, and Gloucester and his sons, are entwined and juxtaposed to great effect.

Character types

In his plays, Shakespeare makes frequent reference to the four humours: a well-established means of delineating personality types at the time he was writing. The four types – melancholic, phlegmatic, choleric and sanguine – are based essentially on the four elements of water, earth, fire and air, and their dominant characteristics are, respectively: depression, stolid calm, anger and optimism. References to them recur throughout the plays. It is not necessarily the simple minor characters who are ruled by one dominant humour. You could argue, for example, that Lear's choleric nature and Hamlet's melancholy are obvious and significant character traits; Cleopatra says 'I am fire and air / My other elements I give to baser life' just before she commits suicide. When the Duke in *As You Like It* is described as 'humorous' it doesn't mean funny, it means moody, ruled by passion. Greek tragedies and Roman comedies are full of characters dominated by one ruling passion or quality. Ben Jonson's plays such as *Volpone* and *The Alchemist* create characters who are types in this way, and their names often give the clue to their personalities: Subtle, Justice Overdo, Sir Epicure Mammon, and so on. In many Restoration comedies a similar effect is created: Lord Foppington, Sir Fopling Flutter, Lady Fainall, Aimwell and Archer, for example, as well as Dainty, Fidget and Squeamish from *The Country Wife*.

> ### Exam tip
>
> Although you can make reference to typical character traits, it is always helpful to show that you recognise complexity of character where it is presented in the plays you are studying.

Chorus figures

A chorus is a character or group of characters who help to tell the story of the play, and sometimes act in it as well. Chorus figures have been used from the very earliest Greek drama and are still used today. The chorus makes the audience aware of the context and meaning of the play, and can represent the audience's point of view. Taken together, the characters of the chorus can provide a powerful communal appeal. Examples of individual chorus figures are Tom in *The Glass Menagerie* and Time in *The Winter's Tale*. The peasants in *The Playboy of the Western World* constitute a kind of chorus, as do the women in the final scene of *The Country Wife*, commenting together on the action. The songs at the end of *Serious Money* provide a rousing musical chorus.

Motivation

Why do characters do what they do? Their behaviour should be generally believable, and arise out of the situations they find themselves in. Audiences tend to accept the status quo at the beginning of the play, even if it is rather unusual, and then expect believable behaviour after that. On the whole there are plenty of plausible reasons for characters' behaviour suggested within the text. A character whose motives are discussed endlessly is Iago, in *Othello*. Is he a 'motiveless' character who is just evil, as some have claimed? Or is he fuelled by envy of Cassio or Othello, racism, revenge at being passed over for promotion, anger because Othello has had sex with his wife, and so on? Your interpretation must take account of those clues in the text that you think are important, and you must be able to quote them. Why does Christy embroider the story of his fight with his father so lavishly in *The Playboy of the Western World*? Perhaps because he is enjoying the attention paid to him, particularly by women. In *Who's Afraid of Virginia Woolf* by Edward Albee, George and Martha are cruel to each other, but their complicated games are fuelled by their inability to have a child and the elaborate fantasy they have created, a fact not revealed until the end of the play.

Is there a difference between what the character says about her/himself and what you the audience or reader observe? There may be irony if the character is not fully aware of her/his motives. In *A View from the Bridge*, Eddie is not able to face the nature of his love for his niece Catherine, and feels tortured when his wife forces him to face up to it near the play's climax. Shakespeare's King Lear, for example, is not very self-aware: 'he hath ever but slenderly known himself', says one of his own daughters. In *Much Ado about Nothing*, Benedick and Beatrice are the last to realise the powerful attraction they feel for each other.

Task

If you have access to a group, discuss together the motivation of the characters in the play you are all studying. You will find a great variety of different opinions.

Exam tip

Make sure that you support your interpretations of character by close reference to the text. Many different interpretations are valid, because the approach of Shakespeare and other playwrights allows for different emphasis and perspective.

Conflict and persuasion

It is often said that drama comes from characters in conflict, and this is certainly a valid point.

Task

Find some examples of conflict in the plays you have studied. They can be physical fights, disagreements or the force of two personalities ranged against each other. Discuss what effect each conflict has on the drama.

Sample response

The long scene between Marlene and Joyce at the end of *Top Girls* is a furious personal and political argument, and its aftermath ends the play. The row that erupts between Tom and Amanda after Jim leaves the apartment in *The Glass Menagerie* is the fatal one that sends Tom off into the world away from the family. The argument between Macbeth and Lady Macbeth in which she accuses him of being weak and unmanly pushes him into the murder of Duncan. The many arguments between Antipholus of Ephesus and Adriana in *The Comedy of Errors* are a source of both laughter and reflection.

However, in the relationships between characters depicted by Shakespeare, one of the most enduring images is of persuasion: one character whispering into another's ear, or flattering another to win a point, or speaking seductively to win a lady's hand. Here are some examples:

- Iago pouring poisonous lies into Othello's ear (*Othello*)

- Richard Duke of Gloucester wooing the lady Anne (*Richard III*)

- Lady Macbeth urging Macbeth to murder the King (*Macbeth*)

- Rosalind urging Silvius to be stronger with Phebe. (*As You Like It*)

Parallels and contrasts

One of the most significant structural devices used by playwrights, as you have already seen in unit 37, is the juxtaposition of elements to emphasise and clarify their qualities, and characters are no exception. Sometimes a play's very framework is dependent upon opposing, or apparently opposing, characters who are often, though not always, from the same family. Consider the following:

- The sisters Marlene and Joyce in *Top Girls*: opposites who articulate between them many of the issues faced by women today.
- The Antipholus twins in *The Comedy of Errors*: opposites who may represent two sides of a human personality – the introvert and the extravert.
- Horner and Pinchwife in *The Country Wife*: the witty gallant and the domineering cuckold.
- Edgar and Edmund in *King Lear*: the two sons of Gloucester, one a heroic knight, even a Christ figure, the other a villain.
- Pegeen and the Widow Quin in *The Playboy of the Western World*: foils for each other who both admire Christy.
- Duke Frederick and Duke Senior, or Oliver and Orlando: the paired brothers of *As You Like It* – one good, the other evil, but because the play is a comedy, the evil ones repent and change at the end.

Sometimes two paired, opposing characters can be representative not only of different forms of personality, but of opposing methods of government, and even the succession of one epoch to another (for example Richard II and Bolingbroke in *Richard III*, who represent respectively the medieval and the new era which heralds the Tudors; Marlene in *Top Girls*, who is Thatcherite, and Joyce, who is socialist).

Sympathy and identification

Unless the drama is deliberately alienating, everyone who watches a play will find themselves involved sympathetically in the unfolding situation and identifying with some of the characters and the crises they face. This is only to be expected with characters such as Viola from *Twelfth Night* and Ophelia from *Hamlet*, Orlando from *As You Like It* or Claudio from *Measure for Measure*. Margery Pinchwife is a likeable protagonist in *The Country Wife*. But do you always sympathise with Horner? Or King Lear? What about Shylock? What is it about Richard III, or Edmund in *King Lear*, that fascinates and entertains even though they are such villains? Why do you have such mixed feelings about Caliban? Which of the sisters do you sympathise most with in *Top Girls*? Do you think Tom was justified in leaving his mother and sister in *The Glass Menagerie*? How do you feel ultimately about Christy Mahon – the *Playboy*? Do any of the characters in *Serious Money* draw your feelings of sympathy? Have you a preference for one of the Antipholus twins in *The Comedy of Errors*?

Exam tip

Try to pinpoint the evidence in the text which supports your view of a character, using brief quotation where you can, and remember: the more complex the characterisation, the more likely it is that there will be differing opinions and interpretations.

(39) The language of drama

Plays are written in dialogue that is expressed in poetry or prose (or both) so the analytical skills you have been developing will prove useful. This unit will look at dramatic dialogue and give special emphasis to the language of Shakespeare. Shakespeare was a poet and a man of the theatre, so his plays are both dramatic and poetic in language and structure. However, even a contemporary playwright like Caryl Churchill will on occasion use a poetic form, for example in *Serious Money*.

Exam tip

There is always a question alternative that uses an extract from the play you are studying and asks you to comment on its language, dramatic qualities, development of character or theme and perhaps where it fits into the wider structure of the play. The more detailed the analysis you give, the higher your mark will be.

In this unit the focus will be on the variety of language used by Shakespeare and other playwrights.

Shakespeare the poet

Shakespeare's plays are verse dramas with some sections written in prose. The use of poetry does not mean the characters are poets – it means that the playwright is using the power, descriptiveness and flexibility of poetry to express the thoughts and feelings of many of his characters. (The use of prose is discussed on page 216.) The basic metrical scheme of each line of the poetic speeches is blank verse or the iambic pentameter, which you will remember has ten syllables arranged in five feet, or repeated units of unstressed followed by stressed syllables. Here are a few examples of regular lines of iambic pentameter:

> I will not be afraid of death and bane
> Till Birnam Forest come to Dunsinane.
>> *Macbeth*

> I look'd upon her with a soldier's eye,
> That lik'd, but had a rougher task in hand ...
>> Claudio in *Much Ado about Nothing*

> Most humbly do I take my leave, my lord.
> The time invites you; go, your servants attend.
>> Laertes and Polonius in *Hamlet*

Although iambic pentameter is the basic structure, it is not always easy to find perfectly regular examples of it because the conversational impact of the lines may require some irregularities, however minor.

The verse is also dramatic and needs to be spoken out loud by actors to make sense, not just to scan perfectly.

Task

Find the stressed syllables in the following lines from *Romeo and Juliet* and show how they contribute to the dramatic effect of the speech. Romeo is about to commit suicide, thinking that Juliet is dead.

> O, here
> Will I set up my everlasting rest,
> And shake the yoke of inauspicious stars
> From this world-wearied flesh. Eyes, look your last.

Sample response

This is fairly regular iambic pentameter until the final line, where Romeo's determination to die, and powerful emotion, are made more emphatic by the extra stresses which make the line irregular. I think 'world', 'wearied' and 'flesh' should be emphasised, as well as 'eyes', 'look' and 'last'.

Exam tip

Look closely at the verse for the irregularities which give emphasis to the emotional or dramatic qualities of the speech you are analysing.

In his earlier plays Shakespeare uses rhyme quite extensively, but as his style matures, rhyme disappears apart from the occasional rhyming couplet, often to end a scene emphatically, or to make a really memorable point. Here is an example where Hamlet has been told by his father's ghost to avenge his murder:

> The time is out of joint. O cursèd spite,
> That ever I was born to set it right!

The word 'cursèd' has two syllables because the 'ed' is pronounced; if it were one syllable it would be spelt 'curs'd' or even 'curs't'.

Caryl Churchill

Contemporary playwrights use poetic techniques too. Look at these two examples of rhyming couplets used by Churchill in *Serious Money*:

JACINTA: I tell you I've caught a
Big cocoa importer,
Your deal goes without a hitch.
His school was at Eton
Where children are beaten,
He's a prince and exceedingly rich.

ZAC: The last couple of years in the United States it's been takeover mania
And I guess the deals there have gotten somewhat zanier.
Junk bonds are a quick way of raising cash, but it's kind of hit 'n'
run method, which doesn't go down too well in Britain.

Churchill's use of rhyming couplets in this play can be very witty and amusing: it is difficult not to be amused by a speech which rhymes 'hit 'n'' with 'Britain', and 'zanier' with 'mania'. The first example has a comic effect because it has some of the rhythms of a limerick. The clever rhyme scheme makes these money-obsessed characters sound very shallow, and lends a fast pace to the action, which is highly appropriate for this play.

Shakespeare's prose

Shakespeare uses prose in his plays as well as verse, more often in comedies than tragedies. However, be careful not to make simplistic assertions about this.

Exam tip
Many exam candidates claim wrongly that prose is only used by Shakespeare for the lower classes: servants and peasants. This is not so. Beware of making this false claim yourself.

Prose *is* used for lower-class characters, true. But it is also used by the nobility, both in tragedies and comedies. Sometimes the scene moves from prose into verse even when the same characters are speaking. This is usually to indicate that the emotional quality of the action is becoming more intimate or intense. However, there are also examples of longer prose speeches which are forcefully emotional. You do need to look closely at each instance, rather than rushing into a generalising comment about the use of prose.

Task
Try to find examples from several plays, especially your set play, to indicate the varied use of verse and prose. Look particularly for scenes where both are used and suggest what special effects are created thereby.

Sample response

1 In Act 2 Scene 3 of *Macbeth*, the Porter, a serving man, Macduff and Lennox speak in prose, but when Macbeth enters, the scene moves into blank verse as the tone becomes more intense and they speak of the King, Macbeth knowing that he has murdered him and trying to act as a normally loyal subject would.

2 In Act 1 Scene 3 of *As You Like It*, the princesses Celia and Rosalind are speaking in prose, but when Duke Ferdinand enters to banish Rosalind the scene moves into verse. This is one of the most serious and potentially threatening sequences in the play.

3 In Act 3 Scene 1 of *Hamlet*, Hamlet has just delivered his 'To be or not to be' soliloquy when Ophelia comes in. After a few lines of verse dialogue the scene moves into prose, but it is passionate and strongly expressed ('Get thee to a nunnery ...'). Then, when Hamlet goes out, Ophelia's speech about his former nobility is in verse, as is the rest of the scene.

Dialogue

When characters speak to each other, the interplay of the contributions to the scene is known as **dialogue**. Sometimes when the scene is in verse, the characters speak alternate lines. Here is an example from *The Comedy of Errors*:

LUCIANA:	What, are you mad, that you do reason so?
ANTIPHOLUS:	Not mad, but mated; how, I do not know.
LUCIANA:	It is a fault that springeth from your eye.
ANTIPHOLUS:	For gazing on your beams, fair sun, being by.
LUCIANA:	Gaze where you should, and that will clear your sight.
ANTIPHOLUS:	As good to wink, sweet love, as look on night.

This gives the impression that the characters are intimate, but there is something comically neat about it, especially when rhymed, as here. Luciana thinks this is her sister's husband misbehaving, not realising it is his identical twin: her shock and his besotted wooing are well served by the dialogue form of single lines uttered by alternate speakers, which is known as **stichomythia**.

Characters sometimes even share the lines with each other, and this suggests a particularly close interaction between them.

PROSPERO:	What is't thou canst demand?
ARIEL:	My liberty.
PROSPERO:	Before the time be out? No more!
ARIEL:	I prithee
	Remember I have done thee worthy service ...

In this dialogue between Prospero and Ariel the first two speeches form one line and the second two speeches form one line, showing their intimacy even though they are disagreeing. This device has the even longer name of hemi-stichomythia.

Task

Find some more examples of this device in the play you are studying and try to work out the relationships of the characters involved and the dramatic effect of the scene.

Realistic speech patterns

In contemporary drama some playwrights have striven to create the effect of real-life speech with all its repetitions, interruptions and unfinished sentences. Churchill uses a method in *Top Girls* to capture the way people interrupt each other, using a slash (/) to show the point of interruption. Here is an example from Act 1:

JOAN:	The day after they made me cardinal I fell ill and lay two weeks without speaking, full of terror and regret. / But then I got up
MARLENE:	Yes, success is very ...
JOAN:	determined to go on. I was seized again / with a desperate longing for the absolute.
ISABELLA:	Yes, yes, to go on ...

Similarly, Churchill shows characters continuing to speak right through another's speech (typical of real life) or responding to an earlier speech than the one immediately preceding:

GRISELDA: I'd seen him riding by, we all had. And he'd seen me in the fields with the sheep.*
ISABELLA: I would have been well suited to minding sheep.
NIJO: And Mr Nugent riding by.
ISABELLA: Of course not Nijo, I mean a healthy life in the open air.
JOAN: *He just rode up while you were minding the sheep and asked you to marry him?

Here 'in the fields with the sheep' is the cue for both Isabella's 'I would have been…' and Joan's later 'He just rode up…'.

Soliloquy

Soliloquy is a dramatic convention in which characters are alone on the stage and speak their thoughts aloud to the audience. Some plays have very few such long speeches; others, like *Hamlet,* have many. Often the character is confronting some truth about her or himself or her or his life. Macbeth speaks his soliloquy reflecting on the meaninglessness of life when he hears of his wife's death:

Tomorrow, and tomorrow, and tomorrow,
Creeps in this petty pace from day to day
To the last syllable of recorded time,
And all our yesterdays have lighted fools
The way to dusty death. Out, out, brief candle!
Life's but a walking shadow, a poor player,
That struts and frets his hour upon the stage.
And then is heard no more; it is a tale
Told by an idiot, full of sound and fury,
Signifying nothing.

In *The Glass Menagerie* Tom Wingfield, the narrator as well as a major character, speaks directly to the audience in soliloquy at the beginning and end of the play, as well as before Scene 3 begins. This is part of the final speech of the play:

> Then all at once my sister touches my shoulder. I turn around and look into her eyes ...
> O, Laura, Laura, I tried to leave you behind me, but I am more faithful than I intended to be!
> I reach for a cigarette, I cross the street, I run into the movies or a bar, I buy a drink, I speak to the nearest stranger – anything that can blow your candles out!

Task

Compare the kinds of images used by Macbeth and Tom and assess their effectiveness for evoking each character's mood at this point in the play.

Sample response

Both writers, centuries apart, use the image of the candle and its transient flame to represent the delicate, fleeting quality of life. But Macbeth's dreary, desperate tone is very different from Tom's emotional outpouring. Macbeth has destroyed everything that makes life precious and meaningful, rendering the passage of time a 'petty pace' that simply takes him step by step towards oblivion; the imagery suggests that life is like an unconvincing actor in a meaningless play, with only a brief scene before he disappears for ever. Tom's raw emotion pays tribute to his feelings about his sister. He knows what matters but he has walked away from it, caught between his desire to leave home and become independent and his devotion to his sister.

Task

Find a soliloquy in the play you have studied and consider what sort of effect it has in the play at that point. What kinds of characters are given soliloquies by the playwright?

Exam tip

The word 'soliloquy', like the word 'tragedy', is often misspelled by candidates in their exam essays. Try to make sure that you can spell words such as these, which are central to a study of literature.

Wit combats

In comedies in particular, there are many examples of scenes in which characters are shown having witty dialogues with each other. Here is an example from Oscar Wilde's play *The Importance of Being Earnest*:

LADY BRACKNELL: ... Is this Miss Prism a female of repellent aspect, remotely connected with education?

CANON CHASUBLE: (*somewhat indignantly*) She is the most cultivated of ladies, and the very picture of respectability.

LADY BRACKNELL: It is obviously the same person. May I ask what position she holds in your household?

CANON CHASUBLE: (*severely*) I am a celibate, madam.

This wordplay, revealing opposite values, is delightful for the audience, who are by now familiar with the two speakers and Miss Prism. In Shakespeare's comedies characters try to score points by outdoing each other's puns. These are not so much funny scenes as admirably clever, and an audience would have to be very quick to catch every nuance of the witty interchange between the characters. Here is a short sequence from *As You Like It*:

JAQUES: I thank you for your company; but, have good faith, I had as lief been myself alone. (**had as lief** would rather)

ORLANDO: And so had I; but yet, for fashion sake, I thank you too for your society.

JAQUES: God buy you; let's meet as little as we can. (**buy you** be with you)

ORLANDO: I do desire we may be better strangers.

JAQUES: I pray you mar no more trees with writing love songs in their barks. (**mar** make marks on)

ORLANDO: I pray you mar no more of my verses with reading them ill-favouredly.

JAQUES: Rosalind is your love's name?

ORLANDO: Yes, just.

JAQUES: I do not like her name.

ORLANDO: There was no thought of pleasing you when she was christen'd.

JAQUES: What stature is she of?

ORLANDO: Just as high as my heart.

JAQUES: You are full of pretty answers. Have you not been acquainted with goldsmiths' wives, and conn'd them out of rings?

ORLANDO: Not so; but I answer you right painted cloth, from whence you have studied your questions.

JAQUES: You have a nimble wit;

In the play, Orlando the lover has carved Rosalind's name on the trees in the forest; Jaques the cynic is against love but enjoys talk and philosophising. Here at the beginning, each professes to dislike each other's company and says he is only being polite because it is fashionable to do so. Jaques has already shown he is witty in the play, but Orlando holds his own: his quick-witted retorts impress Jaques as he admits at the end rather grudgingly. Notice that both accuse the other of getting their jokes from another source – carved on a ring or out of a cloth book. Originality in wit, if not plots, was much prized.

Verbal wit also runs throughout Restoration comedies such as *The Country Wife*, but it is not only a feature of comedy. Hamlet is savagely witty and his pun on the word 'kind' in 'a little more than kin and less than kind' sums up one of the great paradoxes of the play: that your kin – your family – are not always kind – well-disposed – towards you, a point already noted in unit 36.

Songs

Songs, set to music, are used by playwrights to enhance the atmosphere of a scene, especially in comedies. Such verses are rhymed, and they often have a refrain or a repeated line, as songs usually do. Caryl Churchill ends each of the two acts of *Serious Money* with rousing, raucous, scurrilous songs that encapsulate the supremely confident and careless atmosphere of those whose greed makes them masses of money in the City of London. Lady Fidget's song in *The Country Wife*, though lively and witty, has a serious point to make about men's treatment of women. In each case the words of the song point to a theme of the scene or play as a whole. Sometimes they are jolly and cheerful, but not always. In *Twelfth Night*, for example, the song sun by Feste the Clown in Orsino's court dwells on the tragic potential of unrequited love:

> Come away, come away, death;
> And in sad cypress let me be laid;
> Fly away, fly away, breath,
> I am slain by a fair, cruel maid.
>   My shroud of white, stuck all with yew,
>   O prepare it!
>   My part of death no one so true
>   Did share it.
>
> Not a flower, not a flower sweet,
> On my black coffin let there be strown;
> Not a friend, not a friend greet
> My poor corpse where my bones shall be thrown;
>   A thousand thousand sighs to save,
>   Lay me, O, where
>   Sad true lover never find my grave,
>   To weep there!

The imagery of this song is conventional in the way it describes the lover's suffering, but it is not just an exaggerated love lyric. Its eloquence reminds us that even in a comedy love can be explored as an experience that causes terrible suffering. You have already seen that it can be shown as a kind of madness too.

Characteristic idiom

The Playboy of the Western World imitates the characteristic speech of Irish peasants and might be difficult to follow if you are trying to read it yourself rather than watching it on the stage:

PEGEEN:	He'll not stir. He's pot-boy in this place and I'll not have him stolen off and kidnabbed while himself's abroad.
WIDOW QUIN:	It'd be a crazy pot-boy'd lodge him in the shebeen where he works by day, so you'd have a right to come on, young fellow, till you see my little houseen, a perch off on the rising hill.
PEGEEN:	Wait till morning, Christy Mahon, wait till you lay eyes on her leaky thatch is growing more pasture for her buck goat than her square of fields, and she without a tramp itself to keep in order her place at all.

Here it is not just vocabulary such as 'pot-boy', 'kidnabbed', 'shebeen' and 'houseen' that might be unfamiliar, but the syntax of sentences, particularly in Pegeen's last speech that sound just right for the character when spoken by an actor, but are more difficult in the study.

Exam tip

It is much easier to understand and appreciate a play if you can see a production of it. For example, the interchange between Pegeen and the Widow Quin above makes complete sense when you can see the two women sparring in front of Christy.

40 Writing on plays for the exam

In this unit you will (a) study a method for close analysis of a scene or extract to help you to answer the passage options in the exam paper and (b) consider how to write an essay on a play.

Analysis of a passage

Plot and context

How is the story, or plot, developed in the passage you are given? Remember that, although you will never be expected to tell the story in an AS or A level essay, it is an essential foundation for all your understanding of, and response to, the play.

One of the commonest mistakes made by candidates in exams is to tell the story of the passage or scene, or to paraphrase it (put the words of the passage into your own words), rather than noting the context of the passage in the play as a whole and analysing how this fits into the wider structure.

Themes

What major concerns of the work as a whole are developed in the passage? How are the play's issues expressed and further explored?

Characterisation

- Are any new characters introduced? If so, how do they fit into the picture so far established?
- Are your impressions of the other characters added to or modified further?
- Is the scene or passage mostly an elaboration of a particular character without much action?
- Are characters spoken of by other characters without appearing themselves? (This is one of Shakespeare's favourite devices, as you have seen.)
- What effect does this have?

Dramatic action

You may not have seen the play you're studying or you may have seen a film or video version. Whether or not you have seen the play, you do need to think about the dramatic qualities of the scene in question:

- Is there any exciting action?
- Are there humorous or farcical interchanges between characters?
- Does anyone have a soliloquy? If so, what effect does it have at this point?
- Where do the climaxes come in the scene?
- Does action seem to be building up and then a change of tempo alters the mood of the scene?
- What would you say by way of advice to the actors playing the parts?

The action is one of the most difficult aspects to consider when you are writing an essay; you need to use your imagination to understand this aspect well.

Features of language

Although plays are written for performance, they are written in words that have been chosen by the playwright to evoke emotion, convey thought or present character. When you are practising for the exam, try to read the dialogue out loud to a friend to bring it alive. Shakespeare was a poet as well as a dramatist, and close attention to his language is essential if you are to appreciate the significance of what is happening. J. M. Synge wrote *The Playboy of the Western World* in a particular Irish dialect, but his interest in language shows in the combination of local idiom with more imaginative use of language.

First of all, with the help of your teacher or a good edition of the play with helpful notes, try to tease out any parts in the passage that are difficult. Then consider questions like these:

- What unusual words, imagery and descriptive language are used and by which character?
- If the passage is from a comedy, are they any 'wit combats' where characters are trying to outdo each other in their cleverness?
- Is it funny?
- Is it passionate or tragic?
- Are there sequences of intensely emotional utterance?
- In Shakespeare, has the playwright used poetry or prose for the scene?
- Do songs feature and, if so, what do they add to the atmosphere or themes of the play?

Quotation

Don't forget to make a note of useful **quotations** – highlight them so that you can find them easily later when you are working on an essay. Never quote more than two lines; a few apt words are even better!

Task

Read the following very short scene (Act 2 Scene 2) from *As You Like It*, one of Shakespeare's comedies, and analyse it using the headings above.

Enter Duke Frederick *with* Lords.

DUKE F: Can it be possible that no man saw them?
            It cannot be; some villains of my court
            Are of consent and sufferance in this.
1 LORD: I cannot hear of any that did see her.
            The ladies, her attendants of her chamber,
            Saw her abed, and in the morning early
            They found the bed untreasur'd of their mistress.
2 LORD: My Lord, the roynish clown, at whom so oft
            Your Grace was wont to laugh, is also missing.
            Hisperia, the Princess' gentlewoman,
            Confesses that she secretly o'erheard

> Your daughter and her cousin much commend
> The parts and graces of the wrestler
> That did but lately foil the sinewy Charles;
> And she believes, wherever they are gone,
> That youth is surely in their company.
>
> Duke F: Send to his brother; fetch that gallant hither.
> If he be absent, bring his brother to me;
> I'll make him find him. Do this suddenly;
> And let not search and inquisition quail
> To bring again these foolish runaways.
>
>   *[Exeunt.]*

Even a short scene or passage (of 21 lines in this case) can be analysed using the check lists above.

Sample response

Plot and context

Duke Frederick, the wicked Duke, has learned that Celia, his daughter, and her cousin and best friend Rosalind have run way from the court with the court jester, Touchstone. (Duke Frederick had banished Rosalind, saying that she was a traitor like her father, his brother Duke Senior, a good man who had been supplanted by the wicked Duke Frederick before the action of the play begins.) One of his courtiers reports that Celia slipped away unnoticed and another says that one of her maids overheard the two girls praising Orlando, a young man whom they had met previously and with whom Rosalind had fallen in love at first sight. The angry Duke sends for Orlando's brother to help to search for them. Because this scene is early in the play it is part of the exposition, and so the plot here seems detailed and complex. [Remember that you do not need to summarise the plot in an exam answer; this activity is to help you get your bearings.]

This scene is both a parallel and a contrast with the previous scene, where the usurped Duke Senior is also being attended and advised by his lords, as his brother is here. The whole atmosphere is completely different though: Duke Senior was in the Forest of Arden, which contrasts with the court, and his men were entertaining each other and behaving courteously and good-humouredly. The idea of two brothers, one good and the other bad, is a favourite of Shakespeare's, here represented in the two Dukes and the two brothers, Orlando and Oliver (who end by marrying the two princesses, so much does Shakespeare love these patterns in his comedies). This court scene is one of a number of brief court scenes at the beginning of the play which gradually disappear as the action in the Forest of Arden assumes greater importance.

Themes

One of the play's main concerns is the contrast between the court and the countryside. Here the court under Duke Frederick is shown as a treacherous place where even the Princess's maid spies on her and overhears what she says. The Duke is very ready to blame 'some villains' of his court, and promises 'search and inquisition' to bring the runaways home. From this scene alone you get a very clear sense of why the two girls would want to run away! The love theme in the play is reinforced too by the mention of Orlando, whom the audience met earlier and feel great sympathy for. However, it is such a short scene that the audience might suspect that the play's villainy will be short-lived, and this is proved to be the case. The play is a comedy, and although it has serious themes, the wicked Duke has a religious conversion at the end, and another unpleasant character – Orlando's brother – reforms too.

Characterisation

The Duke is rather a stereotypical villain, as befits a comedy, and you can easily see his rage and unreasonableness as well as his corrupting influence on the court. The Lords are not important as characters – they are just 1 Lord and 2 Lord – but what they say is useful (and sometimes Shakespeare uses a nameless lord or gentleman to make a speech of great importance, rather like the chorus in a Greek tragedy). Although there are only three characters in the scene, seven others are referred to: Celia, Rosalind, Touchstone, Hisperia the maid, Charles the wrestler, Orlando who beat him in the wrestling match and his brother Oliver. This helps to add to the impression of the court as a busy, gossipy place. Shakespeare characterises many of these missing characters with a brief description: the clown is 'roynish' (a scurvy fellow), the wrestler is 'sinewy', Orlando is a 'gallant', the two runaways are 'foolish'. These all help to depict the characters as well as to establish the Duke's impatience and sarcasm.

Dramatic action

Although brief, this is a dramatic scene, which creates suspense in the audience because they expect repercussions of an extreme nature from the Duke. Although the two princesses are not with Orlando, we expect them to meet again shortly too, a more pleasant kind of suspense. The suspicious and brooding atmosphere of the court could be imaged in a dark, stifling room with heavy curtains, perhaps, reminding the audience that people spy on each other and overhear private conversations (a favourite Shakespearean motif in both comedy and tragedy). The scene is only 21 lines and yet Shakespeare has packed in action, description and atmosphere very effectively.

Features of language

This short scene is entirely in verse, which suits the intensity of the situation and the status of the Duke. [See unit 39 for the use of verse and prose in different contexts.] His language is threatening and imperative. He is used to being obeyed and to making harsh decisions: 'let not search and inquisition quail'. Celia's precious quality is imaged in the metaphor about the maidservants: 'They found the bed untreasur'd of their mistress' – Celia in her bed is like a jewel in a setting, but the jewel has been stolen.

Quotation

[Any of the words or phrases already quoted would be useful ones if writing about this scene. You should always try to quote briefly.]

Task

The following short scene comes from *The Glass Menagerie* by Tennessee Williams. Use the same method to analyse the different aspects of the sequence.

AMANDA: You *will* hear more, you –
TOM: No, I won't hear more, I'm going out!
AMANDA: You come right back in –

TOM:	Out, out, out! Because I'm –
AMANDA:	Come back here, Tom Wingfield! I'm not through talking to you!
TOM:	Oh, go –
LAURA:	(*desperately*) Tom!
AMANDA:	You're going to listen, and no more insolence from you! I'm at the end of my patience!

(He comes back toward her.)

TOM:	What do you think I'm at? Aren't I supposed to have any patience to reach the end of, Mother? I know, I know. It seems unimportant to you, what I'm *doing* – what I *want* to do – having a little *difference* between them! You don't think that –
AMANDA:	I think you've been doing things that you're ashamed of. That's why you act like this. I don't believe that you go every night to the movies. Nobody goes to the movies night after night. Nobody in their right mind goes to the movies as often as you pretend to. People don't go to the movies at nearly midnight, and movies don't let out at two a.m. Come in stumbling. Muttering to yourself like a maniac! You get three hours' sleep and then go to work. Oh, I can picture the way you're doing down there. Moping, doping, because you're in no condition.
TOM:	(*wildly*) No, I'm in no condition!
AMANDA:	What right have you got to jeopardize your job? Jeopardize the security of us all? How do you think we'd manage if you were –
TOM:	Listen! You think I'm crazy about the *warehouse*? (*He bends fiercely toward her slight figure.*) You think I'm in love with the Continental Shoemakers? You think I want to spend fifty-five *years* down there in that – *celotex interior*! with – *fluorescent – tubes*!

Sample response

Plot and context

This short sequence (not a complete scene) is a part of a row between Tom and his mother Amanda. Laura, Tom's sister, is present and tries to intervene once, but without effect. It is a perennial row: Tom wants to go out at night to escape from the drudgery of his everyday routine and the pressure of the domestic situation; his mother nags him and tries to make him behave more conventionally because she is anxious about the security of his job, which is keeping them afloat financially. She is also anxious that he might run away more permanently.

Themes

Tom is described by Williams as 'a poet with a job in a warehouse'. His desire to escape from the everyday world of the warehouse, where he works at a boring job, and his home, where his mother nags him, are in conflict with the close emotional bond he feels with his shy, withdrawn sister. Here his desire to escape to the fantasy world of the movies is made very clear as is his mother's anxious determination to keep him in a steady job. She does not really understand him or, if she almost does, she tries hard not to face up to it. The scene reveals the domestic tension which will finally erupt so that Tom does in fact leave the family at the end of the play, following another row like this one, where Amanda accuses him of being a 'selfish dreamer'.

Characterisation

No new characters are introduced here and indeed all three of the Wingfields behave characteristically: Amanda trying to tell Tom what he should and should not do, Laura's mute desperation and Tom rejecting the life his mother is trying to impose on him. Significantly the audience tends to sympathise with Tom, especially if it contains young people who find restrictions and expectations of their elders limiting and demeaning. But Williams is always responsive to Amanda, whose concerns for her children, while maddening to them, are understandable in the light of their financial situation.

Dramatic action

This is a highly dramatic passage which starts at the peak of a family row and the two protagonists are shouting at each other at the beginning. Emotions run high throughout the quoted sequence. Following this extract, Tom tries to storm out, shouting at Amanda and insulting her, breaking some of Laura's glass collection as he does so. This action prefigures the destructive effect his final abandonment of the family will have, at the same time as making the abandonment very understandable to the audience, who have sympathy for all three of the family in different ways.

Features of language

The row is expressed in repetitive language with many exclamations, rhetorical questions and unfinished sentences (for example the first few lines). Williams captures very effectively the tone and atmosphere of a family row which has happened before. Repeated words emphasise themes powerfully as well as creating the angry mood. 'Out', 'movies', 'nobody' and 'jeopardize' all chime repetitively, hammering out their point. Amanda's utterance becomes poetic as she expresses Tom's return home, 'stumbling. Muttering', and his imagined behaviour at work: 'Moping, doping, because you're in no condition.' But even this has less passion than Tom's furious outburst against the warehouse, with its celotex interior and fluorescent tubes, a wholly artificial and ugly interior, a place that he only endures because he has to make enough money for the family to survive.

This scene parallels the later one which forms the play's climax when Tom has finally had enough and leaves home and job. But it is in contrast to the more tender moments of the play involving his sister, the more resigned and mutual conversations with his mother and the last poignant lines when he remembers sadly what he has left behind.

Exam tip

This pattern of headings should not be followed slavishly when answering a passage question. They are just to help you to organise your thoughts and would naturally be invisible within the final essay. However, don't forget the importance of close critical comment and analysis which includes the elements above, particularly the language used and its contribution to characterisation, action, tone and atmosphere.

Writing an exam essay on a play

Once again, revise the discursive essay in units 19 and 20 and remind yourself of the importance of organising your ideas logically.

Read the essay below on *Macbeth,* written under exam conditions. You do not need to have studied this play to appreciate the clear structure of the essay. If you have studied the play, you will have other ideas about the topic that this particular student did not include. For example, you may want to have said more about Banquo's ghost. However, this is an important reminder of the multiple possibilities for selecting material from complex texts to create an argument in answer to a question. As long as you can support your points with close textual reference, your opinion is valid and will be rewarded.

Sample essay

What is the importance of the supernatural in *Macbeth* in your opinion?

Macbeth is a play filled with supernatural events and references and the supernatural is clearly a very important aspect of the dramatic effect of the play on the audience. At the time that Shakespeare was writing, the audience would have been more superstitious than we are today, but a modern audience is still fascinated by the supernatural aspects of the play, which emphasise its themes and characterisation.

The first important feature of the supernatural is the way in which the disorder in the kingdom is mirrored in the stormy weather and strange behaviour of animals on the night when Duncan is murdered. 'Strange screams of death' were heard, and the earth 'was feverous and did shake'. The sky becomes unnaturally black: 'dark night strangles the travelling lamp' and Duncan's horses 'turned wild in nature … as they would make war with mankind' and began to eat each other. These completely unnatural and alarming events are symbolic of the way in which the murder of the king will affect the kingdom. It was believed that a king had a sacred right to rule and his death would have major repercussions on society, symbolised by the supernatural events in nature and the cosmos.

But the supernatural is also used to show that Macbeth himself is not just a murderer, but a man with a vivid imagination. Just before doing the terrible deed of murdering the king, he sees a dagger floating in the air in front of him, drawing him onward to do the murder. It is possible that this is not a ghostly dagger but 'a dagger of the mind, a false creation, / Proceeding from the heat-oppressed brain', a weapon which has 'gouts of blood' on its handle. Whether supernatural or not, what it does remind us is that Macbeth does not find it easy at this point to be the hard unfeeling man murdering to advance his career. He seems genuinely overwrought and has, in the scene before, even had second thoughts about doing the murder at all, which Lady Macbeth soon overturns by her powerful persuasions.

Lady Macbeth may indeed be persuasive, but she is a human woman of apparently strong character, not a supernatural agent. Possibly the most memorable and striking examples of the supernatural in the play are the three witches, who also persuade Macbeth, but they use riddling and ambiguous statements to do so. Their scene opens the play, immediately arousing a sense of curiosity in the audience as to why they have singled Macbeth out, especially when in the next scene he is praised for his valour, loyalty and nobility. They represent evil and overturn the values of goodness; they make this clear when they say, 'Fair is foul and foul is fair.' The audience gets a shock when the first words of Macbeth seem to echo this statement: 'So foul and fair a day I have not seen' – a verbal echo which seems to link him mysteriously with the witches and prepares us for the effect they will have on his stability.

The witches' meeting with Macbeth influences him profoundly. Because they promise him that he will be Thane of Cawdor and 'King thereafter' and he is immediately and unexpectedly given the first title, his mind starts to churn, imagining the possibility of becoming King. Although he does have some misgivings at different points, he starts to plan to murder Duncan and make the witches' prophecy happen. He describes their words as 'supernatural soliciting', but who actually suggested the deed of murder? They did not tell him to make it happen, they just said he would be king, and fate might give him the throne without him lifting a finger. But his own ambition and his wife's strong prompting lead him along the fateful path that will end eventually with his own death. The witches may represent supernaturally those events in life which unexpectedly knock us off course and lead us to making the wrong decisions. On the stage they are terrifyingly evil and influential.

Another very dramatic example of the supernatural is the apparitions conjured up when Macbeth visits them later, having murdered Banquo to prevent his children becoming King as the witches had also promised. But the apparitions only confirm that the issue of Banquo will be kings and his will not. Moreover, they give him prophecies that are true but so ambiguous that he misunderstands them (that Birnam Wood will move to Dunsinane before he will be caught; that he will die at the hand of one not born of woman). This suggests the way in which we make assumptions about the future on the basis of misunderstandings.

Ultimately the presence of the supernatural in the play is part of the framework of good and evil upon which it is structured, and which is reflected in the language, with mentions of deeds, angels, darkness and light. There is supernatural goodness at work too, in the English King who has the gifts of healing and prophecy. The ghost we see, Banquo attending the feast, was a good man whose spirit is haunting the guilty Macbeth, one of the most exciting moments in the play. But the real interest of the play lies in the character of Macbeth himself, who is not just an ambitious 'butcher', as he is described at the end, but an imaginative and intelligent man who could perhaps have chosen good, but is persuaded into evil by his wife and the three weird sisters.

Comment

This essay is well organised and each paragraph deals clearly with one topic. There are connective words and phrases linking paragraphs to show the direction of the argument, and the many close references reveal familiarity with the text. It reveals a sense of theatre too, which is important in this section of the examination. Overall it gains a high mark.

Exam tip

Look at the question and jot down relevant ideas. Make them into a logical plan and write your essay, using apt references to the play to support your points. You will need to be selective because one hour is not enough time to say everything.

(41) A guide to exam questions

In this final unit, you will look at the wording of examination questions so that you understand exactly what you have to do when faced with a particular requirement. Each instance of wording is accompanied by an example and a comment on what you need to do in each case. The examples are from poetry, prose and drama.

1 Discuss

The word 'discuss' is often used for essays at this level. Revise unit 19 on discursive essays in the Language part of the book. Discussion of a topic means that you must consider all the important aspects of it, analysing and debating the issues that you think are important.

Example Discuss Shakespeare's use of images of light and darkness in *Macbeth*.

Comment You will need to cover what the images are, how they are used in specific situations and what they add to the play overall. Some consideration of the contrast between them would be helpful too. You should be able to quote several examples directly, and analyse them, as well as making more general points.

Example Discuss [the writer's] presentation of [character/setting/idea] and what it adds to the [novel/play] as a whole.

Comment You would not be given the first part of this question without the second, because you might otherwise be tempted just to describe the person, place or theme, without showing its importance in the whole work. For example, a character could be used to contrast with the main character; a setting could be used to symbolise a particular culture or way of life; and an idea might be one of the writer's main concerns in that work. 'Presentation' means how the writer has used language, tone and structure to represent the character, setting or idea.

2 How far... or To what extent...?

'How far...' and 'To what extent...' give you the freedom to pitch your response on an imaginary scale: it could be completely, not at all or something in between.

Example How far do you agree with Amanda Wingfield that her son Tom is a 'selfish dreamer'?

Comment You are free to argue as you wish: that Tom is selfish, that he isn't, or that he partly is and partly isn't. You will need to argue carefully to support your case from the play, but there is not a 'right' answer here. An essay arguing that Tom is a selfish dreamer can gain as many marks as an essay arguing that he is sensitive to others and realistic about his life.

3 In what ways… (or By what means…) and How effectively… ?

'Ways' and 'means' are the methods used by the writer to communicate her/his ideas. If they are effective, then the reader is moved to realisation, understanding or appreciation of the idea.

Example In what ways and how effectively do two poets in your anthology write on the passage of time?

Comment You need to look closely at the poetic methods used and decide if you find them effective at communicating the ideas to you.

4 What importance or significance… ?

The question is asking you to argue how far and in what ways an episode, character or idea adds meaning to the work as a whole.

Example Discuss the significance of images of pregnancy and childbirth in the poems of Sylvia Plath in your selection.

Comment A selection of images must be analysed and their importance assessed against other kinds of image; then a judgement must be made as to their importance.

5 Comment closely, comment in detail, with close reference to the text, focusing on…

Analyse the language of a passage or poem, looking closely at…

6 Concerns

'Concerns' are themes or ideas.

7 Methods

'Methods' are the means used by the writer such as imagery or symbol or characterisation.

Example Comment closely on Hardy's concerns and methods in the following poem.

Comment Don't neglect any aspect of the themes and style of the poem within the constraints of the timing of the exam.

8 Effects

'Effects' result from the writer's employment of particular methods.

Example Looking closely at the effects of the dialogue and other narrative methods, show how this passage helps you to understand Emma's characterisation in the novel.

Comment You need to look closely at how you respond to the way Austen at times offers only dialogue, without authorial comment, and at other times uses reported speech and description of characters' states of mind. One of the effects of dialogue without comment is irony, because the reader can imagine the effect this talk is having on other characters, for example when Emma is flirting with Frank.

9 Dramatic

The word 'dramatic' is used to remind you that you are studying a play, with action, tension and dialogue. 'Dramatic significance' means importance to the play as a whole; 'dramatic contribution' means contribution to the play; 'dramatic effects' are, for example, action, climax, characters in conflict, sudden changes of scene, surprises or denouement for the audience. Don't be frightened by the word 'dramatic' – plunge into the passage and look for the excitement!

Example Discuss the dramatic function of the witches in *Macbeth*.

Comment You will have your own ideas about the function of the witches, for example as instigators of Macbeth's downfall. Make sure that you also give plenty of evidence of their effectiveness on the stage: refer to their stirring the cauldron and producing the apparitions, as well as their parallels/contrasts with Lady Macbeth and their ambiguous, riddling speeches.

10 Language, imagery, tone, atmosphere

Although imagery is part of language, it is often highlighted separately in the question to remind you to look for figures of speech such as metaphor. Don't forget images of the senses such as sight, hearing, touch, taste, smell and movement. If you are asked to comment on tone in a passage of drama, it suggests that there are significant features of tone for you to identify: someone is angry, another is evasive, someone else is trying to calm them down. If the passage is a poem, perhaps the poet's tone is striking in some way: especially sad, or aggressive, or nostalgic. Atmosphere is created by all the many effects of language in a poem, play or novel. If you have analysed closely, you will feel the atmosphere and will be able to refer to it.

Example With close reference to the language and tone of this passage, discuss how effectively Ngugi presents the character of John Thompson.

Comment Ngugi's critical portrait of Thompson lends a cool and unsympathetic tone to most of his descriptions which effectively present a hard, unfeeling character. To answer this well you will need appropriate examples from the text, which will be printed in the examination paper.

Acknowledgements

Thanks are due to the following for permission to reproduce copyright textual material: pp.4, 9, *1914–18 in Poetry: An Anthology*, selected and edited by E. L. Black, University of London Press, 1970; pp.4, 9, 'Beaches' by Ken Wilkie, *Holland Herald Magazine* (KLM) 2002; pp.5, 9, 'We will be free' Melina Mercouri (Washington, January 1968) from *The Penguin Book of Twentieth-Century Speeches*, edited by Brian MacArthur, copyright © Melina Mercouri 1968; pp.5, 9, *The Remorseful Day* by Colin Dexter, Macmillan 1999; pp.5, 9, 98, *Long Walk to Freedom* by Nelson Mandela, reprinted by permission of Time Warner Books UK and Time Warner Books NY, copyright © Nelson Mandela 1994; pp.12, 22–3, *Chocolat* by Joanne Harris, published by Doubleday, copyright © 1999 by Joanne Harris, used by permission of Viking Penguin, a division of Penguin Group (USA) Inc; p.13, 'The Colours of Rice' by Delphine Barbier St Marie, *Going Places Magazine* (The Inflight Magazine of Malaysia Airlines) 2002; p.15, *Memoirs of an Infantry Officer* by Siegfried Sassoon, 1966, copyright © Siegfried Sassoon by kind permission of George Sassoon; pp.20–1, *As I Walked Out One Midsummer Morning* by Laurie Lee (Penguin Books Ltd), first published by André Deutsch 1969, reprinted by permission of Carlton Publishing Group, copyright © Laurie Lee 1969; p.26, *When We Were Orphans* by Kazuro Ishiguro, reprinted by permission of Faber & Faber Ltd; pp.27–8, 'Rail Travel' by David Bowden, *Going Places Magazine* (The Inflight Magazine of Malaysia Airlines) 2002; p.30, *On Tracks to Lose Weight, The* (Glasgow) *Herald*, Saturday April 20, 2002; pp.31–2, 'Let freedom reign' Nelson Mandela (Pretoria, 10 May 1994) from *The Penguin Book of Twentieth-Century Speeches*, edited by Brian MacArthur; p.37, Scottish Tourist Board © VisitScotland.com; pp.41–2, Letter from America, BBC © Alastair Cooke; pp.43–4, 164, *The God of Small Things* by Arundhati Roy, reprinted by permission of HarperCollins Publishers Ltd and David Godwin Associates, copyright © Arundhati Roy 1997; p.46, *Boots Health and Beauty Magazine*; pp.52–3, 'Best Foot Forward', *Skylines Magazine*, copyright © Barney Spender; p.55, *Period Piece: A Cambridge Childhood* by Gwen A. Raverat 1952, reprinted by permission of Faber & Faber Ltd; pp.56–7, 'A Modern Constitution' Tony Blair (Blackpool, 4 October 1994) from *The Penguin Book of Twentieth-Century Speeches*, edited by Brian MacArthur, reprinted with permission of The Labour Party; p.57, *After You'd Gone* by Maggie O'Farrell, copyright © Maggie O'Farrell 2000, reprinted with permission from A. M. Heath & Co. Ltd; p.58, 'Football World Cup', *Times Educational Supplement* 19 April 2002 © Sean Coughlan; p.59, *The Cone Gatherers* by Robin Jenkins, originally published by Longman, reprinted by permission of Pearson Education; pp.68–70, *Twenty-One Stories* by Graham Greene, originally published by Heinemann 1954, reprinted by permission of David Higham Associates; pp.71, 73, 'Secrets' from *Secrets and Other Stories* by Bernard MacLaverty (Penguin Books), first printed by Blackstaff Press Ltd 1977, copyright © Bernard MacLaverty, 1977, 1984, reproduced by permission of the author c/o Rogers, Coleridge & White Ltd, 20 Powis Mews, London W11 1JN; pp.72, 74, *Don't Look Now and Other Stories*: Daphne du Maurier, Penguin 1981, reprinted by permission of Curtis Brown on behalf of the Estate of Daphne du Maurier, copyright © The Chichester Partnership 1981; p.74, *Original Sin* by P. D. James, Faber & Faber Ltd, © P. D. James 1994, reprinted by permission of Greene & Heaton Ltd; pp.74, 84, *The Millstone* by Margaret Drabble, Weidenfeld & Nicolson (copyright © Margaret Drabble 1965), reprinted with permission of The Orion Publishing Group Ltd and by PFD on behalf of Margaret Drabble; pp.82–3, *The Comfort of Strangers* by Ian McEwan, published by Jonathan Cape, copyright © 1981 Ian McEwan, reproduced by permission of the author c/o Rogers, Coleridge & White Ltd, 20 Powis Mews, London W11 1JN; pp.85–6, 158, *The Great Gatsby* by F. Scott Fitzgerald (Penguin Modern Classics), reprinted by permission of David Higham Associates; p.95, *The Diary of Anne Frank*, Heinemann 1990, copyright © first published 1947 in Holland by Contact Amsterdam, translated from the Dutch by B. M. Mooyart-Doubleday and published 1953 by Vallentine, Mitchell & Co. Ltd, reprinted with permission of The Anne Frank Foundation, Switzerland; pp.96, 199–200, 'A View from the

Bridge' by Arthur Miller, Penguin 1981, reprinted by permission of ICM, NY; p.97, *Graham Greene, Friend and Brother* by Leopoldo Duran, HarperCollins 1994; p.115, 'In a Station of the Metro' from *Personae* by Ezra Pound, reprinted by permission of Faber & Faber Ltd and New Directions Publishing Corporation; p.118, 'Thistles', reprinted by permission of Faber & Faber Ltd from *Wodwo* by Ted Hughes; pp.118–19, the quotations from 'Church Going' by Philip Larkin are reprinted from *The Less Deceived* by permission of The Marvell Press, England and Australia; p.120, 'The Waste Land' from *Collected Poems 1909–1962* by T. S. Eliot, reprinted by permission of Faber & Faber Ltd; pp.121, 140, 'Two Sisters of Persephone' and 'Metaphors', reprinted by permission of Faber & Faber Ltd from *Collected Poems* by Sylvia Plath; p.124, 'Not Waving but Drowning' from *Collected Poems of Stevie Smith*, copyright © 1972 by Stevie Smith, reprinted by permission of New Directions Publishing Corporation; p.127, 'Haiku', *The Haiku Hundred* by James Kirkup, Iron Press, reprinted with permission of the author, copyright © James Kirkup; pp.128, 137, 'Everyone Sang' from *Collected Poems 1908–1956*, reprinted by kind permission of George Sassoon, copyright © Siegfried Sassoon; p.139, 'A Summer Night' by Douglas Dunn, reprinted by permission of PFD on behalf of Douglas Dunn from *Selected Poems 1964–83* © Douglas Dunn; p.143, 'The Germ' from *Candy Is Dandy: The Best of Ogden Nash*, selected by Linell Smith and Isabel Eberstadt, published by André Deutsch 1994, copyright © 1935 by Ogden Nash, renewed, reprinted by permission of Curtis Brown Ltd and Carlton Publishing Group; pp.144, 146, 'An Arundel Tomb', reprinted by permission of Faber & Faber Ltd from *The Whitsun Weddings* by Philip Larkin; p.145, 'Epitaph on an Army of Mercenaries' from *The Collected Poems of A. E. Housman*, copyright 1922 by Holt, Rinehart and Winston, Inc; p.147, 'Enemies' from *Selected Poems* by Elizabeth Jennings, reprinted by permission of David Higham Associates; p.148, 'The Seafarer', reprinted by permission of Faber & Faber Ltd from *The Rattle Bag* edited by Seamus Heaney and Ted Hughes; pp.160, 163–4, 173, *Martha Quest* by Doris Lessing, Panther 1966, usage by kind permission of Jonathan Clowes Ltd, London, on behalf of Doris Lessing, copyright © Doris Lessing 1966; pp.160, 173, 179, *A Grain of Wheat* by Ngugi wa Thiong'o, published by Heinemann Educational, reprinted by permission of Harcourt Education; p.160, *The Life and Times of Michael K* by J. M. Coetzee, published by Martin Secker & Warburg, reprinted by permission of Random House Group Ltd; pp.160–1, *To the Lighthouse* by Virginia Woolf © 1927 by Harcourt Inc and renewed 1954 by Leonard Woolf, reprinted by permission of the publisher and by permission of The Society of Authors as the Literary Representative of the Estate of Virginia Woolf; pp.163, 173, *Things Fall Apart* by Chinua Achebe, reprinted by permission of Harcourt Education; p.164, *Underworld*, Picador 1997, reprinted with the permission of Scribner, an imprint of Simon & Schuster Adult Publishing Group, and by Macmillan Publishers Ltd, from *Underworld* by Don DeLillo, copyright © 1997 by Don DeLillo; p.164, *The Go-Between* by L. P. Hartley (Hamish Hamilton, 1953) copyright 1953 by L. P. Hartley, this edition © Douglas Brook-Douglas 1997, reprinted with permission from The Society of Authors as the Literary Representative of the Estate of L. P. Hartley; p.164, extract from *Cloudstreet* by Tim Winton, published by McPhee Gribble, an imprint of Penguin Books Australia 1991; p.168, *The Third Policeman* by Flann O'Brien, HarperCollins Publishers Ltd © 1967 Flann O'Brien; p.170, *A House for Mr Biswas* by V. S. Naipaul (Penguin Books, 1969), copyright © V. S. Naipaul 1961, copyright renewed 1989 by V. S. Naipaul; pp. 179–80, *Alias Grace* by Margaret Atwood, Virago 1997, copyright © 1996 by O. W. Toad Ltd, used by permission of Doubleday, a division of Random House Inc, and McClelland & Stewart Ltd, The Canadian Publishers; pp.205, 218, 225–6, *The Glass Menagerie*, excerpts from Penguin Plays: *The Sweet Bird of Youth, A Streetcar Named Desire*, and *The Glass Menagerie* by Tennessee Williams, copyright © 1987 by Tennessee Williams, reprinted by permission of Georges Borchardt, Inc., for the author; pp.214, 216–17, *Top Girls* copyright © 1982, 1984 and *Serious Money* copyright © 1987, 1989 by Caryl Churchill, Methuen Publishing Limited.